ANARCHISM AND ANARCHISTS

ANARCHISM AND ANARCHISTS

ESSAYS BY
GEORGE WOODCOCK

Quarry Press

Canadian Cataloguing in Publication Data
    Woodcock, George, 1912 —
        Anarchism & anarchists

Includes bibliographical references and index.
ISBN 1–55082–018–4

        1. Anarchism.   I. Fetherling, Douglas, 1949 —
II. Title.

HX833.A52 1992   320.5'7   C92–090046–1

Cover art entitled "Coups sur coups" by Jean-Paul Riopelle,
reproduced by permission of the Art Gallery of Ontario.
Design by Keith Abraham. Typeset by Susan Hannah.

Printed and bound in Canada by Hignell Printing, Winnipeg, Manitoba.

Published in Canada by *Quarry Press*, Inc., P.O. Box 1061, Kingston, Ontario
K7L 4Y5.

CONTENTS

ANARCHISTS

INTRODUCTION

It should be a simple matter to introduce this book, which is being published simultaneously in Canada, the United States, and Britain, because George Woodcock is not only an important political writer but one who has had experience and an audience on both sides of the Atlantic. But the same facts that make him virtually unique as a senior veteran of the British as well as the North American Left also make this task a difficult one.

In Canada, Woodcock is a public figure, famous for his energy and the extreme range of his interests, but he is most conspicuous as a historian and literary critic; readers are aware of his political concerns, but tend to regard them as the glue that binds all his works together. His politics are always noted, sometimes in a reassuring way, but they are seldom discussed seriously or at length. They form a kind of *leit motiv* the way the politics of John Berger, for example, or of Maureen Duffy, must do for contemporary English readers. In Britain, conversely, Woodcock is far better known for his political writings than for his recent ones on history and culture, even among his own generation, which first discovered him as a poet and had the pleasure of his astounding productivity during the first half of his life. In America, however, he is known only in a rather spotty fashion. No more than a handful of his hundred or so books have been published there, though these include some of his most closely read and often cited ones, such as *The Crystal Spirit*, a memoir of George Orwell.

Much of this lack of consensus arises from certain anomalies in Woodcock's biography. He is Welsh but was born in Winnipeg, reared in the Welsh Marches, built his career in London, taught in the American West, and has lived in British Columbia for more than forty years. On a quite different level, it may also be traceable to the cross-cultural and internationalist nature of so many of his recurring subjects and underlying concerns. His agenda has focussed not on economic or partisan issues but on the basic human ones: how men and women might best organize themselves for daily living and working when mutual benefit requires such collective action, yet avoid the tyranny of groups. That is to say, he is an anarchist.

This is a representative selection of his articles and essays on anarchist topics over the past half century. As such, it can easily stand on its own, or it can be taken as an adjunct to, an extension of — perhaps even a commentary on — the most widely known of his books, *Anarchism: A History of Libertarian Ideas and Movements* (another one that has found a place in the United States). In any event, the present collection is best viewed as an organic whole built up over the years by the twin processes of historical enquiry and topical engagement.

Woodcock was born in 1912. An earlier generation found the First World War to be the single great informing event of their lives, just as Vietnam would be for a later age. But for Woodcock and his contemporaries, the events in Spain between 1936 and 1938 were what shaped their dreams and nightmares. One of the significant facts about the Spanish Civil War was the anarchists' support of the Loyalist cause. Never had the anarchists been so prominent, never had they seemed such a cohesive movement. Or put another way, never had misunderstanding about them and what they stood for been so widespread. In the intense heat of the moment, for example, it was perhaps not always clear to what extent the anarcho-syndicalists had been a factor in Spanish politics since the middle of the nineteenth century. The contextual void must have been all the more obvious in view of the way the world's attention was concentrated on Spain. At this great distance one can be forgiven for guessing that it was this situation that set the young Woodcock to work on the anarchist tradition, a labor that has engaged him intermittently ever since.

His mission was not necessarily to inflate the importance of anarchism. In fact, when he published his now famous book it was with the melancholy sense that the movement had come to an end, having served its useful purpose of provoking the victors into acting more compassionately. No one could have predicted that such a work would become, in a quiet way altogether uncharacteristic of the period, one of the signal documents of the 1960s. Nor did he try to make his topic any more respectable a historical phenomenon than it was or is; he himself has always been a pacifist (he was a conscientious objector during the Second World War, for example), but he could not deny the existence of those extremists in the past who themselves had been unable to reject violence. What he sought was simply to convey a better understanding of the subject, particularly the way it developed differently in various countries but following the same basic pattern as the novel, with the Russian and French strains being the most complex and self-confident, the English the most artful and evocative, and the American the most energetic but ultimately the least substantial.

The history is especially important because it is in the nature of anarchism, as the denial of rigid ideology, bureaucracy, and hierarchy, that it must therefore lack the artificial memory built into formal political institutions. Ironically, this weakness has helped to keep it vital by giving it so much of the plasticity that it requires of itself and promises others. Anarchism continues to exist — *flourish* would be too strong a word — in reaction to both authoritarian socialism and slash-and-burn capitalism, yet without having much in common with liberalism save optimism about the future of the human spirit. Proudhon, Godwin, Tolstoy, and those other nineteenth-century figures to whom Woodcock returns us again and again were the ultimate idealists, what with their dream of a free association of equally free individuals acting in their own collective best interests, without the yoke of government or other manmade institutions. Their faith in the essential goodness of human nature has never been surpassed; it can hardly be equalled without lapsing into organized (indeed corporate) religion — a superfluous progression given the vernacular religious impulse that often underlay those classic anarchists of old.

The Taoists' complaint about the Confucians was that the Confucians, in giving definition to the concept of morality, had therefore made immorality inevitable. So too did centralized administration make anarchism inevitable when it eclipsed the idea of the tribe and other small organic self-governing bodies. This basic notion of counterpoise is what gives anarchism its flexibility and therefore its resilience.

Another Canadian critic, Northrop Frye, has reminded us how the Bible was promulgated in order to supplant the ancient mother-goddess religions, which were based on the idea of an all-powerful matriarchal figure at the center of Nature, with the Christian concept of a patriarchal God who urges reliance on human institutions rather than on objects and forces found in the natural order: an essential theme of Judaism and Islam as well. Anarchism is a tiny voice of corrective protest, urging that old harmonious arrangements be re-evaluated at the expense of artificial grids. This is why it has been so easy for anarcho-feminism and eco-anarchism to become the most important new forms of anti-authoritarian thought in recent years, important to anarchism itself and to the larger movements of which they are part. Constant renewal of the premise gives anarchism its ability to adapt to present realities. That might almost be Woodcock's message in a single sentence. He would tell us: To appreciate Bookchin, first study Bakunin. But to acquire the context, a chorus might answer, go and read Woodcock.

Douglas Fetherling

ESSAYS ON ANARCHISTS

1

The Advent of Anarchism and the Revolutions of 1848

January 12th, 1848 the people of Palermo came out into the streets in rebellion against the despotic rule of Ferdinand of Naples, later to become notorious as "King Bomba" for his brutal bombardment of the rebel city of Messina. This rising was the prelude to a whole series of revolutions, involving not merely Italy, but also France, Germany, Austria, Hungary, Bohemia, Transylvania, and all the small Slav peoples who were then the "inferior" races of the vast Austrian Empire. Even in England and Ireland, under the stimulus of continental examples, there were extensive riots and abortive revolutionary movements.

The events of 1848 represent in reality at least two different movements. In France, ever since the deposition of the legitimate Bourbon king, Charles X, in 1830, the big business men had ruled under the pretence of a constitutional government by Louis Philippe, 'The Citizen King." The rising in France represented an attempt by the lower middle class, supported by the workers, to gain their share of power, and, in consequence, it had prominent social revolutionary elements.

The risings in the rest of Europe, on the other hand, were directed largely against the power which was wielded by the old conservative, Metternich, who, since 1815, by his direct domination over the whole of Central Europe and Italy, and his influence on the remaining continental rulers, had contrived to maintain, in spirit if not in name, the Holy Alliance of reaction and obscurantism as the main force in Europe. Assisted by the Pope, the princelings of Germany, and the rulers of those parts of Italy which, like Tuscany and Naples, were nominally independent, he had maintained as far as possible an almost absolute form of dynastic government, based on an aristocratic society. Austria, from which his power stemmed, was governed in the most despotic manner, and was known as "the China of Europe," since it was isolated by the most severe of censorships. No newspapers could be published, and books, whether printed internally or imported from abroad, were subjected to the most rigorous examination before the citizens of the country were allowed to read them. Even the mildest radical or reformist propaganda was forbidden, and an efficient political police system assisted the control of Metternich and the Emperor Ferdinand.

The remainder of Germany was, in theory, a federation of large and small sovereign states, under the suzerainty of the Emperor. In fact, these States were completely under the reactionary domination of Metternich, who quickly called to order any prince daring to defer to liberal pretensions. Where a principality, like Baden, began to show the least sign of yielding to progressive tendencies, Metternich was quite prepared to interfere directly in its internal affairs. The only State in the German federation that really challenged the power of Austria was Prussia, but this was merely a dynastic struggle, and the Hohenzollerns were in complete agreement with Metternich over his policy of suppressing the democratic movements within Germany.

Within Austria were included, not only the small country which now bears that name, but also territories that today form parts of Czechoslovakia, Poland, and Yugoslavia. In these areas all nationalist or democratic movements were carefully suppressed, the native languages were, as far as possible, forbidden, and all the key posts and services in the public administration were in the hands of Germans from Austria.

Among the subject territories was also the northern part of Italy, which, after the first fall of Napoleon in 1814, had been occupied by the Austrians, and retained as an Austrian dominion at the peace of 1815. The possession of this area gave the Austrian government strategic control of all Italy. While the native princes had returned to their provinces in 1814, and perhaps enjoyed more real sovereignty than the German princes, the Imperial authorities were careful to allow no democratic excesses even in parts of Italy outside their normal control, and the comparative lack of direct interference was due only to the fact that most of the Italian princes were themselves too despotic to do anything that might displease Metternich. When, in 1821, the people of Naples rose and forced a democratic constitution on their king, the Imperial authorities did not scruple to violate the sovereignty of Neapolitan territory by sending an army to suppress the liberal movement and re-establish the old autocracy. The only state in Italy that possessed any real independence and could afford even the mildest leaning towards liberalism was the kingdom of Piedmont, which also included Genoa and Sardinia. This was due in part, at least, to the fact that Piedmont enjoyed a certain veiled support from both France and the Swiss cantons as a counterbalance to Austrian influence in Italy.

The remaining country over which the Emperor ruled was Hungary. This country was not part of the Empire, and was nominally independent, the Emperor of Austria ruling it as king. But, in fact, since the days of Maria Theresa, it had become dominated by the Emperor's German bureaucracy, and continual attempts had been made to interfere with the rights of the Magyars, the ruling people of the country. But the Magyars were only one race in that sprawling land, which included Transylvania, inhabited largely by Roumanians, and Croatia, with its Slav population, as well as part of Serbia. The Magyar aristocracy, while claiming independence from Austrian domination and equality with Germans within the Habsburg dominions, themselves repudiated and tried to suppress any attempt by either Roumanians or Slavs to claim their autonomous rights, and attempted to maintain their continued suppression under Magyar institutions.

Feudalism persisted throughout Germany and the Austrian subject territories, with the exception of northern Italy, which had been freed of this particular institution by the Napoleonic rule, and the peasants were subjected to the tyrannies of the local landowners as well as those of the centralized bureaucracy. Unlike France and England, these countries had as yet no large class of industrial workers, and the middle class was only just emerging into a condition of political consciousness, much retarded, in the small states at least, by the general economic dependence on princely and aristocratic patronage. Nevertheless, the opening of communications and extensions of commerce with the outside world, as well as the emergence of an industrial revolution in parts of Germany, were welding the bourgeoisie into a conscious class, of whom the more prosperous were feeling the manifold disadvantages of the division of Germany into thirty principalities, with as many frontiers, customs barriers, and codes of local law, and were beginning to join the liberals in their demands for a united democratic Germany.

The first, and also the most bitterly fought revolution of 1848, was that which began in Italy in January of that year. The Italian revolutionary movement was essentially and predominantly nationalist. The middle classes were opposed to the separatist ideas of the various princes, who were concerned mostly with their own immediate local or dynastic interests. Having enjoyed a temporary unity under the Napoleonic government, the Italian bourgeoisie were not slow to see that, however irksome that dictatorship may have been, it gave them more commercial opportunities than the return to eighteenth-century conditions. They looked to the unity of Italy in a bourgeois democracy. Some, like Mazzini and Manin, wanted a republic, but the majority of the Italian liberals would have been content with a kingdom, and they looked towards Charles Albert of Savoy, the

King of Piedmont, as the possible future king of a united Italy. Generally speaking, in the early part of the nineteenth century, there was a remarkable unity among Italians of all classes in their desire to get rid of native rulers as well as foreign oppressors, so heavily did the yoke of Austrian police tyranny, Papal obscurantism, and the cruelty and corruption of the petty kings and princes weigh upon burgess, peasant, and artisan alike. Thus the risings of towns and districts often showed an amazing unanimity, aristocrats, tradesmen, workers, farmers, and even priests and monks playing their part in the movement for a revolution that would free them from the intolerable oppression and corruption they had to endure.

The prelude to the risings of 1848 came when Gregory, one of the illiberal Popes, died and, owing to the dissensions within the College of Cardinals, the timid Pius IX, Pio Nono, was elected. Pius was not wholly hostile to the liberal cause in Rome, and the month after his election he conceded a partial political amnesty, and granted permission to form a civic guard in the city of Rome. From that time onwards Pio Nono became, like Charles Albert, an unwilling figurehead of the Italian revolutionary movement. He was regarded as a liberal opponent of the Austrians, which he certainly was not, and his minor concessions gave a great impetus to the movement for constitutional government and Italian unity, and helped to prepare the way for the risings of 1848.

Significantly, the first risings took place, in January, 1848, in Milan and Palermo, the former city in the center of the provinces subjected to the hated Austrian rule, the latter in the most disaffected part of the dominions of the King of Naples.

Neither of these risings was immediately successful, but they were followed by riots in all the principal cities, and during February the leading sovereign princes of Italy, the Pope, the King of Naples, and the Grand Duke of Tuscany yielded in terror to the demands of their peoples, and promised constitutions.

The revolutionary initiative now passed to France. The political trickery and attempts at absolute rule of Louis Philippe and his minister Guizot, the French Metternich, the corruption that permeated the whole administration and more or less sold France to the big financiers who supported the Orleanist cause, the restricted suffrage which gave participation in the Government to a very tiny minority of the population, all combined, by the end of 1847, to produce a widespread movement for constitutional reform, and the opposition to the inept rule of Louis Philippe spread to all classes, even including the big financiers, who were being hit by the economic crisis, which during 1847 and the early part of 1848, caused very wide distress, particularly among the industrial workers, many thousands of whom were unemployed in all the large towns.

Guizot and his fellow ministers promised reform and then went back on their word; in the end the disgust with their maneuvres was so great that a general demand arose in Paris for the dissolution of the Government. The ministerial majority in the Assembly dwindled until it was only preserved by the fact that many seats were held by government functionaries.

The final clash came over an apparently minor issue, as is often the case in revolutionary upheavals. The Liberals, led by Odilon Barrot and Thiers, had adopted as a propaganda device the idea of holding political banquets throughout the country, at which they hoped, by the numbers of their supporters, to impress the few electors into returning a vote hostile to the Government.

The increasingly general discontent, and the apparent success of the Liberal campaign, led the King and his advisers into an act of panic which provoked a wholly unexpected resistance. A great banquet in Paris was announced for February 22nd, and the Government decided to forbid it. Much feeling was aroused over this question, and on the appointed day the people of Paris came out into the streets to display their solidarity with the cause of reform. The Liberal leaders did not hold their banquet, but the barricades began to rise in the working-class streets. Before this popular indignation the King agreed to dismiss his ministry, and it is possible that the whole affair might have ended in a change of government and some mild electoral reforms, if a party of regular soldiers had not fired on a crowd of demonstrators and killed a number of them. All Paris rose in protest; barricades were erected in every quarter, and the workers, led by the moderate socialists like Ledru-Rollin and Louis Blanc, as well as by such extremists as Blanqui and Barbés, joined the bourgeois National Guard in a general uprising. The regular soldiers were mostly sympathetic towards the insurrection, and made no important resistance. Within two days the King abdicated and the revolutionaries invaded the Chamber of Deputies to demand a Republican Provisional Government. In the Chamber Lamartine, one of the Republicans, announced a list of Liberal members to form the new Administration, while at the offices of the revolutionary paper, *La Réforme*, another list was drawn up, consisting of Socialist politicians, and even one worker, Albert, while the Socialists seized the Prefecture of Police and the Post Office. Eventually a compromise was reached by the combination of the two lists. But the final result was a government with a right-wing Republican majority, and this fact was in due course to affect profoundly the course of events in the 1848 revolution in France.

At first there was almost complete unity among the revolutionaries, and in the early days the workers exercised a quite considerable influence, partly through the Socialist representatives in the Government, but more significantly through the innumerable revolutionary clubs which, under the leadership of men like Blanqui, Barbés, Cabet, and Raspail, carried on the various Socialist ideals of Baboeuf, Saint-Simon, Fourier, and Louis Blanc, and gave focus to the revolutionary aspirations of the people. Most of the working-class demonstrations during 1848 in Paris sprang at least partly from the discussions of the clubs, yet it is significant that, with the exception of Blanqui, most of the club leaders lost their influence in the years following the failures of 1848, and more influence was eventually wielded by a man who had never sought to set himself up as a group leader, P.-J. Proudhon, the most energetic and independent political journalist of 1848.

The Provisional Government immediately set out to conciliate the workers by a number of reforms. A ten-hour working day was decreed, and a somewhat vague "recognition of the Right to Work" was propounded. Undercutting of wages rates by prisons, convents, and other institutions was forbidden, and the community accepted responsibility for industrial accidents, the Tuileries being set aside as a hospital for this purpose. Sub-contracting was abolished, and the old trade guilds were replaced by organizations of workers and employers for conciliation purposes.

But these mild reforms were overshadowed by the initiatives of the workers themselves. They had at first demanded a Ministry of Labor; this was refused by Lamartine and the other Republicans in the Government, but, through the intervention of Blanc and Albert, a "Commission for the Workers" was set up at the Luxembourg. Delegates were elected by each trade, and a kind of Soviet of three or four hundred members assembled, providing, for a time at least, a center for working-class industrial activity of a radical nature, as opposed to the purely political aims and methods of most of the clubs, with their doctrinaire leaders and orators. By intervening to support strikers, the Luxembourg Commission managed to obtain minimum-wage rates in a number of industries. It encouraged the formation of trade unions among the workers, and also the very wide movement of voluntary co-operatives of producers, which sprang up in many Paris trades. Finally, it issued programs calling somewhat vaguely for the replacement of capitalist control of industry by a kind of mutualist Socialism, and encouraged workers to offer themselves as candidates in the elections for the Assembly.

Undoubtedly the vigor and power of this organization aroused much disquiet and jealousy among the bourgeois members of the Government. The reactionaries began to gather in order to combat what they justly regarded as this new threat to their interests, while early in March the right-wing members of the Government set up a scheme to counter the influence of the Luxembourg Commission by regimenting the unemployed into National Workshops, where they were drilled into a force which the Government hoped might be used against the independent and more militant workers grouped around the Luxembourg Commission. Once, indeed, the workers of the *Ateliers Nationaux* helped to break up a popular demonstration organized by the workers of the Luxembourg, but later, in the June days, they were to join very actively in the rising against the Government.

As an additional means of countering the influence of the Socialist revolutionaries, Lamartine formed, from the youths who had taken a somewhat hooligan part in the February Revolution, a kind of Janissary corps, the *Garde Mobile*, who were paid, drilled, and disciplined to counter popular demonstrations or risings of the type by which he himself had come to power. This corps was to have a somewhat sinister place in French social history, and even today remains the most unpopular body in a country where nobody likes the police. Thus already, after the first few days of enthusiastic brotherhood in the February revolution, that clash of forces which later brought a sorry end to the revolution was already becoming evident.

Meanwhile, however, the news of the Paris revolution had an electric effect on the radical movements in the rest of Europe. The French revolutionaries maintained an internationalism, merely theoretical in the case of the middle-class liberals, but practical in the case of the more extreme Jacobins and Socialists. Lamartine, as Minister of Foreign Affairs, issued a manifesto to the other countries of Europe, which was guardedly internationalist, while at the same time showing a nationalist trend by denouncing the clauses of the 1815 treaty. But in practice the Provisional Government took a very cautious attitude, and Lamartine gave nothing more than fraternal phrases to the many deputations of European revolutionaries who came to petition him. Paris was full of foreign political refugees, and the revolution brought others flowing into this left-wing Mecca. Although small expeditions of refugees were organized in France and crossed the frontiers into Italy, Germany, and Belgium, they were not assisted in any material way by the Provisional Government, and their own plans were even frustrated by its acts. Only in the case of occasional individual agitators, like Bakunin, was any assistance given, and that was usually done secretly and in order to get rid of an embarrassingly subversive person.

However, although the French Republic never gave any material encouragement to insurrections abroad, the example of the February rising had a really stimulating effect throughout Europe between the Pyrenees and the frontiers of Russia. In Germany the discontent of the middle class began to manifest itself in action. In Italy the existing revolutionary movements were impelled to really desperate activity.

The previous year had already seen a stirring of organized opposition to the various German governments. In the Rhineland there were small groups of Socialists and Communists, among whom Marx was already prominent as the editor of the *Neue Rheinische Zeitung*. But Marx and his associates played a very minor part in the revolutionary movements of 1848, which were essentially liberal and Pan-German in character. The German revolutionaries were divided into Moderate and Republican camps. The Moderates, led by von Gagern and Mathy, aimed merely at a federation of the German States which would not interfere with the sovereignty of the existing dynasties, and some kind of democratization of their individual governments. The Republicans, led by Hecker and Struve, who had held a conference at Offenburg in November 1847 put forward a more radical but essentially similar program. They asked for a German parliament elected by universal suffrage, for freedom of Press and conscience, for trial by jury and a graduated income tax, for the responsibility of ministers and the abolition of privileges. To these demands they added a number of aspirations so imprecise as to be virtually meaningless, such as "Comfort, education and instruction for all," "Protection of labor and the right to work," and "Adjustment of the relations between capital and labor." Their chief characteristic was a certain swashbuckling wordiness, but for all practical purposes their program was essentially a liberal one of the most cautious kind.

These groups had succeeded in organizing very little really effective resistance, and it may be doubted whether, without the impetus of the Paris rebellion, they would have gone far beyond vague discussion and fruitless resolutions.

But the news from Paris stirred them into action. On February 27th, von Gagern, leader of the Moderates, brought forward a resolution in the Darmstadt Chamber for a German National Parliament. Mathy persuaded the Grand Duke of Baden to grant a democratic constitution, and the rest of the smaller princes followed suit. The mood of the German people was still so cautious that these moves effectively forestalled the Republicans.

But the really great events in the German revolution were to come later in the month. On March 13th in Vienna, the very stronghold of the Empire, the people — burgesses, students, and workers together — rose and overturned the seemingly undefeatable régime of Metternich. That statesman went into exile for ever, remarking to his wife, "Yes, my dear, we are dead." The Emperor conceded the people's demands for constitutional government. A National Guard was formed, and on the day after the revolution the great censorship machine of the Empire was destroyed, while the Diet was summoned to meet shortly.

From Vienna the revolt spread to the other great stronghold of German reaction, and on March 18th the barricades went up in Berlin, the troops retired from the city, and the King made haste to submit to the demands of the revolutionaries. The Prince of Prussia, who was regarded with hatred by the population, fled to join Louis Philippe and Metternich in comparatively untroubled England, and the King granted the usual constitutional demands and a political amnesty, while a Liberal ministry was installed under Camphausen. On March 20th the King of Bavaria abdicated and Lola Montez fled from Germany; the first stage of the German revolution, so far as it went, was complete. The customary democratic freedoms and safeguards had been granted, the burden of feudalism was removed from the peasants, and German unity seemed to be carried a step nearer by the meeting on March 31st of the Vorparliament from the Estates of the various principalities. This body decided to convoke a National Assembly, based on universal suffrage, which it was expected would become the federal organ of the German nation, with the power to over-ride the will of princes, whether large or small.

In Italy the Paris revolution gave the impetus to a new wave of resistance. On March 10th, after wild demonstrations in the streets of Rome, the Pope granted a constitution and called in a government where churchmen were no longer preponderant. A few days later, when the news of the Vienna revolution reached Italy, the people of Milan rose in arms, and, after five days of very bitter fighting, drove the Austrians back to Verona. Venice rose on March 23rd, declaring a republic and taking possession of the Austrian arsenal and navy in their city. Willing to gain what he could from a unification of Italy, fearful of insurrection among his own subjects, and anxious to avoid trouble with the neighboring revolutionaries in France, Charles Albert of Piedmont declared war on Austria and sent his army into Lombardy. Forced on by the demands of their subjects, even the Pope and the King of Naples sent expeditions to help the Piedmontese, though both of them later went back on their word, as soon as it seemed convenient to accept Austrian influence in preference to the revolutionary tendencies among their own people.

Meanwhile, even England had its revolutionary movement, though it assumed a somewhat farcical character. Chartism had been moribund for six years, since the failure of the Petition of 1842, but the news of the rising in Paris stirred up the remaining Chartists to new activity, and the existence of a certain amount of economic distress led the people in many parts of the country to express their discontent in riots and demonstrations, which reached very formidable proportions in Glasgow and Edinburgh. A new Convention was called, in order to present a further petition, and the creation of a revolutionary National Assembly was even proposed. But popular support for the Chartists had shrunk more than either their leaders or the Government imagined.

A great demonstration to present the petition was planned for April 10th, and the authorities, with their minds full of the examples of Paris, Vienna, Berlin, and Rome, made elaborate and frightened precautions, calling many troops into London and recruiting from among the wealthier classes a great mass of special constables for duty on the day of the demonstration, among whom was Prince Louis Napoleon, very soon to become the final destroyer of the achievements of 1848 in France.

The demonstration, however, proved a complete fiasco. A small crowd gathered to hear the speeches, and the procession allowed itself to be halted by the cordons of police and troops at the Thames bridges. The day reached a silly conclusion, when the petition was delivered to the Houses of Parliament in three hansom cabs and was found on examination to contain less than two million names instead of the five or six million boasted by the Chartist leaders. Moveover, many of the signatures were clearly bogus, since, it appeared, Queen Victoria and the Duke of Wellington were both signatories, the latter no less than seventeen times!

Thus the English revolutionary movement ended in an ignominious atmosphere of bathos and hoax, and the Government had no difficulty at all in suppressing the few physical-force Chartists who still tried to arm and drill themselves for an insurrection.

Similarly, the Young Ireland movement received an illusory impetus from the February rising, with almost as poor a conclusion as that of the Chartist movement. There was a great deal of revolutionary talk, and the various nationalist newspapers published inflammatory articles calling for armed rebellion against the alien masters, and giving detailed instructions in the technique of insurrection and the manufacture of weapons and explosives. But the Irish population was as yet unprepared to give adequate support to a revolutionary movement. In June the most active of the revolutionary leaders, Mitchel, was arrested, and the movement soon collapsed, the remaining rebels

of any importance being picked off by the authorities and transport-
ed. A few isolated riots and armed clashes took place, but these were
completely frustrated by the weakness of the leaders, who preached
fiery revolution but were, in general, too scared to carry it out or
encourage it in others.

The revolutionary impetus in Europe was of no long duration, and
within two months it became evident that the upper middle class,
having installed themselves in power, were unwilling that the revolutionary movements should go any further, and were not averse, in
order to gain this end, from allying themselves with those remaining
reactionaries who were not yet completely discredited.

Already, in France, a demonstration of the Left, led by Blanqui
and other club orators, was dispersed because Louis Blanc, the veteran Socialist, intervened on the side of "order" and persuaded the
majority of the demonstrators to go home in peace. Blanc's right-
wing associates regarded this as a triumph for their ends, and a fort-
night later they issued a document, the *Piece Tascherau*, which purported to show that Blanqui had given information on subversive
movements to the Orleanist police. If one considers Blanqui's inflex-
ible character, as demonstrated in his single-minded and almost reli-
giously fanatical career of conspiracy and repeated imprisonments, it
is difficult to believe that this paper was anything other than a
forgery, particularly as no evidence has been produced in corrobora-
tion. But it had the desired effect of alienating many revolutionaries
from the individual whom the Liberals feared most, and this effect
was assisted by the personal animosity which existed within the revolutionary ranks between Blanqui and the equally influential Barbés,
his former friend.

The early part of April was devoted to a systematic propaganda
against the revolutionary Left. The middle-class elements were consolidated, the working-class "fifth column" was fostered in the
National Workshops and the Garde Mobile. By the middle of April
the revolutionary tide in France had definitely turned. On the 16th

of that month the workers' delegates of the Luxembourg organized a large but very peaceful demonstration to the Hotel de Ville. The authorities called on the National Guard and the men from the National Workshops, who appeared in large numbers and broke up the demonstration shouting slogans against the "Communists." Another veteran Socialist leader, Ledru-Rollin, told the deputation which waited on him to go home and cause no more trouble, and thus, like his associate Louis Blanc, played his part in frustrating the movement which he himself claimed to lead.

A few days later the elections took place, and the Right secured a large majority of the seats, particularly in the peasant districts. The Party of Order, a heterogeneous combination of royalists and conservative republicans, gained the ascendancy, and they were not slow to pursue their advantage. When the workers of Rouen held a demonstration four days later to complain of the manipulation of the polls, the National Guards shot them down. The Parisian revolutionaries were incensed by this act, but the new Assembly went so far as to elect as its own vice-president the officer responsible for the massacre. It was furthermore decreed that no more petitions should be presented.

The Parisian workers were disgusted at the trend which events were taking, and, after the Luxembourg Commission had held its last meeting on May 13th, they began to think of open demonstrations of their discontent. Two days later, the clubs organized a demonstration, ostensibly to present a petition for aid to Poland, but really to make a show of strength in the Paris streets in defiance of the Assembly's ban. After invading the Chamber and proclaiming its dissolution, the demonstrators went back to the Hotel de Ville, where they elected a new Provisional Government. The various versions of the list included the names of all the leading figures who stood in opposition to the Assembly, such as Blanqui, Barbés, Caussidière, Flocon, Ledru-Rollin, Proudhon, Cabet, Raspail, and Louis Blanc, but it is unlikely that all of these willingly allowed their names to be used, particularly as Louis Blanc and Ledru-Rollin still tried their best to compromise with the Right, while Proudhon always held himself aloof from the leaders of the clubs, whose names made up the list. The Provisional Government was short-lived, for Lamartine and his associates called out the bourgeois National Guard, who dispersed the unarmed demonstrators and arrested their leaders. Caussidière, head of the Paris police, and Courtois, general of the National Guard, were dismissed because they did not attack the demonstrators.

The conflict between the two sections into which the movement of February had split now became more intense than ever. The Assembly, thinking that it had completely consolidated its ground and, by arresting the club leaders, eliminated the possibility of any further rising, proceeded to attack the National Workshops, which it was felt had served the purpose intended by Lamartine and his associates and could now be regarded as a mere waste of money. On May 24th, Trélat drew up instructions that all workers who refused to join the armed forces or to take work with an outside employer should be dismissed from the workshops. Emile Thomas, the director of the workshops and himself an enemy of the Socialists, protested against the folly of such a decree, but he was silenced by the simple device of kidnapping and transporting him secretly to Bordeaux. After a month's delay the decree was finally issued, with additional provisions abolishing the bureau for giving assistance to the needy and the medical service for workers.

Naturally, the workers who had fought for the revolution in February were not likely to accept such an attack on their livelihood without any protest, and on June 22nd a deputation of them waited on the Government. They received threats in answer, and returned to the working-class areas to prepare for insurrection. By next morning the barricades had risen all over the eastern part of Paris, and the workers, without any leader, had begun the fiercest struggle up to that time in the revolutionary history of France.

Cavaignac, the commander of the Government forces, had withdrawn his troops from the disaffected quarters, with the deliberate intention of allowing the insurrection to grow to its greatest proportions in order to crush completely and finally the revolutionary Left. He then mounted an irresistible attack with large contingents of the Army, as well as the National Guard and the Garde Mobile. The struggle lasted four days, and the workers fought by themselves, with no allies among the middle classes or even among the Socialist leaders, most of whom were in prison or, like Louis Blanc, had no great desire to become too actively involved in real revolutionary struggle. A hostile French historian, de la Gorce, has said of the insurrectionaries:

> To whatever side we turn we find no general direction. The engineers of La Chapelle, who were hidden in the Clos St Lazare, the brigadiers of the National Workshops, who could be seen behind the barricades in the Faubourg St Antoine with their cards in their hats and their ribbons in their buttonholes, the old Montagnards, assembled in the Faubourg du Temple or the Faubourg Saint-Jacques, a few deluded old soldiers who loaded the weapons of the least experienced insurgents and commanded the firing on the troops — these were the leaders of sedition, subordinate and unknown leaders, selected for the most part by chance — yet not therefore contemptible, since, unlike more famous demagogues, they had the merit of knowing how to die.

The slaughter was enormous, and the brutality with which the victors acted was extremely savage, prisoners being shot in batches without trial or examination. The Socialist revolution was defeated, and it would be many years before the working class again played any significant part in French affairs. The Assembly could return in peace to its work of undoing the achievements of February.

The June days represented a major setback to revolutionary aims throughout Europe. Everywhere the more conservative elements began to take the lead. In Germany the princes and their ministers gained confidence; in Italy such reactionaries as the King of Naples began to resume their despotic power and to revoke the constitutions they had granted when the popular uprisings first made them retreat in panic. The most significant effect was that, after June, the European revolution began to lose its social character and to become more nationalist. The nationalist revolutions in Hungary and Italy survived for more than a year after the Paris revolution, with its social basis, had virtually ended.

From June onwards the interest shifts almost wholly to the Austrian Empire and its spheres of influence — Germany, Italy, and Hungary — and becomes increasingly centered on the attempt by the Emperor and the petty despots of Germany and Italy to regain the power which they had lost in the fall of Metternich.

The radical movement in Germany began to decline as soon as the inspiration of Paris was removed. In April Hecker had made another rising in Baden, but was again defeated, and in May there had been demonstrations in Vienna which forced the Emperor to promise a constitution and depart to the safety of Innsbruck. But when the Frankfurt Assembly finally met on May 18th, its conservative character soon became evident, and this was confirmed when the Archduke John of Austria was elected Regent of the German empire. Very soon the Frankfurt Assembly was encouraging nationalist aggressions against the Danes, and supporting the Emperor in his campaigns against the Italians, the Hungarians, and the Slavs. During its whole life, this Assembly devoted itself to wordy discussion and achieved almost nothing; when at last, in March 1849, it awoke and announced its constitution to be the law of Germany, the gesture was many months too late, and its Rump, deprived of the conservative majority, died uselessly on its ignominious expulsion from Wurtemberg in June 1849. Nevertheless, while in itself the Assembly was almost completely useless, it has some historical significance as a precursor of the later movements for a united Germany which ended in the hegemony of Prussia — an event anticipated by the Assembly when it offered the crown of Germany to the Hohenzollerns.

The various subject races of the Austrian empire were late in joining the revolutionary movement, and their role was for the most part reactionary in its effect. In Hungary, as we have said, the revolution remained in the hands of the landowners and the upper middle class, and it was to a Diet of noblemen that the Emperor granted a constitution after the March rising in Vienna had made him feel insecure enough to wish to placate any potential ally. And, for the time being at least, this act stood him in good stead, since during its early days the Hungarian movement remained monarchical and the Republican agitation of men like Perczel had little effect. Indeed, so loyal were the Hungarians to the Emperor, and so little were they willing to understand other peoples who fought for national freedom, that in June, 1848, they actually sent an army to assist in subjugating Lombardy and Venetia.

The acquisition of partial autonomy only increased the nationalist tendencies of the Magyars, and made their rule more intolerable to the Serbs, Croats, and Roumanians included within their territories. In May 1848, there was a general rising of these peoples, of a racial rather than a social character, and for the rest of its existence independent Hungary was beset by revolutions among its subject peoples which might have been placated by a less haughty treatment on the part of the ruling race. But, as it was, the Slavs and Roumanians, incensed by the treatment they received, allowed themselves to be used as tools by the Austrian Government, which maintained a pretence of impartiality towards the differences between the Hungarians and their subjects, but which in fact secretly encouraged all these races, and particularly the Croats, in their rebellion.

The Slavs, in fact, play an unhappy part in the history of the European revolution. There was, indeed, one genuine Slav movement of revolt against the Austrian Government, when, on June 15th, the morrow of a Pan-Slav conference, the people of Prague, supported by a number of Polish and Russian revolutionaries, including Bakunin, who happened to have reached that city during

his travels, rose and drove out the Austrian troops. But the revolt
was soon crushed, and from that time the Slav movements fell into
the hands of bourgeois nationalists who were willing to play the
Emperor's game of divide-and-rule, in the hope of gaining some kind
of autonomy, which, in fact, they never achieved.

During the late summer of 1848 the Emperor began to feel suf-
ficiently confident to return to autocratic methods, so much did
events appear to have turned to his advantage. On August 5th Milan
had fallen and Charles Albert had withdrawn his forces to Piedmont,
leaving the Venetian Republic as the only unconquered part of
Northern Italy. Less than three weeks later a clash between the
National Guard and the unemployed workers in Vienna had shown
that the Austrian revolutionary movement was suffering from a similar division to that which had destroyed the revolution in Paris. In
September, the Croats, with the tacit approval of the Emperor, began
to advance into Hungary, and on October 3rd Ferdinand announced
the annulment of the Hungarian constitution and appointed
Jellachich, Ban of Croatia, the military ruler of Hungary, a calculated
insult to the pride of the Magyar aristocracy, who had always regarded the Croats as an inferior race. Austrian troops began to assemble
for the expedition against Hungary.

But Ferdinand had calculated without one factor, the citizens of
Vienna, who stand out in the history of 1848 as the only people who
were willing to sacrifice themselves for the freedom of another revolution. On October 6th the workers and students rose, the Minister
of War was hanged from a lamp post, and the Emperor fled in terror.
But the next day Windischgrätz began to collect an army of Slavs, and
by October 23rd he had surrounded the city. The Hungarians made a
half-hearted attempt to relieve the Viennese, but were defeated outside the walls, and there followed a general assault on the rebel garrison, which was terminated by the fall of Vienna on November 1st and
the end of the Austrian revolution. Austria returned to its autocratic
government, and, after Ferdinand's abdication in December and the
accession of Francis Joseph to the imperial throne, the Diet, which

had maintained a nominal existence for some months, was dissolved in March 1849, and Austria retired temporarily from German affairs. Nevertheless, the revolution had not been wholly fruitless, for, unlike the German States, the Austrian authorities made no attempt to re-impose feudalism on the peasants.

At the same time, the current of events led the King of Prussia to adopt a changed attitude towards the Assembly to which he had previously deferred, and, supported by the Liberals who had climbed to office in the revolution earlier in the year, he decided to dissolve this institution. The members of the Assembly made a show of resistance, but, when Wrangel's troops appeared before Berlin, they were allowed to enter the city without hindrance, and the Assembly was finally dispersed, its members recommending a campaign of non-payment of taxes which met little response.

The revolution was in full retreat, for the following month Louis Napoleon, after a demagogic campaign aided by the excesses of the Royalists and the right-wing conservatives, became President of France, supported largely by the votes of French workers who had lost trust in Socialists like Ledru-Rollin and who mistakenly thought that by voting for Napoleon they were avenging themselves on Cavaignac and the Right. In this, as in many other points, the career of Napoleon resembled those of the modern dictators.

The early part of 1849 saw a new reversal of fortunes for the Austrian Empire. From January to March the Imperial armies fighting in Hungary met with continual defeats, while new insurrections broke out in Italy. On February 6th the people of Tuscany rose, and, after the flight of the Grand Duke, proclaimed a republic. Three days later there was a rebellion in Rome, the Pope fled to Neapolitan territory, and the Republic was founded. The Roman rising was somewhat different from the previous insurrections, since it was inspired by Mazzini, the great idealist of the Italian revolution, who had never before enjoyed the chance of putting his ideas into practice. Mazzini was not a socialist, but he strongly opposed large-scale capitalism and landlordism, and his movement had such deep roots in the working class that in later years he was a serious rival of Marx and Bakunin for influence in the International. During the six months of the Roman Republic, Mazzini's disinterested administration and Garibaldi's dashing defensive tactics brought about a unity among the Roman people which was only equalled by that of the sister republic of Venice.

The events in Tuscany and Rome led Charles Albert of Piedmont to decide that if he wished to retain any influence in Italy he must act quickly, and on March 12th he again declared war on Austria and advanced into Lombardy.

The new insurrections in Italy and the successes of the Magyar armies in Hungary and Transylvania led the Emperor of Austria to the desperate measure of calling in the assistance of his fellow autocrat, the Tsar of Russia, to re-establish the integrity of his Empire. This signaled the beginning of a really concerted attack by the new alliance of autocrats and the upper bourgeoisie on the remnants of the revolutionary achievements in Europe. The Austrians, assisted by the Russians in Hungary, were enabled to defeat the Piedmontese at Novara and thus suppress once again the revolution in Lombardy. Meanwhile, the French sent an expedition to Italy. Nominally, this was to assist the Roman Republic and halt the southward march of the Austrian troops, but in fact it represented a move against the Republic, and this was made clear by General Oudinot's aggressive actions. De Lesseps was sent to enquire into complaints concerning Oudinot's conduct, but, when an even more reactionary Assembly was elected on May 29th, de Lesseps was recalled and Oudinot's role in Italy became clear. After desperate fighting in the outskirts of Rome, the French army entered the city on July 3rd, and on the 15th of that month the Papal Government returned to Rome. The French Republic had destroyed the Roman Republic and installed an autocrat in its place.

Encouraged by the general tendency, the princes of Germany began to attack what remained of the revolution in their territories. On April 12th, as I have already mentioned, the Frankfurt Assembly performed its one act of real defiance by declaring its constitution to be the law of Germany. The Chambers of Prussia, Hanover, and Saxony decided to uphold this decision, and were immediately dissolved by their respective rulers, the King of Prussia calling on all the States to revise in an autocratic direction the constitutions which had been granted during the risings in the previous year. The German upper bourgeoisie had already consolidated their position as allies of the old aristocracy, and it was left for the petty bourgeoisie to make what resistance they could. In April there were risings in the Rhineland and Saxony, both of which were crushed by Prussian troops. Dresden put up a stubborn defence, among the fighters being Richard Wagner and, once again, Bakunin, who was arrested here and began his decade of rigorous imprisonment in the dungeons of Saxony, Austria, and Russia. Dresden fell on May 9th, and the next day there began a revolt in Baden and the Palatinate. A Republic was declared in these provinces, and for more than two months the rebels resisted; it was the first time that any really effective resistance had been made to reaction in Germany, but it also failed when the last citadel of Rastatt fell on July 23rd, and the German revolution was at an end.

The months of August and September saw the two desperate last stands of the 1848-49 revolutionaries. The first was in Italy. After the revolutions in every other part of that country had been crushed, the Republic of Venice continued to fight on, maintaining, under the leadership of a Jewish lawyer, Daniele Manin, a great unity of classes in the struggle to retain its ancient independence. Cut off from the rest of Italy and from any hope of assistance from outside, the Venetians resisted until it was no longer physically possible, until the last day's food had been eaten, the last ammunition had been consumed, and cholera had reached epidemic proportions. No city showed such an unanimous desire to maintain its essential liberties as did Venice throughout the whole period of the 1848-49 revolution; it seemed as if the spirit of the medieval free cities had been here re-born and brought to a late flowering.

If Venice represented the last stand of the democrats in 1848, in Hungary the nationalist aristocracy carried on for a month longer. In April 1849, the Hungarians had finally declared their independence of the Austrian Emperor, and formed themselves into a Republic under the leadership of Louis Kossuth. The circumstance that led a revolution of landowners to abandon their dynastic loyalties had been what seemed to them the final treachery by which their King had called in a foreign autocrat to help in their suppression. For some months they carried on a great campaign of cavalry warfare, but in the end they were no match for the alliance of Austrians, Russians, Roumanians, Croats, and Serbs. Moreover, they were split by internal dissensions, since many of their leaders, including the commanding general, Görgei, found it hard to give up their monarchical ideas, and seem to have fought half-heartedly after Hungary became a republic. On August 11th the Provisional Government abdicated, and Kossuth fled the country, to enter on a life of picturesque exile in England. Two days later the main army, under Görgei, surrendered at Villagos, and the Austrian General Haynau, who had already made himself notorious for his barbarities in Lombardy, instituted a rigorous process of shooting and hanging. Isolated bands of Hungarians continued to carry on a hopeless struggle against their enemies, and it was not until September 26th, six weeks after the collapse of the main forces, a month after the capitulation of Venice, that the last stronghold of the revolutions of 1848-49, the Hungarian fortress of Komorn, fell to the Imperial armies.

The period of revolution was ended, and a new period of reaction began in Europe, with Napoleon III and Bismarck taking the places of Guizot and Metternich. Some of the political movements of 1848 were to achieve a partial though twisted fulfilment at the hands of these new autocrats. German unity was achieved in a subordination of the remaining provinces to Prussian hegemony, an end hardly desired by the original Pan-Germans. Slav unity was to become a

political weapon in the hands of the Russian Tsars. Italian nationalism resulted in a unification of Italy under the Piedmontese royal
house which did not accord with the original ambitions of Mazzini
and Garibaldi. Most of the demands of the Chartists were gained in
the ensuing century, but their attainment has not eliminated the need
for radical struggles in other fields.

But the actual insurrections of 1848 do not loom so large in our
vision today as the political and social tendencies which the revolution initiated. The movements of 1848, frustrated as they may have
been in their achievements, were accompanied by a crystallization of
the political ideas which were later to become foundations for important social movements. Here it is sufficient to sketch them briefly.

The appearance of Marxist Communism, as a clearly defined
political creed and the basis of a social movement, dates from 1848,
for Marx's *Communist Manifesto*, although it may have been written
late in 1847 and published a month before the outbreak of the Paris
rising, was essentially motivated by the same spirit of revolt as provoked the various European uprisings. Neither Marx personally nor
the *Communist Manifesto* had any great influence on the events of
1848; their time was to come in the following years when the workers had largely turned away from Jacobinism towards a more specifically working-class creed. Marx's influence was at first strongest
among the German workers, but even there it was shared by another
Socialist, who gave active sympathy to the risings of 1848, Ferdinand
Lassalle, the founder of the Social-Democratic movement in
Germany.

In the Latin and Slav countries the influence of Marx was late in
becoming evident, and here the characteristic movements of the latter half of the nineteenth century stemmed from the ideas of other
participants in the 1848 risings. In France the revolutionary movement subsequent to 1849 was divided mostly between the supporters of Blanqui, the founder of a species of extreme Babeuvism and
advocate of revolutionary dictatorship (he initiated the idea of the
"dictatorship of the proletariat") and those of Proudhon, who, as an

independent journalist, had subjected the events of 1848 to an acute criticism in his successive newspapers, all in their turn suppressed by the authorities. Proudhon denounced governmental institutions, and demanded the elimination of accumulated property. Under his influence a large mass of the French workers turned aside from political conspiracy into industrial organization, and Syndicalism owed much to his teaching. During the Paris Commune of 1871 the rebels were mostly divided between the followers of Blanqui and those of Proudhon, while in its early days the Proudhonians were as influential in the First International as the Marxists.

Proudhon was the first continental anarchist, but the creation of an organized anarchist movement, which later played a very great part in social unrest in Latin Europe, Russia, Bulgaria, and the United States, was undertaken by another active participant in the 1848 revolutions, Michael Bakunin. Although Bakunin had already absorbed Proudhon's ideas during 1848, his main preoccupation in these days was a kind of revolutionary pan-Slavism. When, however, he escaped to Europe after his decade of imprisonment, with his ideals of 1848 still unharmed, he entered the revolutionary movement of the 1860s as a declared anarchist, and led the strongest opposition to Marx in the International. This organization eventually split into Marxist and Anarchist wings, and the anarchists remained the most important group in Spain, as well as for many years playing an influential part in the French, Italian, Russian, and American working-class movements.

Another Russian whom 1848 set irrevocably on a revolutionary course was Alexander Herzen. A confirmed sceptic, and a very ironical observer of the shortcomings of the 1848 revolutionaries, Herzen almost unwillingly retained his ideals, and in the following decade founded a Russian emigré paper, *The Bell*, through which he wielded a greater influence than any other single person on the development of a Russian liberal and revolutionary movement against the Tsarist autocracy.

In Italy the influence of Mazzini was for some years very great in the revolutionary movement, but after the unification it gave place to the more definite social ideas of the socialists and anarchists.

In Ireland the farcical failure of 1848 prepared the way for a stronger nationalist movement, which, under the Fenians, brought a really effective opposition to the British rule. In England, with the discrediting of Chartism, the workers turned back to the Trade Union ideas which had been so influential in the 1830s and for a long period, except for the comparatively slight activities of the Christian Socialists, the discontent of the working class was directed into channels of industrial organization.

But, if the influences of 1848 are to be found in all the left-wing movements of today — in Socialism, Communism, Anarchism, Trade Unionism — they are also present among the Right. Napoleonic Caesarism sprang from 1848, and Louis Napoleon became the first of the modern dictators, by the use of methods which closely anticipated those of Hitler and Mussolini. The nationalist movements of 1848 found their perverted conclusion in Nazism and Fascism, the pan-Germans, in particular, being almost as violent as the Nazis in their denunciation of the inferior races and their desire to maintain the German hegemony over a whole range of subject peoples.

A century of crowded political events has passed since "the year of revolutions." Yet we still live under the influence of the happenings of that time, and still, in our own day, are witnessing the fulfilment, usually in an ironically perverted form, of the ideals for which the men of 1848 fought, often futilely, and never more than half-realizing the significance of their acts.

1948

2

Anarchism Revisited

There are still thousands of anarchists scattered thinly over many countries of the world. There are still anarchist groups and anarchist periodicals, anarchist schools and anarchist communities. But they form only the ghost of the historical anarchist movement, a ghost which inspires neither fear among governments nor hope among people nor even interest among newspapermen. Clearly, as a movement anarchism has failed. In almost a century of effort it has never even approached the fulfilment of its great aim to destroy the state and build Jerusalem in its ruins. During the past forty years the influence it once established has dwindled, by defeat after defeat and by the slow draining of hope, almost to nothing. Nor is there any reasonable likelihood of a renaissance of anarchism as we have known it since the foundation of the First International in 1864; history suggests that movements which fail to take the chances it offers them are never born again.

S o I wrote in 1961 in a book called *Anarchism* which was largely a reckoning with my own youth. For more than a decade, from the early 1940s to the early 1950s, I had served my radical time working with anarchist groups in Britain, France, the United

States; I was for a time an editor of the British anarchist papers *War Commentary* and *Freedom*; my *Now* was the main organ of the literary anarchists who gathered around Herbert Read and Alex Comfort during the 1940s; I contributed regularly to Dwight Macdonald's *Politics* when Dwight too considered himself an anarchist; I compiled a jejune manual of anarchist tenets, *Anarchy or Chaos*, as narrowly sectarian as a Trotskyite tract, which Kenneth Rexroth used as a text in his pre-beat gatherings of San Francisco poets during the late 1940s; I was considered unpleasant enough by the State Department to be refused an immigration visa in 1955, a good four years after I had abandoned any kind of connection with organized anarchism. Whether in the changed circumstances of the 1960s that ban still holds I cannot say. My pride has not let me test it again, and in any case I feel it is primarily the business of Americans if their regulations means that, alone among the frontiers of the world, a libertarian finds those of the United States and China closed against him.

During that decade of activity in the dwindling rump of the historic anarchist movement, I received a sustained exposure to the ideas of a series of libertarian thinkers, from seventeenth-century Gerard Winstanley through William Godwin and Pierre-Joseph Proudhon down to Georges Sorel and Peter Kropotkin, which I have found a lasting gain; I received also an education in the history of the labor movement somewhat different from that of the average Old Leftist, since it was sharply critical of Marx, and this I have found invaluable in assessing reactionary developments in socialist and communist countries, which seem to surprise others far more than they do me; I met some intelligent people, of whom a few were charming and one was beautiful, and some of them are still my friends.

But I also lived at that time in the atmosphere of dense and parochial fanaticism which is characteristic of the remnants of dying movements. I watched bitter factional feuds over minor points of anarcho-syndicalist doctrine which history had in any case made irrelevant; I even took part in them. I witnessed, with a horrified excitement, one group of English anarchists turning bandit and carrying out an armed raid to raise funds; the victims were not wicked capitalists, but other anarchists with whom the raiders had quarrelled over the ownership of a printing press, and whose code of honor they knew would not allow them to report the raid to the police. And I found myself agreeing more and more (against my will) with George Orwell, whom I met at this point and who — despite his own libertarian tendencies — pointed out the danger that anarchist intolerance might create a moral dictatorship which would imperil the very freedom for which anarchists claimed to fight. I knew already that within anarchist groups pressures to orthodoxy of belief existed; the more dedicated a militant, the more priggish and intolerant he was likely to be. I felt the infection touching me, knew it would probably ruin me as a writer, and stepped aside to become a free-wheeling radical of my own kind. I have never been forgiven, particularly by those who fawned most upon me when I was a young and promising writer who also appeared to be a true believer. But that is nothing exceptional; it is the experience of all intellectuals who became involved, in whatever direction, with the sects of the Old Left.

The distinction I have emphasized — between what I gained positively from studying the writers and the history of the generative period of anarchism, and what I wasted in time and energy (though perhaps not finally in experience) by becoming too deeply involved with the conservators of a movement which had lost its relevance because it lost its constituency among the peasant and artisan masses of the Latin and Slav countries — is closely related to a point I made in *Anarchism*, where, after tolling a knell for old-line forms of anarchist organization, I went on to say:

Here of course we must distinguish between the historical anarchist movement that sprang from the efforts of Bakunin and his followers, and the anarchist idea which established it.

The idea, in various forms and under various names, was alive more than two centuries before the historical movement began, and since ideas are more durable than organizations and causes, it is possible that the theoretical core of anarchism may still have the power to give life to a new form under changed historical circumstances.

And later, as I moved into the last page of my book, I found "a purpose and a function" which anarchism may possess in the modern world:

If human values are to survive, a counter-ideal must be posed to the totalitarian goal of a uniform world, and that counter-ideal exists precisely in the vision of pure liberty that has inspired the anarchist and near-anarchist writers from Winstanley in the seventeenth century. Obviously, it is not immediately realizable, and since it is an ideal, it will probably never be realized. But the very presence of such a concept of pure liberty can help us to judge our condition and see our aims; it can help us to safeguard what liberties we still retain against the further encroachments of the centralizing state; it can help us to conserve and even enlarge those areas in which personal values still operate; it can help in the urgent task of mere survival, of living out the critical decades ahead until the movement of world centralization loses its impetus like all historical movements, and the moral forces that depend on individual choice and judgment can reassert themselves in the midst of its corruption.

Anarchism, published in 1962, has enjoyed a modest continuing popularity, with editions appearing in Italy, Sweden, now Japan, which I suspect has had as much to do with the fortunes of the doctrine it discusses as with the book's own merits. For anarchism, as a doctrine rather than as a movement, has had a revival during the last few years of the kind I thought possible. The old revolutionary sect has not been resurrected, but in its place has appeared a moral-political movement typical of the age. The development began about a year after my book appeared, but that particular link is accidental.

Let me begin with facts. One reached me only recently. A political science teacher in a Canadian university wrote me of the curious results of a quiz on political preferences which he had given to the one hundred and sixty students in his class on Contemporary Ideologies. Ninety of them chose anarchism in preference to democratic socialism (which came next with twenty-three votes), liberalism, communism, and conservatism. Most of the voters seemed as square as students run in the late 1960s; only a small minority were overt hippies or New Leftists.

That was a fact for December 1967. Part of its background was of course the unparalleled academic interest in anarchism during the past decade. Since 1960 more serious and dispassionate studies of anarchism have appeared than during the preceding sixty years of the century; apart from my own book, these have included James Joll's excellent *The Anarchists* (1965) and some very good paperback anthologies of key libertarian texts, of which the best is probably that edited by Irving Horowitz, which is also called *The Anarchists* (1964). The French have been somewhat ahead of us in this; Jean Maitron's definitive *Histoire du mouvement anarchiste en France* appeared in 1955, and the first excellent volume of the never-completed *Histoire de l'anarchie*, by Alain Sergent and Claude Harmel, in 1949.

The interest of historians is sometimes the equivalent of a death certificate. All is safely past and ended and can be entombed in books without the fear of a knock in the coffin. The interest of the press, on the other hand, is usually a sign of life in the subject, and during the past few years anarchism has been popping in and out of newspapers on both sides of the Atlantic because of the new role it has been playing as an element in contemporary youth movements.

I first became aware of this trend in 1963, when newspaper accounts began to reach me describing the Easter demonstrations in London, following on the annual Aldermaston march against nuclear armament. I read that behind the banner of the London anarchists five hundred young men and women marched twenty abreast. "The London anarchists came ringleted and bearded and pre-Raphaelite," enthused one reporter. "It was a frieze of non-conformists enviable in their youth and gaiety and personal freedom." In the 1940s the anarchists in London had not taken part in street demonstrations for fear of revealing the smallness of their numbers; we would have thought ourselves lucky to assemble fifty behind the tattered red-and-black which had been preserved from Spanish Civil War days, and half of these would have been veterans — now dead — who bored one with reminiscences of Kropotkin and Edward Carpenter. And nobody would have talked of us as enviable in our gaiety. The Old Left was solemn through and through. At parties we might take down our unringleted hair, but in public we were as earnest as any of the steel-toothed Trotskyites with whom we competed to sell a few dozen papers every Sunday at Marble Arch.

Perhaps, I began to think as I read of those hundreds of gay comrades, perhaps I had been rash in so officiously burying the historic anarchist movement. But this was in fact no knock in the coffin. The anarchists of the 1960s were not the historic anarchist movement resurrected; they were something quite different, a new manifestation of the idea.

The anarchists of the 1940s had been bellicose barricaders, dreaming inoffensively of the violent overthrow of the state, and identifying themselves with the great assassins like Ravachol and Emile Henry as a hearth cat might imagine himself a lion. Only a minority of us followed the pacifist revolutionary line and, provided we were allowed an occasional say in *Freedom*, we did not obtrude our point of view. The tradition of Bakunin and the syndicalist cult of romantic death still hung heavily over the movement; our yesterday was Spain.

In 1963, it was evident, things had changed. The new anarchists who marched ringleted and pre-Raphaelite had forgotten Spain and had no use for the old romanticism of the *dynamitero* and the *pétroleuse*. They were militant pacifists. They represented a trend which had appeared from outside Old Anarchism. It had come into being through radical protest drives against nuclear warfare like the Campaign for Nuclear Disarmament and the Committee of 100. Among the leaders of the Committee of 100, in particular, were older libertarians, unorthodox anarchists like Herbert Read, Alex Comfort, and the pacifist activist Laurie Hislam. Within the Committee and its groups of supporters grew up a philosophy of direct action and defiance of the state which created anarchists without traditions, and in the English provinces especially scores of small groups sprang up and maintained largely autonomous existences; their anarchism was pacifist in nature and concerned itself little with the dogmatic disputes of the past. Glancing through the announcement columns of *Freedom* in 1967, one realizes these groups are still numerous and widely scattered, representing many times the number of individual supporters the anarchists could muster twenty years ago.

One of the great sustaining influences on this youthful neo-anarchist movement in Britain has been the intellectual quarterly, *Anarchy*. *Anarchy* has kept a level higher than that of any anarchist magazine I know of since the French 1890s, escaping from old ideological disputes to discuss practical radical approaches to a great range of current problems; its contributors have included men as various and vital as Colin MacInnes, Alan Sillitoe, Alex Comfort, Paul Goodman, Maurice Cranston; it has been influential in the universities, where mushroom anarchist magazines have also been founded in many places by the students, usually going out of existence after a few issues, but giving expression in the meantime to the local form of the general ferment.

All this (hundreds of new anarchists marching through London, one good durable magazine, a lot of ephemeral ones) might seem to mean very little if Britain's reborn anarchism had not lost the holy isolationism of the past, and become allied with all the radical youth trends in present-day Britain, which it influences by its libertarian approach. Thirty years ago in Britain the leaders of the community were shocked when sons and daughters joined the Communists (the poet laureate among them, singing "Why do we all, seeing a Communist, feel small?"); today one is more likely to hear a sigh of resignation when young David or Sybil comes home to announce that he or she has become an anarchist. Mark the change. Becoming rather than joining. A change of heart rather than a party ticket. That is how the young tend to see their revolutionism, with a stress on feeling and faith that would have aroused derision among past ideologists.

Britain is not the only country where, in a loose way, the new anarchists maintain a link with the remnants of the Old Anarchist Left. In Holland the Provos, rebels against the welfare state who have stirred smug Amsterdam to the depths of its canals with their demonstrations, happenings, and occasional riots, are frankly anarchist in orientation, paying tribute to the Dutch pacifist anarchists of the past (Domela Nieuwenhuis and Bart de Ligt), and giving revolutionary doctrines a new twist so that the despair at ever attaining the libertarian paradise becomes in its own way a weapon, to be used in goading governments into showing their most brutal faces. The weak provoke; the strong unwillingly expend themselves. "Through provocation," says one Provo manifesto,

> we force authority to tear off its mask. Uniforms, boots, helmets, sabres, truncheons, firehoses, police dogs, tear gas, and all the other means of suppression they have lined up for us, must be produced. The authorities must be forced to rage, threatening us right and left, commanding, forbidding, condemning, convicting. They will become more and more unpopular and the popular spirit will ripen for revolution. A revolutionary feeling will once again be in the air: crisis.

A crisis of provoked authority.

Such is the gigantic provocation we call for from the International Proletariat.

In North America, in all the kaleidoscope of New Radical organizations, with names compounded of initials impossible to remember, there is no such obvious revival of anarchism as one finds in Britain and Holland. But only if one seeks explicit statements of anarchistic loyalties. In practice many observers regard anarchism as an important and central element in the pluralistic spectrum of New Radical thought. Probably the best study of the movement from the inside is Jack Newfield's *A Prophetic Minority* (1966), and Newfield has no hesitation at all in placing anarchism, with pacifism and socialism, as one of the three basic influences on the New Left. Sometimes the influence becomes a long but concentrated beam stretching across centuries; that of seventeenth-century Winstanley, for example, on the modern Diggers. In general, however, it is hard to find North American New Radicals who have read an anarchist classic as recent as Kropotkin's *Mutual Aid* or *Memoirs of a Revolutionist*, though many have read that surviving but untypical Old Anarchist, Paul Goodman. In general, the basic ideas of anarchism, like those of traditional socialism and pacifism, have come down to the New Radicals (that generation of voluntary semi-literates) not through direct reading, but in a kind of mental nutrient broth of remnants of the old ideologies which pervades the air of certain settings in New York, the Bay Area, Los Angeles, Vancouver, and Montreal. But the key tenets that have been on anarchist lips for generations are there: the rejection of the state, the abandonment of the comfortable in favor of the good life, direct action, decentralization, the primacy of the functional group, participation.

Where neo-anarchists — avowed or unavowed — flourish, one notices at least two important differences from the Old Anarchists in their heyday. The historic movement that died in Barcelona sprang from the poorest classes, the illiterate and wretched peasants of Andalusia and the Ukraine, the hard-run French and Lombard factory workers of the turn-of-the-century, the marble cutters of Carrara, dock-workers of Ancona, watch-makers of the Jura; a few aristocrats (Bakunin and Kropotkin), unfrocked parsons (Godwin and Nieuwenhuis), and working-class intellectuals (Proudhon and Weitling) were among their leaders; neo-Romantic painters and poets (Courbet and Pissarro and Signac, Octave Mirbeau and Oscar Wilde) skirmished on their flanks. Now the conscience-stricken noblemen and priests have been replaced by the conscience-stricken middle class, and these, with the vastly increased bohemian contingent, have almost completely displaced the old anarchist constituency of the peasants and the poor.

In 1962 the British anarchist magazine *Freedom* conducted a survey of the backgrounds of its readers. Out of four hundred and fifty seven who answered the questionnaire, forty were engaged in industry, but of these six were managers. Twenty-three worked on the land, but eight ran their own farms and holdings and one was an estate manager. Nineteen worked in communications and transport. And that — fifteen per cent when one had counted out the managers and owners — was about the total of those who belonged to the traditional groupings of workers and peasants. On the other hand, there were fifty-two teachers, thirty students, twenty architects, sixteen journalists and writers, twenty-three in the arts and entertainments, twelve in the book trade, twenty-five in scientific research and twenty-five in health and welfare; forty, finally, in various administrative and clerical posts. The preponderance of white-collar workers was striking. So was the predominance of youth. Anarchists in the 1940s included a high proportion of the elderly, but of this batch sixty-five per cent were under the age of forty, and if the count were taken again now it would show an even higher proportion. Even more significant was the stronger class shift among the young. Forty-five per cent of those over sixty were working-class, as against twenty-three per cent of those in their thirties and ten per cent of those in their twenties. The new anarchists in Britain — and this applies as much to the Provos in Holland and the New Radicals in the United States — are a movement of dissident middle-class youth.

The historic anarchist movement was strongest in countries which, apart from France, were technologically and socially backward and where authority took on a reactionary and half-feudal form. The new anarchism, on the other hand, is strongest in countries where the state has assumed a bland welfare face, and where its pervading influence on daily life rather than its brutality affronts the young.

Perhaps, in this situation, the failures of anarchism, splendid and comic as they have variously been, speak in its favor. Anarchism can claim, almost alone among modern ideologies, the equivocal merit of never having really been tried out. Not having come to power, it was never discredited in power, and in this sense it presents an untarnished image, the image of an idea which, in practical terms, has had nothing but a future. Success has not sullied it, and with the young in their present mood this is a unique and powerful advantage. "Flowers for the rebels who failed," the Old Anarchists used to sing. The flowers are descending on their successors.

Though its ideas were originally framed in situations totally different from those in which the young of today find themselves, anarchism — with its cult of the spontaneous — has always shown a strikingly Protean fluidity in adapting its approach and methods to special historical circumstances. Winstanley in Civil-War England concentrates on direct action to cultivate the wastelands; Godwin at the height of the Enlightenment interests himself in the spread of discussion groups; Proudhon works through the pioneer credit unions (his People's Banks); Bakunin's romantic insurrectionism is balanced by Kropotkin's scientific-sociological approach, from which arose some seminal insights on the relations between town and country, industry and agriculture; the tragically flamboyant gestures of the Terrorists in the 1890s gave place to the syndicalists' myth of the regenerative general strike; the Andalucian peasants in the early months of the Spanish Civil War set up communes of idyllic and altruistic simplicity. The means were always fluid, adapting to changing social norms, but always keeping close to the ground, to the ideal of a society deep at the roots, and always keeping away from ordinary politics, away from power.

None of these specific phases of the anarchist past seems to matter greatly to the New Anarchists; unlike their predecessors, they do not have the historic urge which loved to relive past battles and to dwell on what birds might lodge on the libertarian family tree between Zeno and Sir Herbert Read. What mainly concerns them in ideas is applicability to their own situation, and here anarchism certainly seems to have a great deal to give them.

Consider that situation. They are in full revolt against a society dominated by material goals, by established power. They are facing — perhaps more realistically than their elders — the great revolution which automation will wreak within a few years on our concepts of the dignity and necessity of toil; they see at the same time that the world which provides material security and leisure for tens of millions, leaves — even in North America — other millions in poverty and alienation, to which there appear at present no certified cures. They see the most condemned war in their country's history being fought in their name and, for many of them, with their blood. But they cannot even applaud unreservedly the other side, since only the most naively gullible among them believe that the Vietcong is really better than its enemies. They see the traditional great American and Canadian parties concerned with despicable goals of power and material reward. They revolt against the hierarchic institutionalization of revolutionism by the Old Left, which is why, despite the fantasies that crowd the mind of J. Edgar Hoover, the Communists have never made any appreciable headway among them. They see the unions concerned almost wholly with money; labor radicalism is dead, and its one great manifestation in the American past revives for a grotesque and ghostly Sabbath each year when the few surviving veterans of the I.W.W. gather to shout old slogans at the annual convention in Chicago and to sing old songs of defiance to an unlistening world.

What the anarchist tradition has to give the radical young is perhaps, first of all, the vision of a society in which every relation would have moral rather than political characteristics. The anarchist believes in a moral urge in man powerful enough to survive the destruction of authority and still hold society together in the free and natural bonds of fraternity. Recent events — the civil-rights campaigns, the revolts in the negro ghettos, the behavior of have-not countries towards their prosperous benefactors — have shown that even in a materialist culture, non-materialist values will make an irrational but convincing clamor. The relations among men are moral in nature, and politics can never entirely embrace them. This the anarchists have always insisted.

Within such a non-materialist attitude they have posed, against the T.U.C. and A.F.L.-C.I.O. drives to bring the workers into line materially with the rich, the ideal of a dignified poverty. Paul Goodman has written a great deal on this, but we should not forget those magnificently poetic passages of *La guerre et la paix* in which Proudhon draws the distinction between pauperism and poverty. Pauperism, he contends, is destitution; poverty is the state in which a man gains from his work just enough for his needs, and this condition Proudhon praises in lyrical terms as the ideal human state, in which we are most free, in which — masters of our senses and our appetites — we are best able to spiritualize our needs. In material terms anarchists have never asked for more than the sufficiency that will allow men to be free. One has only to read the moving accounts of Gerald Brennan and Franz Borkenau to realize how deeply the peasant anarchists of southern Spain felt their freedom; they were willing to give up not merely alcohol and tobacco, but even tea and coffee, so that their newly communized villages could escape more completely from the golden chains of the money system.

The great anarchists — and here I am not considering the embittered last-ditch defenders who represented the historic movement in the 1940s — laid a constant stress on the natural, the spontaneous, the unsystematic. For them individual judgment held primacy;

dogmas impeded one's understanding of the quality of life. That life, they believed, should be as simple and as near to nature as possible. This urge towards the simple, natural way of life made men like Kropotkin urgently concerned over the alienation of men in modern cities and the destruction of the countryside, themes that are dear to New Radicals. The anarchists were ever conscious of the danger of rule by experts. Bakunin was frankly hostile to professional scientists. Even Kropotkin, scientist by training, stressed the great role of the amateur in scientific development, and when it came to the organization of a trade or a village or a city quarter to fulfill its material needs, he believed that responsibility should lie with those nearest to the problem. People must learn to make their own decisions. This strong sense of the appropriateness of those directly concerned deciding on all matters affecting them alone became the basis for Proudhon's federalism. He saw society organized in functional groups, industrial and social in character, in which people would decide what should be done at their place of work or their place of living; above these primary levels, and dependent always upon them, would be constructed — in the most loosely federal manner possible — the few national and international institutions that might be necessary. At every level the people would participate as widely as possible, but at the lowest level, in workshops and living areas, participation would be complete.

It is easy to see how such views may appeal to New Radicals today and, indeed, how far New Radical views derive half-consciously from those of the anarchist past. But perhaps the way in which the anarchists have most interestingly anticipated the preoccupations of the young today is in their concern over what they firmly believed would be the death of the relation between man and his work as we have known it. As long ago as 1793, writing his *Enquiry Concerning Political Justice* (the first major anarchist text), Godwin foresaw with great accuracy the age of automation and forced leisure which today seems almost upon us:

At present, to pull down a tree, to cut a canal, to navigate a vessel requires the labour of many. Will it always require the labour of man? When we look at the complicated machines of human contrivance, various sorts of mills, of weaving engines, of steam engines, are we not astonished at the compendium of labour they produce? Who shall say where this species of improvement must stop? . . . The conclusion of the progress which has here been sketched is something like a final close to the necessity of human labour.

With a daring that seemed more astonishing 175 years ago than it does today, Godwin ventured the prophecy that one day man might have to work no more than an average of half an hour a day. The rest he could devote to the cultivation of his nature.

Peter Kropotkin, writing almost a quarter of a century later in *The Conquest of Bread,* was more cautious than his predecessor, merely making a suggestion whose fulfillment is now almost upon us in the Western world; the physical comfort of society might be assured, he ventured, if all men worked "five hours a day from the age of twenty or twenty-five to forty-five or fifty." But Kropotkin also realized what is becoming steadily more clear to us today, that the small amount of work necessary in the near future will be of far less concern than the long hours away from the factory and the office. We are faced with the problem of what happens — to borrow phraseology from that other old libertarian, William Morris — when Useless Toil is eliminated and we have to find Useful Work. Kropotkin believed optimistically that when the problems of excessive toil had been solved, men would adjust themselves, creatively.

Man is not a being whose exclusive purpose in life is eating, drinking, and providing a shelter for himself. As soon as his material wants are satisfied, other needs, which generally speaking may be described as of an artistic nature, will thrust themselves forward. These needs are of the greatest variety;

they vary in each and every individual, and the more society is civilized, the more will individuality be developed, and the more desires be varied.

So Kropotkin wrote in 1892. I think New Radicals today would see the problem in exactly the same way, though I doubt if many would be as optimistic.

To a great extent I still share many of the libertarian attitudes I have been describing, though I answer to no whip and accept no label. I am not seeking converts to them; my propagandist days are ended. But I am, as a historian, extremely interested in the phenomenon of a group of ideas, which only a decade ago seemed tied to the dying animal of a nineteenth-century working-class movement, but which today have taken on new company among the young and the middle class, and which seem to be giving the young at least some of the answers they want to the questions of the age.

I am also interested in the absence of some of the elements which were part of classic anarchism. There is no longer much talk of barricades and revolutionary heroism, and while "direct action" is a phrase continually on the lips of New Radicals, it means something very near to Gandhian civil disobedience, which Old Anarchists would despise ostentatiously. I believe all these changes are to the good, since they represent the liberation of useful libertarian ideas from many of those elements of the historic anarchist movement which its critics, with a degree of justification, condemned. The anarchists of the past were too much inclined, despite their fervent anti-Marxism, to accept the stereotypes of nineteenth-century left-wing thinking: the idea of the class struggle as a dominant and constructive force in society, the romantic cult of insurrectionism and terror, and even — though this they rarely admitted — a vision of proletarian dictatorship, particularly among the anarcho-syndicalists who envisaged a society run by monolithic workers' unions. Those who openly or unwittingly advocate anarchistic ideas today have mostly shed these outdated concepts, together with much else of the ideological baggage of the Old Left. The revolutionary tactics of Bakunin are as dead as if they were buried with him among the solid burghers of Berne. It is unlikely that we shall see the revival of a movement dedicated to pursuing them, however far libertarian ideas and impulses may spread among the young and influence their social and moral concepts.

As to the kind of society their efforts might lead to, the anarchists were never great utopians; they liked to keep the future flexible and felt that elaborate plans laid burdens on generations which had not made them. I am sure most New Radicals would agree. But there was nevertheless an unbending rigidity about one aspect of the Old Anarchist view of the future. It was a hard, no-compromise view; either the completely non-governmental society, or nothing at all. The Old Anarchists never came within light years of attaining such a goal; hence the glorious record of unsuccess which is now so much to anarchism's advantage.

Today I doubt if anyone in the West seriously believes in the possibility of creating a uniform society of any kind, and I suspect the Russians too are fast abandoning such a hope. We no longer think terminally, thanks paradoxically to the threat of nuclear destruction. The future is open-ended, open-sided, and as far as we can see ahead we are likely to be involved in pluralistic permutations that will embrace many philosophies, many institutional patterns, many nuances of approach.

The anarchists, in other words, will never create their own world; the free society of which they have dreamed is as pleasant and as remote a myth as the idyllic libertarian society William Morris portrayed in *News from Nowhere*. The material and social complexity of the modern world obviously precludes such simplistic solutions. But this does not mean that the ideas which have emerged within the libertarian tradition are — outside the context of an anarchist utopia — irrelevant in the real world. Taken individually, as I have suggested, they often have a striking relevance to current problems. At the same time, it seems to me, they can only become useful if those who respect the positive aspects of anarchist thought are willing to make a number of radical admissions.

Classic anarchists — for instance — believed that the destruction of an authoritarian society must precede the creation of its libertarian successor. But history in the past 50 years has shown that the revolutionary destruction of an authoritarian society tends to create a more efficiently coercive society in its place. The liberalization of a society is, in fact, an evolutionary and not an apocalyptic process, and can only be attained by concentrating on piecemeal changes. These changes are to be attained not by rejecting all laws, since some restraints are manifestly necessary in any foreseeable future society, but by searching out those areas in which authoritarian and bureaucratic methods have manifestly failed or over-extended themselves, and by endeavoring to give practical application to libertarian concepts of decentralization, voluntarism, and direct participation in decision-making. Such an admission implies that it is time for those who still find some virtue in basic libertarian teachings to recognize that, despite the moralistic pretensions of past anarchists, anarchism has never been genuinely non-political; it has always represented politics carried out by other means; a recognition of this kind would free those who hold libertarian convictions to seed the social changes they think necessary within an existing political framework which, needless to say, is also changeable.

Finally, one must accept a more existential view of nature than the historic anarchists upheld. They believed that — even if man was not naturally good — he was naturally social. Such an assumption presupposes impossibly ideal circumstances; given freedom and sufficiency and time to heal their psychic wounds, men would perhaps begin behaving with perfect sociability. But this, again, is a utopian vision, unlikely to be realized. We live in the present, where most men are probably better fitted for responsibility than the pessimists assume, and where a few are more chronically anti-social than the optimists wish to admit;

this, impossible to define as it may be, is the only human nature we know from experience. We must therefore accept its existence, and limit anti-sociality where it impinges on the lives of others. Our aim should be to preserve as much freedom as possible for men as they are, rather than dream of a hypothetical total freedom for men as they at present are not.

What I have left, I can hear my old comrades complaining, is no longer anarchism. Perhaps not. But it is an attempt to bring the constructive insights of anarchist thinkers, too often neglected in the past because of the tactics they were wedded to, into a context where they may at last wield some positive and beneficial influence in the shaping of society. The fact that we are now thinking in political and social matters more openly and more pluralistically than in the past makes it possible for the ideas that emerged within the libertarian tradition to play a vital part in shaping, not an anarchist utopia, but a world that will really exist as the product of the vast technological changes of our age. But this can only happen if, as Paul Goodman does so admirably, libertarians are willing to make their social criticisms and their proposals for reform relevant to our concrete and rapidly changing present and not to some idealized future.

1968

3

Democracy, Heretical and Radical

"When we use the word democracy we do not or should not mean any particular form of political structure; such matters are secondary. What we mean or ought to mean is the completely open society . . . We have in fact no choice at all; we have to adapt ourselves to an open society or perish." Such words do not seem out of place today, but they were spoken in 1941; the speaker was the poet, W. H. Auden. Both facts are significant. By 1941 the dream of the thirties had died as a major casualty of the Spanish Civil War, and among the first to realize the implications of this destruction of an almost purely political ideal was the poet who had once seemed its laureate.

Auden's brief statement prefigures a vital shift in the way we now regard democracy, a shift with implications that began to manifest themselves clearly in the 1960s. Until the mid-twentieth century, the heart of the democratic ideal was supposedly that it put political power in the hands of the people. From this limited preoccupation arose movements for majority rule and universal suffrage, concerns radical in appearance but conservative in effect. "Universal Suffrage is the counter-revolution," cried the French socialist Proudhon, and where universal suffrage has been that and nothing more, events have usually proven him right.

Whenever the right of the people to rule was considered, too few theorists considered the relevance of the question: "What shall the people rule?" The rule of people over persons — the rule of the majority over a minority — is surely, as anarchists have always argued, a special form of tyranny. It is the rule of people over things that is true freedom. Radical democrats are at last becoming aware of this fact, in the latter half of the present century. We have reached the point when radicals and revolutionaries can, without inconsistency, all begin thinking of themselves as democrats, a point at which the great socio-political currents of the past — liberalism, libertarian socialism, anarchism, pacifism — can at last be united in a conception of democracy that, in all its aspects, embraces nothing less than the open society of which Auden spoke. On the other hand, not to reflect on those currents from the past that led to the democratic ideal would be tragic nihilism. We need to know all they can teach us, as well as all our own inventiveness can conceive, if we are to salvage from the undirected technological and social revolutions of the modern world a society worth living in — or any society at all.

Seen from the historical point of view, the development of the notion of radical democracy is a history of heretics. It is the history of a vision of freedom always emergent, never complete, and above all, never tied to the merely political. Auden contrasted narrow political democracy with the open society; today the contrast is most frequently described as being between representative democracy and participatory democracy. I prefer Auden's phrase as the more inclusive, but both conceptions assert a growth and broadening of democratic conceptions. They also presage the flowing into the idea of democracy, like tributaries coming into some vast Amazonian river, of many doctrines, theories, intuitions, and experiences of a libertarian nature that even a quarter of a century ago might have been regarded as outside and even opposed to it.

In the gentler mountains of eastern Switzerland lies the Canton of Appenzell. Its capital is a former village with the cozy reek of cow-dung still hanging in its streets. Here political democracy survives in its most pristine form. Appenzell offers its few thousand citizens something more, and less, than representative democracy: it offers direct democracy. On the last Sunday of every April, around an ancient lime tree, the male Appenzellers over the age of twenty meet, as they have done most Aprils since 1408, in a plenary assembly to determine their laws. A council is elected to wield the executive power over the coming year, and to recommend laws for the assembly to accept or reject. Any citizen of Appenzell can also propose a law and have it put to the vote by the assembly.

The advantages of the Appenzell system over a representative democracy are obvious. Government lies far more securely in the hands of the people than in either the federal United States or parliamentary Great Britain. But the limitations of democracy in Appenzell are equally evident. The people meet only once in a year, so initiative rests mainly in the hands of the council. The fiat of the majority is still imposed on the minority, no matter how large that minority may be. Women have no part in deciding the laws that will affect them. Finally, although the constitution of Appenzell provides for political democracy, notions of social liberation and regeneration have no place in it.

Appenzell represents in fact a high point of medieval democracy; it is a relic of one of the few successful peasant revolts, preserved almost unchanged for five and a half centuries. In 1408 the people of Appenzell wanted to rid themselves of their overlords, regulate their own affairs, and having shed their tax burden, prosper on their farms. Land was plentiful, and the society was industrially and technologically primitive, so there was no need to complicate their constitution with social overtones. Mountain barriers, good farming, and the steady flight of the young to the cities have enabled them to preserve, almost untouched, a political idyll, a beautiful fossil of a former struggle for liberty.

Appenzell stands a little less than a quarter of the way back in time to classical Athens, where our ideas of democracy were first articulated. Despite the 18 centuries that divide Appenzell's original rebellion from the high point of Athenian democracy, the two have much in common. The Athenians had a modified form of direct democracy, with considerable power reserved for an assembly of citizens, while political officeholders rotated according to a system of lots, which avoided some of the greater flaws of the elective system. To the women who in modern Appenzell are second-class citizens, the Athenians added a great company of slaves who had no hope of becoming citizens. Athenian democracy was strongly territorial, as Swiss cantonal democracy remains, and at one time in Athens only those who could prove the local descent of both parents were allowed to vote.

But in spite of its xenophobia, its caste system, its anti-feminism, Athenian democracy did find a reasonably successful solution to a major problem that concerns modern theorists of democracy. Though many Athenians were hard-working farmers or craftsmen, there were others for whom slavery had eliminated toil, as machinery and technology promises to free us. For these, Athenian democracy, within its limitations, was able to provide outlets for creative leisure. Their masterpieces survive, fragmentarily but still magnificently, in philosophy, history, political thought, and such great dramas as Aeschylus' *Prometheus Bound* and Sophocles' *Antigone*, which still speak in clear voices to modern man of the difference between justice and human law, and of the right of the individual to oppose his conscience to arbitrary power. Civil disobedience, which we today recognize as an essential mechanism of true democracy, found moving expression in these tragedies performed more than two thousand years ago. The voice of Antigone still strikes our hearts when she cries out, "I cannot share in hatred but in love," and dies in defiance of a vindictive political authority.

The five centuries from the time Appenzell came into being in 1408 and now have been a period of increasingly rapid socio-political evolution. Compared to them, the centuries from Athens to Appenzell seem like a broad desert in the history of freedom, spotted with scattered oases, traversed at immense distances by small rivers that lose themselves in the sand. To these we now turn.

In Rome in the third century, B.C., the plebeians gained some measure of political identity when, by massive civil disobedience, they won a Tribunate of the People. But the real governing power still lay with a patrician oligarchy that survived to the despotism of the Caesars. In Greece the schools of Stoics, Epicureans, and Cynics put forward egalitarian and internationalist doctrines that criticized both the institution of slavery and the xenophobia of Athens. The Cynics mounted an anarchist attack on the rigidities of political institutions in general, and taught that a true philosopher must opt out of politics and live beyond the law. But such doctrines influenced only a small minority, and certainly did not bring about the abolition of slavery, the destruction of the state, or international brotherhood. In fact, it was during the period of these schools that Macedonian and Roman rulers carried an insanity of power to the extreme of declaring themselves gods as well as kings.

Probably a more solid advance in the direction of human liberation was made, not by the philosophers, but by the mystery religions that emerged from the East and the more primitive regions of Greece to provide the poor and disaffected with cults that did not bow to god-kings or the interests of the privileged, as did the city cults. In these mystery cults, the only real distinction was between novice and adept; once initiated, citizens and foreigners, slaves and women, were regarded as equals. The story that Nero was refused initiation into the Eleusian mysteries because the fact that he was Emperor did not compensate for his moral wretchedness may be apocryphal, but the very fact that it was told indicates that social iconoclasm of a kind was a recognized feature of the mystery religions.

Of these mystery religions the greatest was Christianity, which borrowed from the Orphic cult a recognition that all men were equal, in the sight of God, from the Stoics internationalism, and from the Essenes a stress on brotherhood, community, and mutual aid. Christianity also added a dynamic of its own, the hope of Heaven, which broke the ancient world's obsession with cyclical time and set men's thoughts forward to the millennium instead of backward to an ever-repeated Golden Age.

For centuries the spirit of egalitarianism, brotherhood, and internationalism implicit in Christianity remained encysted in monastic orders, while its forward-looking dynamism was astutely diverted by Saint Augustine into a search for the spiritual City of God. But the chiliastic dream of an earthly kingdom of God, of a literal fulfillment of Revelation's promise that Christ would rule for a millennium, held its own. As the Church attempted to crystalize the medieval social order, the most powerful heresies were always those that promised more freedom to the downtrodden classes. By the eleventh century the great Catharist movement had swept westward from the Balkans into the heart of Europe. The Catharists objected to the episcopal power structure of the Church and to the hierarchical political structure of the feudal kingdoms. Their criticism of contemporary society passed from the political to the social when they denounced the materialism of their age, and advocated either a holy poverty for all men, or a simple communitarianism where work and goods were shared. Because of the Inquisition's assiduous suppression of every trace of Catharism, we know very little of the links between this movement and later religio-political movements of rebellion. It may well be, however, that the tradition of democracy in the post-Greek world had its obscure roots among the Catharists.

Catharism stimulated a flowering of culture in medieval Provence, but it vanished underground in the bloody repression of a Crusade led against the heretics by Simon de Montfort in the name of the Pope and the kings of Europe, who feared for their very existence if the movement were allowed to spread. But by then the medieval order itself was beginning to decay, and by the fourteenth century the disintegration was well advanced. The feudal lords forgot their obligations and became mere despots; the Black Death and the flight of peasants from the countryside to the free atmosphere of the cities eroded the institution of serfdom, and the desire for freedom began to take on multiple forms.

Ancient Greece was rediscovered, and Renaissance humanism fostered a cult of the individual in direct contradistinction to the medieval caste-system. Once men were regarded as individuals, the temptation to think in terms of their political and even social equality was irresistible, and a fine fruit of this renaissance humanism, in the late sixteenth century, was Sir Thomas More's *Utopia*. More tried to reconcile the individual's demands for economic equality with his social responsibilities, within a communitarian structure. To a modern libertarian democrat, the political framework of More's *Utopia* will seem pretty rigid (as will that of any utopia except William Morris' highly permissive *News from Nowhere*), but it was a landmark in recognizing that social, economic, and political rights are interdependent. If its negative inheritance has been the welfare state, its positive inheritance has been the long tradition of intentional communities where human beings have experimented flexibly with human relationships. In his day More was an intellectual writing for a very small audience of peers; but he died ironically as a martyr in the cause of a chivalric order whose decay he had recognized.

As the feudal order decayed, a new element of secular revolt — actual proto-democratic movements — were added to the religious radicalism inherited from the Catharists. During the English Peasant's revolt of the fourteenth century people chanted the jingle,

> When Adam delved and Eve span
> Who was then the gentleman?

Although the jingle had biblical reference, because at the time the Bible and history were synonymous, it also embodied quite independently a conception of social equality. And even if John Ball, who incited the rebels, was a heretic priest, the fragment of his famous speech that Froissart quotes shows him as a social agitator putting forward demands for a democracy at once political and social.

"Things cannot go well in England, nor ever will, until all goods are held in common, and until there will be neither serfs nor gentlemen, and we shall be equal." Freedom, equality, community — in other words, the basic elements of modern radical democracy.

Until the eighteenth century there were no important movements of social or political rebellion, no advances in democratic ideas that did not borrow a great deal of their driving force from the dynamism of heretical Christianity. Thomas Muenzer, who led the German peasant revolt, was a religious chiliast, but at the same time he was politically concerned enough to establish, when he ruled Muhlhausen, an ultra-democratic constitution with a senate elected by universal suffrage but directly responsible to the forum of the people; in fact, something very similar to the direct democracy of the Appenzellers. At times the spirit of religious millenarianism perverted the political element, as in Münster when Jan de Leyden proclaimed himself King of Earth and set up an oligarchy of "saints" to usher in the second coming of Christ. But elsewhere radical religious belief went hand in hand with a deepening social and political radicalism. The modern use of the word *dissent*, with its political connotation, records accurately the debt that radical movements today owe to the Reformation and its religious sects with their constant tendency towards fragmentation on the left. Yet by the seventeenth century the most significant, in socio-political terms, among these dissenting sects were the ones that went beyond religious fundamentalism toward deistic rationalism.

At this period the Civil War of the 1640s in England became another source of democratic ideas. The war was fought over the issue of absolute monarchy, though of course the leaders of the parliamentary cause were oligarchs rather than democrats. They sought a political order in which landowners and merchants could order the world to their convenience, and the upshot was the first modern dictatorship under the rule of Lord Protector Cromwell and his major-generals. But on the heretical fringes of the Parliamentary movement — here was a radical and truly democratic thrust. Three men personified it:

John Milton, John Lilburne, and Gerard Winstanley; each demonstrated the extent to which dissent had become political rather than religious.

Milton reveals the shift in perhaps its most ironic form. He spent his old age writing a poem intended to "justify the ways of God to men," but instead he made of Satan a Promethean hero, passionately rebellious, defiant of arbitrary authority, and a symbol of glorified individualism, to be taken up later by Byron and Blake and the whole Romantic school. Milton was probably more aware of being of the Devil's party than Blake imagined, certainly when he campaigned for the right to divorce and above all when, in *Aeropagitica*, he made the first great plea for freedom of speech and the press, the very foundation of the democratic process.

"Honest John" Lilburne was the leader of the Levellers, an extreme political left wing of Cromwell's New Model Army. While the generals were content to establish the principle of parliamentary government (which they shortly abandoned to set up the Protectorate) and had no intention of extending participation to any but men of property, large numbers of the rank and file of the army and even several younger officers — Lilburne was a colonel — believed that in a true democracy all men should take part in government. These people shared with later liberals the illusion that universal suffrage — the right of all men to vote — would ensure this. In fact, the Levellers anticipated the chartist workingmen-reformers of the nineteenth century in demanding for every man maximum participation in a representative democracy, but only a few of them went further to speculate on the relationship between economics and freedom.

At the time, this fell to a group who called themselves the True Levellers, but who have become better known as Diggers. Their leader and principal theoretician, Gerard Winstanley, was a small merchant who had been ruined by the Civil War and whom poverty had set to thinking like a religious and political radical. Winstanley carried his radicalism so far as to declare that God was none other than Reason:

Where does Reason dwell? He dwells in every creature,
according to the nature and being of the creature, but supreme-
ly in man. Therefore man is called a rational creature. . . . This
is the Kingdom of God within man.

It was this indwelling reason, according to Winstanley, that should
dictate a man's social behavior:

For Reason tells him, is thy neighbor hungry and naked
today, do thou feed him and clothe him, it may be thy case
tomorrow and then he will be ready to help thee.

God was reason, but He was also "universal liberty," which led
Winstanley to broaden his concept of democracy and attack economic power as well as political power. He also attacked power politics in the family, warning fathers and husbands that "their wives,
children, servants, subjects, are their fellow creatures and have an
equal privilege to share with them in the blessing of liberty." Finally,
as clearly as any nineteenth-century socialist, Winstanley recognized
how property oppresses and how it destroys freedom. He wrote his
most important pamphlet, *The New Law of Righteousness*, in the
beginning of 1649, and in it opposed to the world he saw around him
the vision of a society where none would lay claim to property or
rule his fellow man:

But every one shall put their hands to till the earth and bring
up cattle, and the blessing of the earth shall be common to all;
when a man hath need of any corn or cattle, take from the next
storehouse he meets with. There shall be no buying or selling,
no fairs or markets, but the whole earth shall be a common
treasury for every man, for the earth is the Lord's. . . . There
shall be no lords over others, but everyone shall be a lord of
himself, subject to the law of righteousness, reason and equity,
which shall dwell and rule in him, which is the Lord.

This anarchist communist vision, which would have warmed Peter Kropotkin's heart if he had read it, Winstanley and his followers almost immediately tried to embody by peaceful and direct revolutionary action. They went — forty of them — to a piece of unused waste land in Surrey, dug and sowed it, and called on the local people to join them and the landless men of England to imitate them. The story of their persecution, their obstinate passive resistance, their final failure, has been often told. The Diggers vanished so completely into the anonymous poor that even the date of Winstanley's death is unknown. But the vision he and his followers had and tried to practice was the most radical and far-reaching notion of democracy that appeared in his time and for generations after.

Unlike the British, the American Revolution was essentially a war of national liberation, and its leaders were much too enamored of fusty visions of the Roman Republic for much of importance in democratic theory to emerge. The principle of federalism (which may yet become the saving element in American political life) was introduced largely as a political expedient to reconcile conflicting interests among thirteen very different ex-colonial societies. And, as events have all too often shown, the powers given the executive have militated against the emergence of a mature and effectively functioning democracy in the United States.

The French Revolution, too, was primarily a political event, a power struggle in which the warring factions were little concerned with democracy as we must conceive it today, though they had their effect, no doubt, on the perversion of democracy over which General de Gaulle presided. Men like Saint-Just and Robespierre created a current of authoritarian, anti-democratic revolutionism that continued through Babeuf and Blanqui, and was incorporated, in various adaptations, by both Leninist communism and fascism.

The people's life in revolutionary Paris was far more truly democratic, and left a more interesting heritage, than the Grand Guignol in which the leaders strutted and bloodily vanished, since it was centered on the Commune, which embodied the principles of federalism much more directly than the American constitution. Paris was divided into sixty sections, in each of which citizens could meet in general assemblies to regulate and administer their affairs directly. Where delegation was necessary, it was done by appointing special commissioners subject to close scrutiny and recall. The institution of the French general assembly has echoed down through French radical history. It inspired the later and more celebrated Paris Commune of 1871, which hoped to establish a federalist society to replace the centralized bureaucratic order that has always negated France's pretensions to democracy. It was taken up by Pierre-Joseph Proudhon, the greatest of French socialists, as the basis for a theory of society where coercion from above would be supplanted by a federal organization developed from the simplest local level upwards, through communes and associations in which the people most involved in a problem would have the right to solve it themselves. In other words, the experience of the Paris Commune of 1793 was translated into the first clear theory of participatory democracy by Proudhon, writing in the 1860s.

In Great Britain, the reaction among writers on the Left to the authoritarian excesses of the French Revolution was not to reject the democratic ideals with which the revolution had begun, but to find a way to effect social change without violence and coercion. The most brilliant and monumental theoretical work to emerge as a result was William Godwin's *Enquiry Concerning Political Justice*, published in 1793. *Political Justice* has long been regarded as one of the canonical works of anarchism, but it has a wider relevance. As one of the most exhaustive studies ever written on the evils of coercive government, it deserves to be recommended reading for all democrats.

Godwin had some extraordinary insights. He foresaw the technological revolution and realized that it might well bring, in his words, "something like a final close to the necessity of human labor," and he regarded this as a liberating trend. He followed Winstanley (though unaware of the fact) and anticipated later libertarian socialist and anarchist movements in recognizing how "accumulated property" helps perpetuate authoritarian politics. The merits of democracy over other known political systems he also recognized:

> Democracy restores to a man a consciousness of his value, teaches him by the removal of authority and oppression to listen only to the dictates of reason, gives him confidence to treat other men as his fellow beings, and induces him to regard them no longer as enemies against whom to be upon his guard, but as brethren whom it becomes him to trust.

Up to now, however, Godwin argues, democracy has clung to elaborate institutional mechanisms. He pleads for progressive simplification, for local governments united in a kind of federalism of autonomous parishes, with juries of arbitration as their only governing bodies, and with national assemblies convened as rarely as possible to deal with matters of common interest to the parishes. Little government, and that directly from the people in their own communities, was Godwin's idea of democracy.

But Godwin remained the theoretician, aloof from the practical task of creating the democracy he envisaged. Robert Owen, to some extent Godwin's disciple, was, on the other hand, an experimenter, and served as a catalyst for a number of movements that sought to give democracy a social and largely non-political base. Owen was disillusioned with the parliamentary reform movement in early nineteenth-century England, but unlike the Chartists, did not regard universal suffrage as the cure-all for political and social ills. He believed that men must begin immediately to build a new society within the old. After experimenting with enlightened factory management in Scotland, in 1825 he funded one of the most celebrated of American intentional communities — New Harmony. Owen believed that such experiments might spread by example and become the nuclei for a new social order.

Except for a few isolated examples, like Winstanley's seventeenth-century experiment, such communities, conceived as a means

to change society, have been nineteenth and twentieth-century phe-
nomena. Religious communities, of course, had existed before, and
in the form of Christian and Buddhist monasteries, and among such
dissenting groups as the Hutterites, still do. But those that survived
were the most austere and authoritarian; in them, an over-riding
desire to withdraw for the sake of personal salvation led to a way of
life quite other than the norm of *l'homme moyen sensuel*. These
communities were sustained — making it possible for those within
to live and work together under a rigid but voluntary discipline —
by an over-riding religious purpose that went far beyond the simple
desire to live together amicably. Community was to them a means,
not an end, and they took it in their stride as that.

The politically oriented intentional communities of the early
nineteenth century were most frequently conceived by European
social prophets, such as Robert Owen, and the French socialists
Cabet and Fourier; but it was in the United States, where free land
was still available, that most of the actual experiments were made. In
all, between two and three hundred American socialist and anarchist
communities were founded, some as late as the Depression of the
1930s, and many thousand people lived in them. Some communities
collapsed within a few months; others survived into a second generation; but the only ones that still exist intact today are those originally
inspired by a religious motive, which held the people together and in
some measure insulated them from the outside world.

Three instances of intentional communities that have appeared
in the present century perhaps deserve special note. The *kibbutzim*
of Israel — the first one was founded in 1909 and still exists — are
probably the most celebrated and undoubtedly the most successful
of all intentional communities, for reasons we shall come to.
Somewhat later, during the Spanish Civil War, many villages in the
anarchist regions of Catalonia and Andalusia formed communes,
socializing all property, abolishing the internal use of money, and
sharing their produce. In one province alone, Levante, there were
five hundred such communities, and there may have been thousands

in Spain. Their history remains to be written, nor can their achievement be easily judged, for after two harvests most were overrun by Franco's armies.

The third notable example of a community movement arose at the outset of the Second World War among English pacifists. More than two hundred communities were attempted, varying in membership from three or four people to more than a hundred. Some lasted only a few months while others survived the war. I lived in two of those communities at the time, and visited many others. My experience and observation lead me to believe that most of them failed for a combination of reasons. The majority were agrarian, but few started with enough funds to farm even half-way efficiently. Few chose their members well, so they usually included some people temperamentally unfit for living in groups, some physically unfit for manual work, and others who were conscientious objectors and regarded the community merely as a refuge. Frugality, even when unnecessary, often became a fetish, and many communities were inefficient simply because of malnutrition. Privacy was virtually non-existent; people slept in dormitories, ate in common dining rooms, and were rarely alone. Generally speaking, the outside world was hostile, which created a feeling of intense isolation. This in turn forced the community to face inward, which, with the lack of privacy, meant that personal incompatibilities were dramatized and resentments became formidable. The bitterest feuds started over trivia that would have passed unnoticed in a normal life.

The communities that lasted longest, I noticed at the time, were those that made the greatest effort to keep in touch with the outside world. In Wales, for example, people were sympathetic to war resisters, and so the communities often succeeded in establishing good local relations. It also helped to develop some strong aim other than merely trying to live together peaceably; groups with a real enthusiasm and a practical aptitude for farming did much better than those who tilled the fields as a kind of discipline in the cause of a better way of life.

Here we come to the reason why the *kibbutzim* have, on the whole, been more successful than other intentional communities. They were conceived not as ends in themselves but as a way to build a whole society. Far from being detached from their immediate world, they existed in a climate generally favorable to their efforts. In all, it seems that at the right time and in the right way, intentional communities may be able to take their place within a larger society, but only if they set out with wider ends and with adequate practical resources, of which dedication to work at this stage is probably the most important.

Returning to the nineteenth century: New Harmony was one of the least successful of hundreds of intentional communities that were established in the United States and Canada then and after. To this day the small intentional community has remained a recurrent feature of libertarian radical movements. But New Harmony's failure did not disillusion Owen, and when he returned to England in 1827, he plunged first into the nascent cooperative movement, and then, in 1834, founded the largest of the early worker's organizations, the Grand National Consolidated Trades Union of Great Britain and Ireland, with a half million members.

In an essay of this length, the history of the cooperative and trade union movements cannot be sketched even roughly, but a few important points can be made. Owen was an impresario, not an originator, in these movements. Both originated among groups of working men, and so represent the arrival in the nineteenth century of the common people at what Proudhon called their "political capacity." Not only did the cooperatives and early trade unions run parallel to existing political institutions; they had more than merely ameliorative aims. They cannot be lumped with modern trade unions or cooperative stores, which have become vested interests and are essentially conservative. The early cooperators saw their modest little shops as generating a spirit of mutual aid that would eventually permeate the whole society. As for the Grand National Consolidated Trades Union, its Rules and Regulations say it intended to bring about "A DIFFERENT ORDER OF THINGS, in which the really useful and intelligent part of society shall have the direction of its affairs, and in which well-directed industry and virtue shall meet their just distinction and reward, and vicious idleness its merited contempt and destitution." Like later labor movements, these early cooperatives and trade unions educated their members, this at a time when state schooling was in its most rudimentary stages. Thus they undertook one of the most vital functions of a mature democracy.

An equally innovative step forward took place in 1864 when English trade unionists, who were distant followers of Robert Owen and French mutualist workingmen, who in turn were direct followers of Pierre-Joseph Proudhon, came together to establish the International Workingmen's Association, better known as the First International. Contrary to a stubborn legend, Karl Marx was not one of its actual founders. But the First International collapsed in 1872 when its libertarian elements — the English trade unionists and Latin anarchists — refused to accept an exclusively political direction from Karl Marx and his central European followers. Marx, despite the recent tendency of the New Left to think otherwise, has a negative place in the history of democracy. It is true that at times he is ambiguous and can sometimes be interpreted as advocating a democratic way towards socialism. But on looking at his actions and those of his followers at the First International, this interpretation becomes impossible. The First International broke apart when Marx attempted to restrict it to political action while the membership had pluralistic ideas which have become an invariable feature in theories of radical democracy ever since.

In fact, since the breakup of the First International it is mainly outside Marxism that we must look for the flexible pluralist trends which alone seem viable alternatives in the world of modern technology. They are trends that emphasize means rather than ends, leaving the future open to those who must eventually shape it. Among them were the trade unionists and syndicalists, who, by insisting on their right to strike, proved that democratic procedure could lie nearer to home than a parliament elected every four or five years. Also the suffragettes and conscientious objectors of the First World War, who showed that civil disobedience could give powerful expression to the views of a dedicated minority, must be included. Then there is Gandhi, who made out of this a weapon to bring about political change in India with a minimum of violence and hatred; and Peter Kropotkin, the anarchist who considered the problems of urban congestion and rural devastation, which concern us so deeply, and who suggested means of integrating rural and urban living. In the early stages of the Spanish Civil War factory workers in Barcelona and the peasants of Andalusia expropriated and efficiently managed factories, transport systems, and rural estates, proving that the management of production by the producers was a feasible form of industrial and agrarian organization. Finally, long before the beats and hipsters came on the scene, the anarchistically inclined artists and writers of the 1890s, so-called decadents, asserted the individual's right to explore experience and develop forms of expression without censorship, whether from government or society. The rapid liberation of literature and art from the shackles of convention has indeed been of prime importance to the evolution of democracy, opening the way to a corresponding liberation in manners and morals. For example, recent legislation in Great Britain concedes the individual's right to certain forms of homosexual behavior and to abortion.

In the last decade, we have at last seen emerging on the Left a pluralist attitude that recognizes the apparently dissident currents of the past as less contradictory than they once seemed. This awareness underlies the heterogeneity of contemporary protest movements, in which socialists and anarchists, liberals and pacifists and Fidelistas, squares and flower children, work together for a variety of causes from civil rights to Viet Nam: causes espoused by a conscience awakened to the fact that in our time rigid orthodox democracy must give way to heretical democracy. "As for adopting the ways which the state has provided for remedying the evil," said Thoreau, greatest of all American heretical democrats, "I know of no such ways. They take too much time, and a man's life will be spent."

The sense that society must become open, so that groups within it — now most urgently blacks and the young — can be accepted on their own terms and forge their own futures, has become integral to the notion of radical democracy. But this sense is only a beginning; the rest belongs to the future, on whose frontier this essay, being concerned with history, ends.

1971

4

The Rejection of Politics

Almost exactly half a life ago I wrote my first book on anarchism, *Anarchy or Chaos*. In many ways it was a naive book, and a few years afterwards I was so embarrassed with what, in my mid-thirties, seemed its juvenility, that I insisted on withdrawing it from publication. At sixty, I have returned to it, and, like my old friend Herbert Read considering the revolutionary writings of his youth, "I now envy those generous occasions." Much in *Anarchy or Chaos* belongs merely to its decade but there are parts which, with a little rewriting, I still find worth reading, and it is as a mosaic of some of these redeemable fragments of the past that this essay emerges. I still believe in general terms what it says.

Politically, modern society is based on the system of government; economically, on the system of property concentrated in the hands of the few. Its political manifestation is the state; its economic manifestation is the capitalist system of production. Its tendency is centripetal, so that political power becomes more and more concentrated in the state, and economic power tends to progress from the system of many small capitalists to monopoly capitalism, which in its turn becomes state capitalism. So the totalitarian state is achieved by the coalescence of political and economic power in the same body. But this identity of the state and capitalism is no new thing. For the state may be regarded as the translation into social terms of the economic form of society. It serves as the executive instrument of those who, by virtue of the economic power conferred by property, are the real ruling class of a country. And as property comes, through the growth and amalgamation of large business trusts, under the effective control of a class which grows progressively smaller and smaller, so the state itself becomes more and more concentrated until the apparent parallels of political and economic life meet in the totalitarian state.

Anarchism, which presents the extreme opposition to this contemporary development, is not a creed of terror and destruction, of social chaos and turmoil, of perpetual war between the individuals within society; it is not nihilism. On the contrary, it is the opposite of all these; a doctrine based on the idea of natural order within society, and of peace between individuals who respect their mutual freedom and integrity. It is the faith of the complete man, growing to fulfilment through social, economic and mental freedom. It is a social philosophy of individual aspirations.

Anarchism is the only logically complete doctrine of freedom, because it denies all external authority, all domination of man by man. It proclaims the sufficiency of the individual human mind and spirit, and the inborn tendency of men towards peace and cooperation when their natural feelings have not been twisted and frustrated by the oppression of authority.

Socially, anarchism is the doctrine of society without government. It teaches that the major economic and social injustices are intimately associated with the principle of government, which inevitably, in whatever form it takes, creates privilege, and a class hierarchy, and however much it may call itself democratic, must base itself on the coercion of the individual, at best to the will of the majority, most often that of the governing minority. An authoritarian society — and every kind of society that bases itself on government is, in virtue of that fact, authoritarian — cannot survive if it does not create a governing class and a series of gradations of responsibility in its hierarchy which must inevitably destroy all forms of equality, whether of wealth, status or opportunity. The governing class, once created, will tend to harden itself into a caste and to gather to itself privileges which give its members substantial advantages over the other members of society. These privileges will first be granted in the name of expediency, but will be continued as a usurped right. Though rulers may set out with the most sincere intentions, the very necessities of maintaining the power they hold will force them to injustice, and the privileges they obtain will accomplish their inevitable corruption. The evidence of history on these points is unvaried.

True democracy cannot exist outside the imagination in a society based on coercion. Yet, even were democracy possible, the anarchist would still not support it, for democracy puts forward the will of the majority as the supreme law, and declares that society must be governed, and the individual, whether he agrees or not, be coerced by that will. Democracy, then, is not based on freedom and differs only in degree from despotism in its negation of the individual. To the individual whose life is frustrated by the law of the state, it does not matter whether that law is the will of one man or the will of a million. What matters to him is that through its existence he is not free and therefore cannot become complete.

The anarchist seeks neither the good of a minority, nor the good of the majority, but the good of all men considered as individuals. He believes that a society based on the great super-individual myth of the state must in the end enslave all its members in the interests not even of the majority but of the privileged few who form its ruling class. Anarchists have often been upbraided as impractical visionaries for their denial of the institution of government. But they contend that impracticality belongs to those who, in the face of the irrefutable historical verdict, still believe that some day a form of government will appear which will not involve the exploitation of the ruled and the corruption of the rulers. These attributes are as natural to government as venom is to the viper.

All anarchists believe that the institution of government and the state and all other coercive instruments of administration should be abandoned, and many believe they can only be ended by the direct action of the oppressed. This destructive side of anarchism has received undue prominence among its enemies and among some of its more irresponsible friends, and has given rise to certain misconceptions, some frivolous and some serious, which have been fostered deliberately by those in authority.

Of the more frivolous is the idea that the anarchist is a man who throws bombs and wishes to wreck society by violence and terror. That this charge should be brought against anarchists now, at a time when they are among the few people who are not throwing bombs or assisting bomb throwers, shows a curious purblindness among its champions. It is true that a few individual anarchists have in the past, and particularly during the last two decades of the nineteenth century, used the weapon of terrorist assassination as a means of carrying on the social revolution. Some anarchists, therefore, certainly have thrown bombs. But so, also, have members of other political groups, and so have governments. And the difference in responsibility lies in this, that while the bombs thrown by anarchists killed those who were considered guilty of the oppression and murder of their subjects, the bombs thrown by governments in war can be numbered in their millions and have slain hundreds of thousands of men and women innocent of crime against their fellows. And it must be remembered that the practice of individual terrorism was virtually abandoned by the anarchists some forty years ago, when the advent of anarchist syndicalism opened up the possibility of the more satisfactory tactic of revolutionary mass economic action.

The anarchist believes that a political or governmental organization of society is incompatible with justice and liberty. He contends that society should be based on the free cooperation of individual men and women in fulfilment of their common functional and economic needs.

Here we reach a second and more serious misconception concerning anarchism, which has arisen among many people with a superficial knowledge of the movement; that anarchism is individualism carried to its extreme conclusion, and therefore admits of no organization of society. A certain support would appear to be given to this notion by the fact that a few anarchist intellectuals have preached this extreme form of individualism by which a man would live independent of all ties with his fellows and concern himself solely with the development of his own personality and his own happiness.

Where, however, anarchism has existed as a social movement, its exponents have always envisaged the necessity for organization, but a free organization rising organically from the needs of man. Anarchism does indeed preach the freedom of the individual man, but freedom cannot be isolated in society. An individual's freedom is reciprocal, depending on the freedom of others, and therefore anarchism teaches that the concept of justice is as necessary as the concept of freedom, for without justice there can be no true freedom, just as without freedom there can be no real justice.

Furthermore, work in common achieves more in a shorter time than solitary work, and a sane division of labor provides both plenty and leisure where otherwise a man dependent on his own two hands would have to toil all his hours for a miserable standard of life. But the benefits of common work and common life cannot be enjoyed in full measure if the vital functions of production are not organized by the people who perform them.

This necessity for social organization has been argued by those anarchist theoreticians who have refuted the contentions of the "pure" individualist anarchists. In 1872 Michael Bakunin, the founder of the historic anarchist movement, wrote the following defence of participation in the First International:

> To whomever might pretend that action so organized would be an outrage on the liberty of the masses, or an attempt to create a new authoritarian power, we would reply that he is a sophist and a fool. So much the worse for those who ignore

the natural, social law of human solidarity, to the extent of imagining that an absolute mutual independence of individuals and of masses is a possible or even desirable thing. To desire it would be to wish for the destruction of society, for all social life is nothing else than this mutual and incessant dependence among individuals and masses. All individuals, even the most gifted and strongest, indeed most of all the most gifted and strongest, are at every moment of their lives, at the same time, producers and products. Equal liberty for every individual is only the resultant, constantly reproduced, of this mass of material, intellectual and moral influence exercised on him by all the individuals around him, belonging to the society in which he was born, has developed, and dies. To wish to escape this influence in the name of a transcendental liberty, divine, absolutely egoistic and sufficient to itself is the tendency to annihilation. To refrain from influencing others would mean to refrain from all social action, indeed to abstain from all expressions of one's thoughts and sentiments and simply become non-existent. This independence, so much extolled by idealists and metaphysicians, individual liberty conceived in this sense, would amount to self-annihilation.

In nature, as in human society, which is also part of the same nature, all that exists lives only by complying with the supreme conditions of interaction, which is more or less positive and potent with regard to the lives of other beings, according to the nature of the individual. And when we vindicate the liberty of the masses, we do not pretend to abolish anything of the natural influences that individuals or groups of individuals exert upon one another. What we wish for is the abolition of artificial influences, which are privileges, legal and official.

This extract represents the attitude of most militant anarchists. They accept the voluntary limitations necessary for reciprocal freedom;

what they do not accept are the limitations imposed from above by coercive bodies such as the state.

Instead of accepting the government of men, the anarchist wishes, in the words of Saint-Simon, to base society on the administration of things. It is on the economic plane alone, in the necessary production of goods consumed by men and in the provision of necessary social service, that he sees the need for organization, not from above but on a voluntary and cooperative basis, among the individuals whose work actually produces the necessities of a civilized life.

From this point the anarchist proceeds to the contention that the functions of the modern state, represented by its paraphernalia of legal codes, bureaucracy, army, and police, would be unnecessary in a society where common ownership had ended privilege and social-economic inequalities. All these appendages of the modern state are intended ultimately not for the well-being of all men and women, but for the protection of the ruling class and the property by whose virtue it rules. In a society without inequality of property, where every man's needs were satisfied, there would be no incentive to crime, except among the pathological, who in any case are no subjects for prison or law courts. Where property rights had vanished there would be no need for codified laws. Customs and not regulations are the natural manifestations of men's ideas of justice, and in a free society customs would adapt themselves to the constant growth and testing of ideas in that society. Under a society of anarchy every man, once he had fulfilled his economic functions, would be free to live as he liked, provided he did not interfere with the lives of his fellows. A free people could be relied on to see that peace was maintained under such circumstances without the need for police or for magistrates.

The economic ideas of the anarchists have found a concrete expression in anarcho-syndicalism. Anarcho-syndicalism is both a technique of social revolution and a theory of the organization of a free society after that revolution. It advocates the organization of workers under capitalism in voluntary economic organizations, the syndicates, which differ from trade unions in being controlled directly by the workers themselves and in having as their purpose, not the winning of reforms under capitalism, but the achievement of radical social change by economic means. The withdrawal of economic cooperation, in the form of the general strike, is the basis of the anarchist conception of the revolution, and in this economic struggle the syndicates would play the vital role of uniting the efforts of the workers. After the social revolution the syndicates would be the basic units of the network of economic and functional bodies intended to organize the satisfaction of the common needs of men and to replace the system of administration by authority and coercion.

Anarchism, it must be emphasized, is not a static and unchangeable social system. It is rather a dynamic philosophy which recognizes the importance of evolution in human society, and the consequent futility of any attempt to plan social advancement on rigid lines.

The anarchist, therefore, deprecates the idea that a just revolution can be planned and carried out through the seizure of power by a disciplined party organization. Instead he contends that the social revolution can arise only out of the spontaneous movement of the people against their rulers, and that in any ensuing struggle the role of the revolutionary would be to maintain in the minds of men the nature of the goal for which they strive. The anarchist may preach freedom, but he considers that the people must take it for themselves.

In the same way, although many anarchists consider syndicalism a practical means of organizing society after a hypothetical revolution, they recognize that it may not present a perfect social pattern. Indeed, they envisage no static blueprint of a future world. For, when men have been freed from social and economic oppressions, the evolution of human institutions will undoubtedly attain forms we cannot conceive. Proposals for future organization must not therefore be regarded as permanent and hence dead, but as the bases of future social evolution.

The anarchist does not expect to achieve a society without flaw. But he does think that anarchism offers the only possibility of a society based on freedom and justice, which will function efficiently and produce a degree of spiritual and material comfort far higher than most men enjoy today. Anarchism may seem utopian to those who are embittered by the corruption and injustice of modern society. But, as Oscar Wilde said, "Progress is the realization of Utopias."

Anarchists do not advocate political freedom. What they do advocate is freedom from politics, freedom from the institution of government, freedom from coercion, freedom from the law's interference in the lives of individual men and women, freedom from economic domination and inequality. The last is perhaps the most important, in that economic freedom, the satisfaction of man's physical needs for food, clothing, shelter, and all the other material needs of a civilized life, is necessary before any man can begin to be free.

By the elimination of property, vested either in individuals or in corporate ruling classes, by the destruction of the state, by the substitution, for a society based on the mechanical and artificial institutions imposed by the dictates of property and governing interests, of a society based on institutions rising organically from the needs of men, the anarchist sees the need for the suppression of individual freedom brought to an end. Only a society based on control from above has need of coercion. A society based on cooperation can do without oppression and restriction because it is based on voluntary agreement among its members. Indeed, it *must* do without coercion, if it is to retain its cooperative basis, and avoid relapsing into a political institution controlled by a governing cabal.

Freedom is as much a necessity for society as it is for the individual men and women who comprise it. Restrictions on liberty naturally produce oppositions within a society. No political unit in the history of civilization has existed without carrying within itself the disruptive forces of discontent — precisely because no political unit has existed which did not base itself ultimately on the ability to force the individuals within it to obey the will of the controlling elements.

On the other hand, social units operated by cooperative and voluntary means have often succeeded in surviving over long periods without destructive internal strife. Their failure has resulted either from the attack of overpoweringly strong external forces or from the cooperative units themselves adopting the authoritarian pattern of external political bodies. (The decline of the English trade unions to the position of subordinate institutions of the state is a notable example of the decay of an originally cooperative institution which adopted a centralized authoritarian pattern.)

An examination of history, the real history of concrete human achievements and institutions as against the semi-mythical history of political institutions, shows that the development of the corporate and individual achievements of men is strongest and assumes its most significant forms in periods and places where political organization is weakened and least centralized. The vitality of human culture appears to run in inverse proportion to the strength of the state. Periods of political stabilization, when authority is held firmly by an efficient centralized government, when the state is deified and the free action of the individual is impeded, are most often periods of sterility, both in the development of organic institutions and the cultural achievements of individual artists and scientists. Times of political disintegration, when social forms are in flux, when the power and efficiency of the government are weak, when the state is regarded lightly and the individual finds room and freedom for development, are periods of institutional and cultural growth. One need only compare Sparta with Athens, the Italy of Mussolini with the Italy of the Renaissance.

1944/1972

5

Anarchy Now

The pacifist's stand against war and conscription is based on a conception of man as a free individual. However law-abiding, however respectful of the political orthodoxies and of civil authority an individual pacifist may be, as soon as he begins to resist war and refuse conscription he is placing himself above the law, he is asserting the primacy of the individual judgment over any authority or code that may be invoked to try and force him into the King's uniform. In this situation, whatever may be his general political creed, he acts as an anarchist, denying the law's right to dominion over his acts.

But does the matter end there, at a single act against the law? It seems to me that, once a man has made his denial of the rights of authority, he cannot halt at any given point, if he is to be at all logical in his actions. The real meaning of his resistance is, that he is willing to accept the law's authority only in matters where his own ideas of right action happen to coincide with it. He does not murder — because he does not want to, not because the law forbids it. He refuses to murder when the law demands, because he places the consistency of his own conscience above the inconsistencies of the law. The implications of this attitude, to my mind, cannot end this side of complete anarchism. I think it is only a lack of full consistency, a failure to apply their attitude regarding war to the rest of their social responsibilities, that prevents all pacifists from basing their whole philosophy of life on the supremacy of the individual idea of right.

I contend that the pacifist is a complete pacifist, a pacifist at all levels of mutual contact, only when he accepts the fact that in no circumstances have we, or the law or the State, any right to demand of a man that he should do what is not right in his own eyes, even less a right to coerce him to do such an act. In other words, pacifism reaches its conclusion in the lawless condition of anarchy, where individual responsibility replaces mass authority as the bond within society.

The pacifist is a potential anarchist. At any moment he is liable to be faced by the situation where all compromise must end and he must take up resistance to authority not, like the patriot, because authority belongs to another nation, or, like the Communist, because it belongs to another party, but because it offends a general principle of human right, because it interferes with the freedom of individual judgment. And at this moment of resistance for a principle he questions the very basis of the rights of authority. He becomes an anarchist even if he does not acknowledge it.

I know there are many pacifists who feel uncomfortable at being told that their beliefs find a logical conclusion in anarchism. It is surprising how long the cloak-and-dagger spectre with the smoking bomb has survived. Indeed, years ago a tiny minority of anarchists did throw bombs — very small ones compared with the atomic monsters thrown nowadays by law-abiding citizens. But, in spite of this historical association, there is no *necessary* connection between anarchism and violence. Still less is there any identity, as pretended by politicians, between anarchy and chaos.

Anarchism is the doctrine of being without government. That is its only fundamental and necessary basis. The anarchist believes that men tend naturally towards "goodness," towards living in mutual aid and tolerance, and that it is only coercion and material inequality, the attributes of government, that have produced the very evils of war and crime which force is supposed to cure. He also contends that by voluntary communal organizations, adapted to the needs of the particular function which must be fulfilled, all the social obligations can be met. Property inequalities and coercion should be replaced by distribution according to need from the common stock of goods and by the voluntary giving of work according to the individual's ability.

An unnecessary utopian ideal? It does not seem so when one considers the practical success of free communal settlements in Spain, in Palestine, even in England. And it is surely an idea of society which seems well fitted to the pacifist belief in brotherhood instead of strife as the determinant in social relations. The anarchist ideal of society is brotherhood carried to a logical extreme, and, far from envisaging chaos, it upholds the idea that man has a natural capacity for mutual aid and voluntary order.

Lastly, to revert to the vexed question of anarchist violence, this aspect has been much exaggerated. There have always been pacifist anarchists; today the influence of non-violent ideas among anarchists is increasing, and those who cling to ideas of violence do so largely through a romantic attachment to the revolutionary traditions of the nineteenth century. Many anarchists, like myself, while realizing that it is necessary to struggle for a free and peaceful society, see the practical futility of violence and advocate methods of action very similar to those set out in that pacifist classic, Bart de Ligt's *Conquest of Violence*. Pacifist methods seem the only way to achieve anarchism, but there is a corollary to this. Anarchist ideas of social change, the abolition of the State and the realization of voluntary communal ways of life, are the only practical means of attaining the conditions for ending war.

We must be revolutionaries and attack the causes of war at their roots. Otherwise, we shall not be thorough pacifists, and, bit by bit, our hopes and opportunities will be whittled away in compromises with the continually growing totalitarian states, which, for all their apparent strength, are dependent finally on the support of millions of individuals, of men and women who can destroy the whole structure of war by taking their destinies into their own hands and refusing to obey the institutions of coercion from which war springs.

1946

6

The Folly of "Revolutionary" Violence

This essay was prompted, to a great extent, by Herbert Read's article, "There Is Now No Other Way," in the October-December 1945 issue of *Adelphi*. But, apart from that, I had long wished to discuss some of the ideas on the futility of revolutionary violence which have steadily impressed themselves upon me in studying the catastrophic history of revolutionary movements.

I start from the assumption that a social revolution is necessary before society can be arranged on a reasonably equitable and classless basis. By this I do not mean merely a physical revolution. George Orwell has remarked very aptly that "Most revolutionaries are potential Tories, because they imagine that everything can be put right by altering the *shape* of society; once that change is effected, as it sometimes is, they see no need for any other." But it should be reasonably clear to anyone who has studied human beings as individuals rather than as political ciphers, that this idea of the efficacy of a merely physical revolution is fallacious. Men must be mentally and spiritually oriented towards freedom before they can translate it into social reality.

Here the corrupting role of violence is clear. A propaganda based on class violence, as elaborated in its extreme form by Georges

Sorel, inevitably results in a coarsening of the moral fibre, a growing unscrupulousness in dealings with other people. The actual use of violence arouses a brutality which infects large masses of people. The terrible cruelties practiced by revolutionary idealists, the executions of the French Terror, the mass shootings in Soviet Russia, the almost indiscriminate slaughters during the Spanish Civil War, show that even the best-intentioned people are capable of the worst deeds when they begin to use violence to achieve their ideals. We need hardly ask, are these men in a fit mental state to become the founders of a golden age of freedom? Clearly, as has been shown by the degeneration of so many revolutions after the hated government has been overthrown, their actions can lead only to a reign of fear more crushing than that which existed before.

Sorel imagined that the reintroduction of class hatred and class violence into social life would lead to moral regeneration. In fact it leads to a degradation of moral values in which the struggle for power becomes more acute and social relationships become blunted and brutalized. Michael Bakunin, another advocate of revolutionary violence, saw this more clearly, when he said, "Bloody revolutions are often necessary, thanks to human stupidity; yet they are always an evil, a monstrous evil and a great disaster, not only with regard to the victims, but also for the sake of the purity and the perfection of the purpose in whose name they take place." It is an object of this essay to contend that, not only are violent revolutions evils which in their nature cannot lead to human liberation, but also that they are unnecessary hindrances in attaining revolutionary objectives.

Much more could be written on the moral aspects of violence, and particularly on the role of violence as a disguised form of power whose needs tend always to convert it into naked power. But my concern at present is to deal with the practicality of violence as a means of social improvement. There still survives so much romantic illusion about the barricades and guerilla warfare that we have to demonstrate, as clearly as we can, that violent revolutions in fact possess none of the qualities assigned to them, and that the genuine self-sacrifice with which they are often initiated and maintained will lead inevitably either to failure in the actual insurrection or to a situation in which its objects will, through so-called "necessities," be lost more irretrievably than before. In this study, certain moral issues will emerge, and the relationship between violence and naked power will be shown by example. These accidental moral aspects will only reinforce the practical arguments.

One of the social factors which becomes steadily more evident is the improbability of an armed insurrection succeeding against armies equipped with modern weapons. We need not even take into account such weapons as poison gas and the atom bomb, for there is a reasonable case to suggest that no ruling class would use such indiscriminate methods in cities where their own adherents might be among the first victims and where the property for which they fight would be destroyed. But even excepting such weapons, the ruling class still dispose of dive-bombers, flame-throwing tanks, artillery, machine guns, etc., which the insurrectionary could not obtain, at least in large quantities. Against such resources the traditional small arms of the revolutionary uprising are useless. Since Haussmann's counter-revolutionary town planning, even street fighting, the former *pièce de resistance* of the urban revolution, is won by the side with artillery and tanks. In the Commune, the artillery methods of Thiers defeated the numerical superiority of riflemen at the barricades, while in spite of ingenious dynamite, grenades and petrol bombs, the Spanish Government troops — who must be considered objectively as fulfilling the role of a revolutionary army — were eventually unable to hold back a superior weight of mechanical weapons. No enthusiasm compensated for an inferior armament.

The classic reply is that the revolutionaries must persuade the soldiers to come over to their side. To this there are several answers. Firstly, if the soldiers were already wholly sympathetic there would surely be no need for violence, since the most reactionary government must have some support if it is to survive. If this support is withdrawn it means a bloodless revolution. Such revolutions can be found in history. But if violence is needed, it means that at least a substantial section of the armed forces remain loyal, which in turn means that the workers do not wholly support the revolution. Among romantically inclined supporters of violence there exists an assumption that *their* bloodshed will be wreaked on "enemies of the workers." In fact, all reactionaries use people of the working class for their defence, and the revolutionary who fights against an army is usually attacking people of his own class. The poor are the principal victims on both sides in any war, national or civil.

It is also somewhat superficial to imagine that governments have failed to give thought to the possible disaffection of their armies. This chance has in fact received very great attention, and has been met in most armies by a process of division by which the troops who man planes, tanks, etc., are selected carefully for their class origin and are given especially favorable conditions of service. Such selected corps have thus a vested interest in the *status quo*. The differences in conditions within the armed forces give rises to antagonisms between various services which are not discouraged by the authorities. Generally speaking, the disunity is such that even if the infantry sided with the insurgents, the really important specialist formations would not follow them. It is impossible to imagine any situation in western countries today in which a wholesale collapse of the army would be likely in the face of an armed insurrection.

In other words, there is little prospect of immediate success for an insurrection. Most likely, it would be suppressed immediately. But, even supposing it attained some initial success, seized certain towns, won over troops, obtained a proportion of heavy armor, it is still unlikely that success would be complete, that there would not remain a great mass of specialist troops armed with the majority of the planes, tanks, and artillery. To win final victory, to "consolidate the revolution," the advocates of violence demand a continuance of conflict. In other words, they advocate a civil war.

But civil wars are fatal to revolutions, whether they are won or lost. In most cases it is a foregone conclusion that the trained military forces will win in a short period, although in special circumstances the struggle may continue for years before final defeat, as in Spain, or even result in victory for the so-called revolutionaries as in Russia. But, in any event, a civil war is always destructive to the ends of a revolution. This is because the successful conduct of war demands forms of organization which negate the revolutionary principles of liberty, equality, and fraternity. There is nothing so effective in degrading a revolution into a dictatorship as a period of military adventure.

It is true that, in the initial rising, guerilla bands may gain sweeping successes which form a basis for the first consolidation of the revolutionary groups. This was the case particularly in Spain in July 1936. But it is observed in all major revolutions that such bands are by their nature unable to carry on war efficiently. Their undisciplined methods, the idea of individual freedom which inspires their organization of production and supply, make them quite incapable of standing up to disciplined and well-armed military forces. The guerillas may be very efficient in their native streets or forests, but in the strategic action by which any war is eventually won they will always be defeated by trained and equipped units. Discipline is essential for the prosecution of war, and that is why, as Simone Weil said in a penetrating article recently published in *Politics*, "revolutionary war is the death of revolutions." Any true revolution demands an increasing realization of liberty, equality, and fraternity. The needs of war demand the destruction of these qualities.

This has been proved time and again in history. The French Revolutionary wars led to the introduction of universal conscription. The Commune began in a libertarian manner, but as the fight continued was forced to become steadily more authoritarian in its conduct. In the Russian civil war the original Red partisans were replaced by efficient military units with strict discipline and inequality of status. The same thing happened in Spain, where the voluntary militias gave way to a conscripted army.

It is the custom of apologists for violence to blame authoritarian "revolutionaries," who are said to have used a war situation in order to seize power. It seems more logical to say that if the undisciplined guerilla forces had been efficient, the authoritarians would never have had their chance. The necessities of war forced the conclusion that a military structure was necessary, and gave an opening to authoritarians like Trotsky and the Spanish Communists.

Mrs. K. C. Chorley, in her learned book *Armies and the Art of Revolution*, makes an exhaustive analysis of the classic revolutionary wars, and comes to the following conclusion:

> . . . it may be said fairly conclusively that all the evidence suggests, first, that radical army reconstruction is almost certainly necessary to fight a serious revolutionary war, and secondly, that this reconstruction, if it is to be efficient, must follow professional army lines. A loose type of military organisation, without responsibility to a central authority, may be adequate and invaluable for the opening phases of insurrection or for guerilla warfare; but for a serious war of siege and manoeuvre against trained troops it is useless. The informal army mentality is essentially anarchistic; soldiers feel themselves free to go home when they wish; officers are apt to be chosen for reasons other than efficiency; commanders of units dislike interference from above. There can be no centralisation of command or administration, no concerted strategy, and therefore no possibility of conducting operations on a large scale.

My own researches have confirmed in my mind the justice of Mrs. Chorley's conclusion, although, of course, the ultimate lesson I draw is somewhat different.

It is evident that the violent revolutionary in civil war is faced with an unavoidable dilemma. Either he must continue with inadequate guerilla methods and accept defeat, or he must adopt the military practices of his adversaries, and so jettison the libertarian and equalitarian ideals for which he fights.

It seems clear that the only way of avoiding this dilemma is a recognition that violence is reactionary in its effects, and that the only hope of achieving a successful social transformation is by the use of non-violent means. I do not propose here to enter into the general question of the efficacy of non-violent methods, as this has been dealt with very thoroughly in such books as Gregg's *The Power of Non-Violence* and the Dutch anarchist Bart de Ligt's *The Conquest of Violence*. But I think it desirable to pay some attention to the role of non-violence in the critical stages of certain revolutions.

The Paris Commune, for example, was initiated almost without bloodshed, by the fraternization of the people of Paris with the soldiers who had been sent to frustrate a possible rising. The Russian Revolution of 1917 began with demonstrations in the streets by strikers and other workers. The demonstrators refrained from using any violence against the troops, although some units fired on them. The effect of such action was that in four days the soldiers began to go over to the insurrectionary workers — the troops who had opened fire being the first to fraternize. Thus the *decisive* phase in the Russian Revolution, which destroyed the whole power of Tsarism, was a non-violent moral victory, based on an appeal to human brotherhood. The entry of violence into later phases, the tragic reversal in which the *soldier resumed his soldiery*, was to bring the destruction of brotherhood and the final erection of a tyranny more formidable than that of the Tsar. One speculates with sadness on what might have been the result if the wonderful example of March 1917 had been followed throughout the ensuing months.

Here we see that the successful opening phases of two important revolutions were initiated by non-violent means and not by violent insurrections. It is a further interesting fact that governments always fear far more thoroughly the fraternization of soldiers and civilians than an actual insurrection. When the soldiers started to fraternize with the Parisians in the early days of the Commune, Thiers immediately evacuated his army from the whole of Paris as the only means of preventing it from becoming completely demoralized by friendship. Similar tactics were used in 1848 by the Austrian generals in Milan and

Vienna, and by the Bourgeois Provisional Government in Paris.

Thus the successful return of Thiers to Paris, of the Imperial forces to Vienna, etc., were secured by segregating the troops from the corrupting influence of a friendly people, and creating a barrier of enmity, so that when the soldiers returned it would be to a hostile city. To take the Commune as an example, Thiers withdrew his troops when they had become demoralized by the friendly attitude of the Paris populace. He reorganized them, and then, after some weeks, returned to attack the Commune. Meanwhile a campaign of propaganda had been conducted both in Paris and Versailles so that the hostility on both sides was accentuated. But the main element in the calculation of Thiers was that the armed forces of the Commune, now organized under Blanquist leadership, would resist violently the invading Versaillese army. He was correct. Had the Communards decided not to resist by military means, there might have been further fraternization, for the troops of Thiers would have felt no more comfortable than those of Bismarck a few months before. But the armed conflict removed the possibility of fraternization, for the Communards now appeared to the Versaillese as enemies whom they had to fight in order to avoid being killed themselves. The armed resistance united the peasants and the middle classes behind Thiers, who had previously been unpopular with them. It gave the excuse for a bloodthirsty repression; the most idealistic social thinkers, the best artisans of Paris, were either killed or driven into a miserable exile, and the possibility of social improvements was delayed for two decades. Thus the Parisians not only lost the bloodless revolution with which the Commune was initiated, but also paid a terrible price in lives and liberties.

In the case of the Russian Revolution, the introduction of violence led to a progressive militarization of life until, although the White Armies were overthrown, the Russian people were also defeated and their revolution destroyed in the regimented domination of a caste of former idealists whom power and violence had turned into tyrants. The history of Lenin's destruction of the anarchists, of

Trotsky's massacre of the libertarian sailors of Kronstadt, of Stalin's persecution of the Doukhobors, show how far the Russian Revolution has deteriorated by participation in violence and the consequent development of a militarist system inevitably inimical to real freedom.

Non-violent action, therefore, is not merely efficient as a social solvent, but it also avoids the loss of freedom which seems the inevitable consequence of civil war. But this is not all. Non-violent action is always attended by a comparatively slight loss of life and damage to social resources. The soldiers and police may fire on demonstrating crowds, there may be some sporadic destruction of plants, but in general such action, if successful, results in a gain that far counter-balances any losses. Civil war, on the other hand, takes a vast toll of human lives — often greater than in a national war. Not only are great numbers of people killed in battle, but civil wars are usually fought with such savagery that many prisoners and suspects are shot out of hand. To these must be added the victims of starvation and epidemics caused by the disruption of services. The number of people who died as a result of the Russian civil war will never be known, but it must be counted in millions. As a result of the Spanish Civil War, it would be a conservative estimate to say that a million men, women, and children died — several times the number of English people killed during the Second World War. Added to this, in both Spain and Russia there was such a vast destruction of factories, houses, transport, and shipping that the standard of living of the survivors inevitably dropped well below what it was before the revolutionary crisis. Let us compare these losses with the undoubted advantages which the Indian people have gained, without corresponding loss, through non-violent pressure on the British government.

During the Second World War in Europe we had examples of violent and non-violent actions which provide an excellent means of comparison. In every country but Denmark, the resistance movement was based on violent methods — assassination, warfare by guerilla bands, etc. The result of these tactics was to change the attitude of the German occupying forces, who during their first year or so had shown a tendency to become softened and corrupted from a military point of view by their life among an at first non-violent population. No sooner had the campaign of assassinations, ambushes, etc., begun, than the German soldiers became hardened by terror, and began to kill and torture. In general, with the exception of the Jews, the hundreds of thousands of people executed by the Nazis in occupied countries were sacrificed to the activities of the violent resistance groups. These groups themselves, through their secret formation, developed an authoritarian, Blanquist character, and the men who came to the top were as ruthless and careless of human life and liberty as the Nazis themselves. Throughout Europe, the concrete achievement of the resistance groups was very slight in comparison with the losses which the people sustained through their deeds. Generally speaking, they had to wait for professional armies to clear away the German occupying forces before they could come out and establish their own terroristic reigns of vengeance and discrimination. Only in Yugoslavia, under peculiar circumstances, did the resistance movement make any substantial gains, and then only because it was able to organize in military formations, which later established a regime of totalitarian repression.

The one country which did not indulge in violent resistance to any great extent was Denmark. The Danes had been despised because they did not offer resistance when the Germans entered their country. Later, when they showed no great signs of taking part in the campaign of murders that was sweeping across Europe, they were again subjected to contempt from all sides. But it was these same Danes who, acting with solidarity and restraint, carried through a great non-violent general strike which completely defeated the Wehrmacht and the Gestapo, and resulted in the only major triumph for freedom gained by any European resistance movement working on its own resources. Moreover, this non-violent victory was achieved at a very slight loss to the Danish people in lives or goods, and Denmark emerged at the end of the war less harmed than any other country.

We have seen, then, the great disadvantages of violent as compared with non-violent revolutionary action. It results in great vital
and material losses to the people, and, far from compensating for
these, its usual course is a deterioration in organization and morality
which involves a loss of the very ideals for which the revolution is
fought. Revolutionary violence is thus self-destructive and therefore
in no circumstances effective.

There remains, however, one argument of the supporter of violence. Many revolutionaries will say: "We do not advocate violence
as desirable, but we regard it as inevitable. In a revolutionary situation violence will occur, and then we must take care to guide it in
the right directions." This is an argument so childish that it would
hardly be worth answering if it were not so frequently used. In fact,
violence is not inevitable in social struggle. The people in general
tend to be pacific in their demonstrations, and such complicated
actions as the General Strike of 1926 have been carried out without
violence. Generally speaking, the more consciousness of the issues
involved exists among the people, the less likely they are to indulge
in spontaneous mob violence. Most of the significant outbursts of
revolutionary violence have been carried out by minorities of organized doctrinaires who forced a violent direction on the movement
of the people. Thus, far from revolutionary violence being
inevitable, it is usually engineered by interested groups. There may
be isolated spontaneous acts of violence, but it should be the duty of
a responsible revolutionary to dissuade people from such acts,
which inevitably play into the hands of the authorities and arouse
resistance among the armed forces, who tend to be sympathetic
towards attitudes of non-violence.

In her essay quoted previously Simone Weil said:

> It seems that revolution engaged in war has only the choice
> of either succumbing under the murderous blows of counter-
> revolution or transforming itself into counter-revolution
> through the very mechanism of the military struggle. The

perspectives of a revolution seem therefore quite restricted. For can a revolution avoid war? It is, however, on this feeble chance that we must stake everything or abandon all hope.

Personally, I do not think the chance is so very feeble. The record of non-violent struggles, of the Indians against the British Raj, of the Doukhobors in Canada, of the Danes against the Nazis, give hope that a self-disciplined movement of non-violent action may bring great achievements in the removal of injustice and the establishment of a classless social order of real liberty, equality, and fraternity. This seems to me the only realistic way towards social revolution. All appeals to violence are romantic and dangerous, for they can only lead us back to tyranny and fear.

1947

7

The Tyranny of the Clock

No characteristic is existing society in the west so sharply distinguished from the earlier societies, whether of Europe or the East, than in its conception of time. To the ancient Chinese or Greek, to the Arab herdsman or Mexican peon of today, time is represented by the cyclic processes of nature, the alternation of day and night, the passage from season to season. The nomads and farmers measured and still measure their day from sunrise to sunset, and their year in terms of seedtime and harvest, of the falling leaf and the ice thawing on the lakes and rivers. The farmer worked according to the elements, the craftsman for as long as he felt it necessary to perfect his product. Time was seen as a process of natural change, and men were not concerned in its exact measurement. For this reason civilizations highly developed in other respects had the most primitive means of measuring time: the hour glass with its trickling sand or dripping water, the sun dial, useless on a dull day, and the candle or lamp whose unburnt remnant of oil or wax indicated the hours. All these devices were approximate and inexact, and were often rendered unreliable by the weather or the personal laziness of the tender. Nowhere in the ancient or mediaeval world were more than a tiny minority of men concerned with time in the terms of mathematical exactitude.

Modern, western man, however, lives in a world which runs according to the mechanical and mathematical symbols of clock time. The clock dictates his movements and inhibits his actions. The clock turns time from a process of nature into a commodity that can be measured and bought and sold like soap or sultanas. And because, without some means of exact time keeping, industrial capitalism could never have developed and could not continue to exploit the workers, the clock represents an element of mechanical tyranny in the lives of modern men more potent than any individual exploiter or than any other machine. It is therefore valuable to trace the historical process by which the clock influenced the social development of modern European civilization.

It is a frequent circumstance of history that a culture or civilization develops the device that will later be used for its destruction. The ancient Chinese, for example, invented gunpowder, which was developed by the military experts of the West and eventually led to the Chinese civilization itself being destroyed by the high explosives of modern warfare. Similarly, the supreme achievement of the craftsmen of the medieval cities of Europe was the invention of the clock which, with its revolutionary alteration of the concept of time, materially assisted the growth of the middle ages.

There is a tradition that the clock appeared in the eleventh century, as a device for ringing bells at regular intervals in the monasteries which, with the regimented life they imposed on their inmates, were the closest social approximation in the middle ages to the factory of today. The first authenticated clock, however, appeared in the thirteenth century, and it was not until the fourteenth century that clocks became common as ornaments of the public buildings in German cities.

These early clocks, operated by weights, were not particularly accurate, and it was not until the sixteenth century that any great reliability was attained. In England, for instance, the clock at Hampton Court, made in 1540, is said to have been the first accurate clock in the country. And even the accuracy of the sixteenth-century clocks is relative, for they were equipped only with hour hands. The idea of measuring time in minutes and seconds had been thought out by the early mathematicians as far back as the fourteenth century, but it was not until the invention of the pendulum in 1657 that sufficient accuracy was attained to permit the addition of a minute hand, and the second hand did not appear until the eighteenth century. These two centuries, it should be observed, were those in which capitalism grew to such an extent that it was able to take advantage of the techniques of the industrial revolution to establish its economic domination over society.

The clock, as Lewis Mumford has pointed out, is the key machine of the machine age, both for its influence on technics and for its influence on the habits of men. Technically, the clock was the first really automatic machine that attained any importance in the life of man. Previous to its invention, the common machines were of such a nature that their operation depended on some external and unreliable force, such as human or animal muscles, water or wind. It is true that the Greeks had invented a number of primitive automatic machines, but these were used, like Hero's steam engine, either for obtaining "supernatural" effects in the temples or for amusing the tyrants of Levantine cities. But the clock was the first automatic machine that attained public importance and a social function. Clock-making became the industry from which men learnt the elements of machine-making and gained the technical skill that was to produce the complicated machinery of the Industrial Revolution.

Socially the clock had a more radical influence than any other machine, in that it was the means by which the regularization and regimentation of life necessary for an exploiting system of industry could best be assured. The clock provided a means by which time — a category so elusive that no philosophy has yet determined its nature — could be measured concretely in the more tangible terms of space provided by the circumference of a clock dial. Time as duration became disregarded, and men began to talk and think always of "lengths" of time, just as if they were talking of lengths of calico. And time, being now measurable in mathematical symbols, was regarded as a commodity that could be bought and sold in the same way as any other commodity.

The new capitalists, in particular, became rabidly time-conscious. Time, here symbolizing the labor of the workers, was regarded by them almost as if it were the chief raw material of industry. "Time is money" was one of the key slogans of capitalist ideology, and the timekeeper was the most significant of the new types of official introduced by the capitalist dispensation.

In the early factories the employers went so far as to manipulate their clocks or sound their factory whistles at the wrong time in order to defraud the workers of a little of this valuable new commodity. Later such practices became less frequent, but the influence of the clock imposed a regularity on the lives of the majority of men that had previously been known only in the monasteries. Men actually became like clocks, acting with a repetitive regularity which had no resemblance to the rhythmic life of a natural being. They became, as the Victorian phrase put it, "as regular as clockwork." Only in the country districts where the natural lives of animals and plants and the elements still dominated existence, did any large proportion of the population fail to succumb to the deadly tick of monotony.

At first this new attitude to time, this new regularity of life, was imposed by the clock-owning masters on the unwilling poor. The factory slave reacted in his spare time by living with a chaotic irregularity which characterized the gin-sodden slums of early nineteenth-century industrialism. Men fled to the timeless worlds of drink or Methodist inspiration. But gradually the idea of regularity spread downwards and among the workers. Nineteenth-century religion and morality played their part by proclaiming the sin of "wasting time." The introduction of mass-produced watches and clocks in the 1850s spread time-consciousness among those who had previously merely reacted to the stimulus of the knocker-up or the factory whistle. In the church and the school, in the office and the workshop, punctuality was held up as the greatest of the virtues.

Out of this slavish dependence on mechanical time which spread insidiously into every class in the nineteenth century, there grew up the demoralizing regimentation which today still characterizes factory life. The man who fails to conform faces social disapproval and economic ruin — unless he drops out into a nonconformist way of life in which time ceases to be of prime importance. Hurried meals, the regular morning and evening scramble for trains or buses, the strain of having to work to time schedules, all contribute, by digestive and nervous disturbance, to ruin health and shorten life.

Nor does the financial imposition of regularity tend, in the long run, to greater efficiency. Indeed, the quality of the product is usually much poorer, because the employer, regarding time as a commodity which he has to pay for, forces the operative to maintain such a speed that his work must necessarily be skimped. Quantity rather than quality becoming the criterion, the enjoyment is taken out of the work itself, and the worker in his turn becomes a "clock-watcher," concerned only with when he will be able to escape to the scanty and monotonous leisure of industrial society, in which he "kills time" by cramming in as much time-scheduled and mechanical enjoyment of cinema, radio, and newspaper as his wage packet and his tiredness will allow. Only if he is willing to accept the hazards of living by his faith or his wits can the man without money avoid living as a slave to the clock.

The problem of the clock is, in general, similar to that of the machine. Mechanized time is valuable as a means of coordinating activities in a highly developed society, just as the machine is valuable as a means of reducing unnecessary labor to a minimum. Both are valuable for the contribution they make to the smooth running of society, and should be used in so far as they assist men to cooperate efficiently and to eliminate monotonous toil and social confusion. But neither should be allowed to dominate men's lives as they do today.

Now the movement of the clock sets the tempo of men's lives — they become the servants of the concept of time which they themselves have made, and are held in fear, like Frankenstein by his own monster. In a sane and free society such an arbitrary domination of man's functions by either clock or machine would obviously be out of the question. The domination of man by man-made machines is even more ridiculous than the domination of man by man. Mechanical time would be relegated to its true function of a means of reference and coordination, and men would return again to a balanced view of life no longer dominated by time-regulation and the worship of the clock. Complete liberty implies freedom from the tyranny of abstractions as well as from the rule of men.

1944

8

Anarchist Living and the Practice of Art

The practice of art — of any art — is one of the modes of anarchist living. When I am asked how the arts can further anarchism, or conversely (as a CBC producer recently framed the question to me in asking for a talk) how an anarchist outlook can liberate the creative impulse, I feel a certain artificiality in the question, because, whichever form it takes, the question is posed in such a way that the two viewpoints — that of the artist and that of the anarchist — are assumed to be separate. In my view they are two facets of the same unity. The practice of art is one of the modes of anarchist living, but anarchism is a projection into existence of the harmonies and also of the dissonances that art reveals.

That I can speak in this way reveals a considerable change during the past generation, not in the essential idea which the word *anarchism* represents, but rather in the way we see it exemplified, in the strategy, so to speak, which in the present generation has shifted from the quasi-political into the cultural, using that term in its broadest scope; anarchists now tend to think less in terms of gaining power or fighting power than in terms of living here and now without power.

In its continuing essentials, anarchism is a doctrine of liberty, but not a doctrine of nihilist license, since it recognizes that human existence, like all life, is subject to natural laws, to the ecological imperatives; it exists in the interface between freedom and necessity, just as art exists on the interface between impulse and form. Anarchists believe in the need to destroy, but only in the sense that, as Bakunin said in his famous aphorism, "the urge to destroy is also a creative urge." (*"Destruam et aedificabo"* as Proudhon somewhat differently — and previously — phrased the same continuing libertarian idea.) But what they wish to destroy are the artificial and anticreative structures of authority and coercion which are most emphatically represented in political laws and above all in the nation-state and which everywhere prevent the free development of natural generative impulses.

Herbert Read was a fine modern poet and aesthetician, but he was also one of the seminal theoreticians of anarchism in our age — seminal precisely because in *Education through Art* he taught that the use of the arts to train the senses and sensibilities was the necessary basis for any system of free education or for any society whose idea of socialism was libertarian. "Anarchism," said Read in his earlier book, *Poetry and Anarchism*, "rejects the man-made systems of government, which are instruments of individual and class tyranny; it seeks to recover the system of nature, of man living in accordance with the universal truth of reality. . . . But the rule of reason — to live according to natural laws — is also the release of the imagination." Hence, of course, the close relationship between the anarchist and the aesthetic impulses. Read goes on to say that in its release of the imagination anarchism offers us two possibilities, "to discover truth and to create beauty." He cautions us not to mix the two, for if we try to create truth instead of discovering it we end with artificial and utopian systems, the authoritarian systems of the left and right, that result in the strangulation of the imagination and hence of the power to create beauty.

More than a decade ago, when I wrote *Anarchism*, I remarked on the durability of the idea and the fortunate fragility of its organizational manifestations. I pointed out that though we could trace a kind of historic anarchist movement, running from Bakunin's faction in the First International down to the massive achievements of the Spanish CNT-FAI in the 1930s, this was perhaps an irrelevant line of study, since anarchism had a curiously Protean quality, and depended on no canon of holy books like Marxism and no apostolic succession of leaders like Lenin.

It was a doctrine whose upholders laid no stress on ideological loyalty or organizational permanence, yet which had its own kind of continuity, behaving rather like water in a limestone country, sometimes flowing abundantly, sometimes vanishing underground only to re-emerge later in full flood. In this way, having remained in obscurity ever since Franco's triumph in 1938, anarchism suddenly re-emerged during the 1960s as an idea that in its various forms appealed to thousands of young people in western Europe and North America, laid its influence on the New Left, played a key role in such crucial events as the Paris insurrection of 1968, and ran in close liaison with contemporary movements in the arts.

This anarchism of the later twentieth century is in many ways a different phenomenon from classic Bakuninist anarchism. The anarchists of a century ago were more politically minded and more millenially inclined than their successors today. They thought often in terms of large mass organizations — the syndicates — which could be wielded so as to create a kind of anti-power that would be a force in its own right; and they developed a desperate philosophy of all-or-nothing, of the revolution as a total and instant break with the past: either we sweep all the evil institutions away in the surge of a great social conflagration and begin anew, or we continue in the same old way, without any escape from being oppressed, deceived and robbed by the politicians and their capitalist allies.

Such an attitude was largely the product of the crudely dialectical ways of thinking that afflicted mid-nineteenth century social activists of many schools; it was perhaps an unrepresentative interlude in the longer libertarian tradition, which from Winstanley in the 1640s down to Proudhon in the 1840s avoided such either-or choices and assumed

that the libertarian society did not have to wait for a great day of reckoning but could begin its changes here and now by changing life-styles
and hence changing the character of institutions so that ultimately
the edifice of power would become as unstable as a termite-eaten
palace.

Even in the mid-nineteenth century there were anarchists who
represented this point of view, such as Proudhon with his efforts to
create free credit systems; Faure and Ferrer with their experiments in
free education; even the syndicalists who conceived forms of strike
in which the workers would continue to operate factories for the
benefit of the community, as in fact they eventually did in practice
for a few months in Barcelona after the initial defeat of the Francoist
generals in July 1936. Contemporary with Bakunin, the novelist
Tolstoy — a non-violent anarchist who projected the same kind of
unsuppressible moral force as Solzhenitsyn in our own day —
reminded his contemporaries, in insisting that "The Kingdom of
God is within you," of the moral and cultural liberation that was
necessary before we could even begin to change society. Perhaps the
key figure in this tendency was Peter Kropotkin, whose really seminal works were *Mutual Aid* and *Fields, Factories and Workshops*, in
which, to simplify him rather brutally, he taught that the impulse to
free oneself from manmade law and to live freely by observing natural laws of cooperation was neither new nor peculiar to anarchism.
He showed that it could be traced in every phase of human history,
particularly among the constantly appearing heretical groups which
represented in century after century man's natural tendency to rebel
against artificial restraints. Even today, Kropotkin taught, afflicted as
we are by the organizational gigantism of the modern state, mutual
aid still represents a living and organic force that constantly changes
society and influences it in the direction of greater freedom, throwing up, in the form of an unending series of voluntary institutions
and local rebellions against centralization, a perpetual succession of
antibodies to the rigidities produced by political authority.

Kropotkin, whose *Memoirs of a Revolutionist* show him to

have been a literary artist of considerable accomplishment, was conscious of the important role which the arts and crafts played in this constant anti-authoritarian ferment; he had reason to be, since literature had been a powerful instrument against tyranny during the Tsarist regime in Russia. At the turn of the century the liaison between anarchists and artists of various kinds was particularly strong, especially in France, where writers like Mallarmé and Mirbeau and Tailhade, and painters like Courbet and Pissaro and Signac and even the young Pissaro, were fascinated by the suicidal daring of anarchist activists. English writers of the time tended to be influenced by Kropotkin's mutualism; among them were William Morris, Oscar Wilde, Frank Harris, and Ford Madox Ford. Wilde's *The Soul of Man Under Socialism*, which later writers like Read and Orwell read with considerable zeal, was one of the earliest attempts to establish from a libertarian viewpoint the links between artistic creativity and the social revolution. Through Ford Madox Ford, anarchist ideas continued to attract writers in the modernist movement. James Joyce and Franz Kafka, for instance, both counted Kropotkin among their favorite authors, and Kafka attended an anarchist literary circle in Prague which was also frequented by Jaroslav Hasek, author of *The Good Soldier Schweik*, that unbeatable satire on the stupidity of authority, whether military or civil. When Aldous Huxley set out to envisage an alternative to the futurist nightmare of *Brave New World*, to sketch a society that would be unacquisitive, peaceful, and conducive to artistic creation and spiritual contemplation, he took as his basic model Kropotkin's vision of a libertarian society where manual and physical work were creatively integrated in a decentralized pattern.

Since that time there have been two trends that have combined to bring art and anarchism together. For reasons which are perhaps best argued by the libertarian Albert Camus in *The Rebel*, anarchists have realized that, as far as recorded history shows, total revolutions produce totalitarian and not libertarian regimes. So modern libertarians no longer look to the sudden transformation of society by a great act of destruction. Instead they are inclined to see the idea of a totally free, organic society less as a likely possibility than as a regenerative myth. To quote Herbert Read again: "The task of the anarchist philosopher is not to prove the imminence of a Golden Age, but to justify the value of believing in its possibility."

This shift in aim has led anarchism to shed much of its quasi-political character and to assume a much more social-cultural aspect, based less on the idea of destroying authoritarian institutions in the future than on building an alternative pattern of libertarian institutions here and now. The experience of the counter culture over the past two decades has led more and more anarchists to conclude that by changing life styles we can slowly and irreversibly change society and create the kind of ambiance in which the solidifying of social forms into authoritarian shapes will become increasingly difficult. Colin Ward, an English anarchist with whom I collaborated long ago in editing *Freedom*, has written a quite remarkable book called *Anarchy in Action*, a bringing up to date of Kropotkin's great treatises, in which he charts how libertarian patterns have been emerging everywhere in western societies during the past twenty years, how they are beginning to reshape both our mores and our daily life; he suggests how we can strengthen them in such a way as to create, by mainly non-violent means, perhaps not an anarchist utopia, but at least a libertarian society in which administration will be progressively decentralized, in which democracy will become increasingly direct and participatory, and in which politicians will atrophy until they join the Dodo in extinction.

Now the direction in society that above all others tends to encourage and also to draw strength from such a libertarian trend is that of art, whether one considers high art or popular art. For the recognition of the permeative character of anarchism in practice has run parallel to studies of the creative process which lead us to assume that its operations may be very similar to those by which individuals liberate themselves socially by means of mutual aid situations. The artist creates most truly when — to use Freudian terminology — he escapes from the superego to plumb and utilize the intuitive forces, the great reservoir of archetypes and images which, to shift into Jungian terminology, we call the collective unconscious. It is true, as the social realists have argued, that art is at its finest when it in some way projects a universal impulse, but the universal impulses are not reached through collective channels of an institutional kind; they come from the artist's individual immersion in the pool of collective experience. In following this process — a process analogous to that of the individual seeking to fulfill his personal economic needs through social groups based on affinity and shared need — the artist becomes an agent of liberation, and the practice of art, as I remarked at the beginning of this article, becomes one of the modes of anarchist living. It sustains that peculiar and vibrant tension between individual creativity and social function which the anarchist sees as the only alternative to real or disguised tyranny. People caught up in the routines of business or bureaucracy often envy artists their freedom, and in this they are right, for the impulses that compel the artist are organic rather than synthetic imperatives, and hence are manifestations of liberty. The Communists are greatly mistaken in branding the artist's desire to express his creative impulses freely as a form of bourgeois individualism. It is, on the contrary, one of the most potent and erosive of revolutionary forces.

1976

9

Anarchism and Ecology

With remarkable, even prophetical insight many 19th century anarchists and their followers foresaw the severe social and environmental problems that we now see clearly to be an inevitable consequence of industrialization and development. Anarchists such as these were therefore the forerunners of contemporary environmentalists who today appreciate that destruction and despoliation of the environment has more to do with a social system that has gone pathologically wrong than with inadequate measures of conservation or pollution control. The majority of anarchists believed that man should live in close harmony with his fellow beings and his environment. With some justification it can be said that anarchists were the first true ecologists.

In 1899 the Russian anarchist Peter Kropotkin, exiled in London, published his *Fields, Factories and Workshops*, a book that should be, if it is not already — one of the canonical texts of the ecological tradition. In *Fields, Factories and Workshops* Kropotkin dealt with many problems that concern the ecologist today. He was disturbed by the centralization of population and industry in large, unhealthy agglomerations; he was disturbed by the wastefulness of both industrial and agricultural production in his time, and he calculated that by using proper means of conserving fertility, England could be made agriculturally self-supporting; he believed in the integration of work and education, so that training in productive processes would give academic learning a basis in the reality of social action; he believed also in the integration of agriculture and industry, so that small production units could be scattered over the land and no worker need feel isolated from rural life or from what survived of the wilderness. Patrick Geddes, Lewis Mumford, and other notable precursors of the contemporary environmentalist movement have acknowledged their considerable debt to Kropotkin, and Mumford's proposals for large-scale decentralization in *Technics and Civilization* were little more than Kropotkin plus electricity.

Unless my *Oxford English Dictionary* is misleading me, ecology was first recognized as a branch of scientific theory in the 1870s, the decade in which Kropotkin became an anarchist and developed his theories of anarchist-communism (most thoroughly discussed in *The Conquest of Bread* — 1906). These theories depended largely on reversing the trend towards political and economic centralization that had been building up since the Renaissance, and they stressed the view that in our calculations of social needs we should proceed not from the top — the state or the industrial corporation — but from the level where people came together in direct personal and working relationships, the level at which human needs could most realistically be discussed and most directly determined.

In fact, in developing anarchist communism, Kropotkin was only refining on tendencies that were evident in anarchism ever since William Godwin wrote the first great exposition of the doctrine — *Political Justice* — in the 1790s. Godwin called the local units parishes; Proudhon and Bakunin were more interested in self-governing workshops and communes; all of them stressed the need to base social organization on natural laws; and Kropotkin reinforced this concept in his *Mutual Aid* (published in 1902 after the material had appeared as a series of essays in *The Nineteenth Century*). There he related the social responsibilities which he found characteristic of men when they were undisturbed by coercive institutions with the sociality he found so widely spread among animals. Kropotkin wrote *Mutual Aid* in a mood of reaction against the fashionable neo-Darwinist doctrine which portrayed nature, in Tennyson's unfortunate phrase, as "red in tooth and claw," and saw the struggle for existence as necessarily a struggle between individuals and species. As a field geographer of considerable experience in eastern Asia, Kropotkin found that a number of field naturalists agreed with him in deploring this essentially competitive view of evolution, and it was actually with the encouragement of H.W. Bates, author of the classic *Naturalist on the River Amazon* and a close associate of Darwin, that he put forward his argument that the struggle for existence was in fact the struggle against adverse circumstances rather than within species, and that one of the most potent forces in evolution and in sustaining the balance of the world of nature was in fact cooperation. Since he was concerned mainly with what happened within species, Kropotkin did not explicitly delineate the complex pattern of mutual dependencies which the modern ecologist sees when he looks at relationships within the natural world, but the existence of that pattern was certainly implied, especially in the extent to which Kropotkin sought to prove that the law of mutual aid was universal in its application, embracing man within the same natural continuum as all the animals and basing his own development as a social being on the same principle as that which ensured the survival of other species from the insects up to the higher mammals.

Thus, since they were aware of the extent to which a healthy life in biological terms was dependent on mutual aid on every level, and saw clearly the analogies between animal and human societies, there is little doubt that the classic anarchists would have been — as their successors are today — deeply in tune with the concerns of modern ecologists. Kropotkin's particular contribution — apart from the theoretical contribution in *Mutual Aid* — was to relate anarchism through concrete proposals for industrial and agrarian reform in books like *Fields, Factories and Workshops* to the movement for conserving the environment in the interests of a richer way of existence, a movement that has come to maturity only in recent decades under the pressure of mounting ecological disturbance and rapidly diminishing resources of fuel and raw materials.

Anarchism, which has been in existence for well over a century as a distinctly identifiable political movement, and which in theoretical form dates from the publication of Godwin's *Political Justice* in the late eighteenth century, has taken many forms during its history, since unlike Marxism it never developed a body of orthodox doctrine or a close organizational structure, both of which would have negated its emphasis on spontaneity as a manifestation of freedom. Some of the forms it took resulted in sensational publicity and aroused extreme hostility; there were times, for example, when fanatical anarchists — like the fanatics of other movements — resorted to the assassination of rulers and to other terrorist acts. But such extreme anarchists were always a small minority, and there were others, like Tolstoy, who believed that the anarchist rejection of coercion meant automatically a rejection of violence; Gandhi called himself an anarchist of this kind.

More important perhaps were the differences in anarchist views of how society should be organized economically and politically, and of how the change from an unfree society could be effected. Essential to all anarchist doctrines was the belief that if man was not naturally good, he was at least naturally social, and that coercive government destroyed this natural sociality. All anarchists have also concluded that massive centralized organizations of all kinds carry within themselves the dangers of coercion, and they have therefore invariably related the voluntary principle to social, economic, and political decentralization. Organization, they argued, should begin at the grassroots level, so that people in small groups and limited localities can control everything that affects them immediately and concerns no one else. As wider interests become involved, anarchists favored not coordination imposed from above, by some remote and over-riding authority, but the application of what they called "the federal principle." By this they meant that the common affairs of a town should be managed by a federation of streets and localities, sending delegates to town meetings, with initiatives starting up in the localities, and that society should be federated upwards, from town to district, from district to region, and so forth, but always with the power of decision rising upward from the simplest level rather than stemming downward from some central power. The relevance of such a view of social organization to the concerns of ecologists will be evident, for the potentiality of environmental disaster is always recognizable first at the local level. Indeed centralized administrations are more likely than decentralized ones to ignore environmental danger signs in the interests of so-called national welfare or even of openly-admitted corporate interests.

Parallel to the constant anarchist emphasis on decentralization one can isolate another attitude (for it can hardly be classed as anything so definite as a theory) that relates the anarchists to modern ecologists. It is an inclination towards the simplification rather than the progressive complication of ways of living.

In theory, the earlier anarchists actually tended to share with nineteenth-century socialists the belief that if the world's resources were properly managed, there was no limit to the physical abundance that human individuals could enjoy; it was such an assumption on Godwin's part that led Malthus to bring forward his celebrated arguments on the limits of natural resources and their likely effect on progress and on population. Because the nineteenth-century world was still — in our terms — scantily populated, and because the expansion of available resources throughout the century was always in excess of the powers of consumption at the current state of technological development, Malthus's warnings went unheeded by the anarchists as they were by most men before the 1960s.

Yet with the anarchists there was a compensating factor. By temperament they were always inclined to favor a modest and even an austere way of life. The reasons for this inclination were complex.

There was a certain essential puritanism in the anarchist viewpoint; they were inclined to regard the rich as victims to be pitied as well as villains to be condemned, a duality of perception not uncommon among the religious fundamentalists to whom the anarchists have always been the closest secular counterparts. At the same time, the anarchists not only felt that human life should be as spontaneous and as natural as possible (and hence as untrammelled by material attachments), but also that the goal of affluence introduced the perils of economic centralization and hence of political authority. For these various reasons anarchist thinkers as far apart in time as Pierre-Joseph Proudhon in the mid-nineteenth century and Paul Goodman in the mid-twentieth advocated the goal which Goodman called "a dignified poverty," the simplification of life which would lead to a simplification of social and economic organization. Anarchists, and libertarian socialists who closely associated with them, such as Tolstoy and William Morris, became deeply concerned with the dehumanizing effects of machine technology, and, while neither Morris nor Tolstoy absolutely rejected the use of machines where there was a question of eliminating some degrading form of menial work, both they and their followers looked towards a future in which the manual crafts would return, and the human and environmental destruction caused by the industrial revolution would come to an end.

In India, where a pre-mechanical village society not only survived into the days of the British Raj, but embraced a great majority of the population, Gandhi — who was greatly influenced by western anarchists like Tolstoy, Kropotkin, and Thoreau — planned to create a village-based society with an economy based on handcrafts and a simple, ascetic way of life. This was not merely an Asian adaptation of anarchism; in Spain, during the early months of the Civil War in 1936, many villages of Andalusia, where the anarchists had a following among the farm-workers, expelled their landowners, communalized the land, and then proceeded to set up self-sufficient local economies in which they sought to simplify their needs in the interests of village autonomy. But, as observers noted, their goals seemed to be moral as well as politico-economic; they welcomed the unavailability of luxuries like alcohol and even of coffee with the feeling that their lives had not merely been liberated but had also been purified.

The important aspect of this tendency is not the latent puritanism it uncovers in the anarchist temperament, but rather the fact that alone among the parties of the left, the anarchists — unlike the liberals, socialists, and communists, and the various nationalist movements — were uncommitted to the goal of constant material progress, to the philosophy of the growth economy. They were willing to consider that the good life, the free life, might not merely be possible, but might even be more attainable and defensible, within the context of a more selective approach to technological development, an approach which did not assume affluence to be a necessary good. They were even willing to accept what in conventional liberal or socialist terms would be regarded as retrogression, provided this brought benefits of a less material kind. And this inclination, it should be observed, was present among anarchists at the same time as they denied or ignored Malthus's arguments regarding the relationship between the pressure of population and the limitations of natural resources.

As a historic movement anarchism did not exactly fail to prove the validity of its scheme of a decentralized libertarian society. It never, in any broad sense, had the opportunity to do so. Because of their distrust of excessive organization, anarchists were slow to adapt themselves to the dominant economic trends of the nineteenth century. Proudhon sought to perpetuate as far as possible a society of independent peasants and artisans, whose land and workshops would be guaranteed to them as lifetime "possessions" and who would exchange their products by a system of labor checks. Only reluctantly did he grant that the development of the factory system and of the railways demanded workers' associations to operate larger units of production and communication. Even when later theoreticians, like Bakunin and Kropotkin, developed anarchist schemes for the collective ownerships of the means of production and distribution (on the basis of the classic slogan "From each according to his means; to each according to his needs"), the individualism and localism of the anarchists was reflected both in their views of political organization (they clung very strongly to the idea of the "commune," which corresponded to the village or the urban quarter, as sovereign both economically and politically) and in their idea of revolutionary tactics, based on the method of individual action by militants (the so-called "propaganda of the deed") which it was hoped would by example induce the populace to rise in spontaneous insurrection, destroy the evil and oppressive structure of the state, and in its place create the natural units of a free cooperative society.

This was essentially a romantic vision, and though the anarchists were powerful enough to challenge the Marxists in the First International, during the 1870s, and to build up strong followings in Latin and Slav countries, they were unable to create stable mass movements largely because their localism permeated even the organization of their movement. After the break-up of the First International into anarchist and Marxist factions, both of which perished quickly, no stable anarchist international organization was created, though there was a great deal of world-wide contact among anarchists, fostered by the wandering of constantly exiled celebrities of the movement like Peter Kropotkin, Enrico Malatesta, and Emma Goldman. Even nationally, only in a few countries like Spain and Italy did anarchist federations show even a modest durability.

Instead of preparing for an apocalyptic revolution, contemporary anarchists tend to be concerned far more with trying to create, in society as it is the infrastructure of a better and freer society.

The repeated failure of anarchist insurrections in Spain and Italy during the 1870s and 1880s, and the hostility aroused by the subsequent wave of individual terrorism, had reduced the anarchist movement by the 1890s to a rump of dedicated militants and of symbolist writers and painters; indeed it seemed little more than one of the many forms of eccentric fantasy in which the morbid mood of the fin-de-siècle manifested itself. (Though even then there were anarchists who in progressive schools and agrarian communities and in various fields of artistic experimentation were developing the more constructive manifestations of the anarchist vision.)

But in fact, at this very time anarchism was on the eve of one of the great resurgences that have punctuated its history. During the later 1880s the mood of reaction that in France had followed the defeat of the Paris Commune of 1870-71 (in which many early anarchists, including the painter Gustave Courbet, had played an active part) was relaxed and not only left-wing political parties but also trade unions were allowed to operate. Since they regarded the delegation of one's responsibility by voting for a parliamentary representative as a dereliction of freedom, the anarchists were little interested in joining or forming political parties aimed at gaining power through elections or even *coups d'etât*. For them — and history seems to have proved them right — power was just as corrupting in the hands of a party of left-wing militants as in the hands of a party of right-wing reactionaries; the anarchists sought the destruction, not the appropriation, of the state. But trade unions — or *syndicats* — were another matter, since they retained a direct link with the elemental process of work. Working-class anarchists entered the French *syndicats* in large numbers, established themselves in key positions, and out of their experience developed the only kind of anarchism that attracted a relatively stable mass following.

This was anarcho-syndicalism, or revolutionary syndicalism. The basic theory of anarcho-syndicalism was that the trade union, provided it remained in the hands of the workers and never developed a bureaucracy of permanent union officials, was the ideal instrument for attaining a free society, since industry was the real heart of any state, and the ability to withdraw their labor power would enable the workers to stop that heart beating. They had only to declare the general strike — the "strike of folded arms" as the French militants called it — for the state to grind to a halt, and then it would be a simple matter for the workers to take over their factories through the *syndicats* and place their products at society's disposal.

Theoretical syndicalists likes Georges Sorel, author of *Reflections on Violence*, treated the general strike as a necessary myth for sustaining the militancy of the workers and hence the vitality of society in general. But the anarchist militants within the *syndicats* took the idea literally, and so did those anarchists, notably Malatesta, who remained attached to the spontaneitist and localist doctrines of anarchist-communism, and who feared that the domination of the movement by the *syndicats* would lead to the creation of monolithic interest groups that would dominate society economically if not politically.

Nevertheless, it was through the anarcho-syndicalist unions that, in the early twentieth century and especially in France, Spain, Italy, and Latin America, anarchism became a powerful mass movement and once again a rival of Marxism. Until after the First World War, the powerful French trade union movement, the CGT, was anarchist-dominated, and so, until Franco's triumph in 1939, was the CNT in Spain, which boasted two million members and was the largest organization ever to admit to being anarchist. Not only were the anarcho-syndicalists more numerous in Spain than elsewhere; it was in Spain also that they were able to prove, in the first phases of the Civil War of 1936-39, that anarchist theories of workers' direct control of industry could actually work in practice, for the factories and transport systems in Barcelona as well as many agricultural estates in Andalusia and Valencia were taken over by workers under the lead of anarchist militants and — as unbiased outside observers bore witness — were run remarkably well.

But those early months of the Spanish Civil War represented the swan-song of historic anarchism. Already the considerable movements in Russia and Italy had been crushed by the Bolsheviks and Fascists respectively, the former after a spectacular resistance by anarchist guerillas in the Ukraine under the leadership of Nestor Makhno. The triumph of the Marxists in the Russian October Revolution of 1917 and the foundation of the Comintern weakened anarchism internationally and especially in France, where the Communists took over the CGT and still control it. In Spain, even before the Civil War ended, the anarchist position had been undermined by their communist rivals, and the spirit of the CNT was so weakened that Franco's troops marched unresisted into Barcelona, which had once been the anarchist Mecca. Anarchism became, in 1939, the ghost of a great movement, sustained by a few refugees in Mexico, Sweden, and the English-speaking countries, and, rather surprisingly, by English and American poets and artists.

When I published *Anarchism* in 1962, the *movement* seemed at its nadir. But even then I pointed to the extraordinary resilience of the anarchist *idea*, which, because of the very absence of anything resembling a monolithic party or an orthodoxy of doctrine, was capable of reviving in different forms at various times in history. Already it had appeared as the rational dissenting Christianity of Winstanley in the seventeenth century, as a way of life to be attained by reasonable discourse in Godwin's vision, as a saving doctrine for peasants and artisans in Proudhon's mutualism, as the romantic revolutionism of Bakunin and Malatesta and the free decentralist communism of the scientist Kropotkin, as the pacifist communitarianism of Tolstoy and Gandhi, and as the practical organization of workers' control by the syndicalists. Each form had contributed to the tradition in its time and in its own way. And thus, in the first (1962) edition of *Anarchism*, I pointed out that although the historic movement which Bakunin had founded and which reached its peak in Spain was undoubtedly dead, the anarchist idea was still very much alive and might well appear in new forms.

As I was able to record in the postscript to the 1974 Penguin edition of *Anarchism*, this has actually happened. During the 1940s and 1950s, anarchism was largely kept alive by libertarian writers, notably, in England, by Alex Comfort and Herbert Read, whose *Education through Art* developed the theory of an anarchist form of education through the cultivation of the sensibilities. In the 1960s anarchist ideas began to spread once again as a result of the agitations of the Campaign for Nuclear Disarmament and the Committee of 100 in England and of the civil rights campaigns in the United States. A renewed anarchism appeared, appealing to the young by its insistence on such ideas as participatory democracy, workers' control, and decentralization, all of which struck at the monolithic establishment which the new generation of radicals regarded as their principal enemy.

What has happened is something quite different from the past, and that of course is in keeping with the mutability of the anarchist tradition. The kind of mass movement at whose head Bakunin challenged Marx in the First International, and which reached its apogee in the Spanish CNT, has not reappeared. What has happened is a wide diffusion of anarchist ideas, largely through the publication of new studies and histories of anarchism and the republication of old texts long out of print, a diffusion that has affected the New Left, the student movement, the ecology movement, and other similar trends of the times. Except for a few dedicated militants, anarchists no longer tend to see the future in terms of conflagratory insurrection that will destroy the state and all the establishments of authority and will immediately usher in the free society. That is now seen mainly as the myth of the movement, the point on the horizon that gives direction to present action. Instead of preparing for an apocalyptic revolution, contemporary anarchists tend to be concerned far more with trying to create, in society as it is, the infrastructure of a better and freer society. In experimental communes, in free schools, in movements among the underprivileged to gain control of their own destinies, the neighborhood initiatives that defy authority and promote decentralization, in struggles for greater workers' control and for union democracy, and often in active support for ecological movements as one way of frustrating the threat by corporate power to man and his environment, they are perhaps moving more surely towards the real transformation of society than their predecessors who by making expectations extreme and demands absolute ensured their own defeat. We may never see the free society of which the anarchists dreamed, but if we do achieve a world that is healthier and cleaner and freer than that we now inhabit, the anarchist idea will have contributed to it, and notably in developing those theories of a decentralized and organically integrated society that Kropotkin most fully set out in *Fields, Factories and Workshops*, the book that Tolstoy and Gandhi and Mumford all read as a seminal work.

1974

10

The Prospects for Anarchism

I am not a devotee of cyclic theories of history, but like many other people I cannot help being impressed by the fact that waves of rebellion, if not of revolution, should have broken out at such regular intervals during the greater part of the twentieth century. With a little chronological juggling one can see a regular thirty-year pattern emerging, particularly if one treats the Bolshevik counter-revolution of October 1917 as the climax to a movement that began in the 1900s with the genuine popular uprisings of 1905 in Russia. Thence a leap of thirty years takes us to the 1930s, the Spanish Civil War and the spread of militant labor unrest in the Americas and in the parts of western Europe not pre-empted by the dictators. Again it was a time of popular rebellion which in the end was used for counter-revolutionary purposes by the totalitarian parties, not only the Stalinists, but also the Fascists and — even more — the Nazis, who rode to power through their skill in manipulating popular discontent.

Superficially, at least, the radicalism of the 1960s seemed of a different kind from that of the 1900s and the 1930s. It was highly sectionalized, with little real cohesion, a revolt of minorities: privileged university-educated youth fighting over moral rather than material questions'; women extending the militant struggle of the suffragettes

in the 1900s; blacks and other racial minorities continuing the abolitionist struggle, now for greater genuine equality; native peoples
demanding a return to the land and the political sovereignty that had
been taken away from them by generations of exploiting whites; dis-
abled people demanding above all their rights to the full dignity of
human beings. Unlike the 1930s, when ideologies of the Left
(Stalinism, Trotskyism, Social Democracy) faced ideologies of the
Right (Nazism and Fascism) in epic antagonism, there were no real
unifying ideologies in the 1960s. The Old Left was as discredited as
the Old Right in the eyes of the militant young and the militant
minorities, and though the civil rights movement early in the decade,
and opposition to the Vietnam war later on, gave rallying cries to the
movement in North America, perhaps the only occasion when one
had a real sense of unity of feeling and outlook was during the few
weeks of 1968 (in some ways a predecessor of events during 1990 in
eastern European cities) when the students, the intellectuals, and the
workers of Paris came together in a struggle that temporarily paralyzed the processes of De Gaulle's government. But even in 1968, as
in Paris at the time of the Commune almost a century before, the
unity of rebellious impulse and action was limited to a single place,
for the rural and small town majority of French people withdrew into
their traditional shell of conservatism, and the days of the Paris struggle, when the black flag of anarchism flew over the Paris bourse,
withered into a romantic memory, a splendid might-have-been.

There are of course important historic links between what happened in the 1900s, the 1930s, and the events in eastern Europe with
which the 1990s are beginning. The emergence of the Bolsheviks as a
significant party during the 1905 "revolution" in Russia began the long
and terrible process by which Marxism-Leninism was put to the test as
a working socio-political program and failed both in ideological terms
and in practical terms of socio-economical arrangement. It offered
bread and circuses at the price of freedom and delivered none of them.

The political rivalries of the 1930s, translated into the con-
frontation of totalitarian order and imperial powers led to World

War II, and the situation in which the Bolsheviks could be both dictators and imperialists and, despite their own failure in Russia, seize
control of eastern European countries from the Baltic states down to
Albania, as well as China and, eventually, North Korea and the countries of Indochina. It was against this background of a world divided
between old and new imperialisms — their conflict manifested and
symbolized in the Vietnam war — that the radical movements of the
1960s emerged.

It would indeed be stretching history somewhat to claim that
what happened in North America and Western Europe during the
1960s had very much influence on recent events in eastern Europe
and China, for the traditions of student rebellion that create the
greatest similarities between the 1960s and the present go far back
into the history of nineteenth-century Europe. It would be a foolish
piece of historicism to treat the present situation except in its own
terms, and indeed what strikes one immediately are two basic differences between events now and events in the 1930s and the 1960s.

First, the rebellions which toppled governments from Warsaw
down to Bucharest (and may well lead before long to the collapse of
that in Beijing) were not "revolutions" according to the Marxist-
Leninist-Blanquist model, led by party elites intent on establishing a
fictional dictatorship of the proletariat or another other elect class.
Indeed, all the so-called revolutionaries were on the wrong side, discredited power brokers. The eastern European insurrections, like the
rising in Beijing of the population in support of the student militants,
were upheavals without visible leaderships, and were as near as one
might imagine to the first stages of a libertarian uprising as envisaged
by Kropotkin and the other old anarchist theoreticians. A major difference from the movements of the 1960s was that now it was no
longer specially aggrieved sections of the population that were
involved, but whole peoples, regardless of age, sex, or, as Romania
dramatically showed, racial background. People of all kinds came
together in the streets in their thousands and hundreds of thousands.
I remember on 1968 looking at the photographs of happenings in

Paris and being thrilled by this uprising of youth in the cause of imagination. I have been even more thrilled in the last few months to see the photographs from Berlin and Prague and Bucharest, which seem to represent whole peoples united in revolt, old women and men standing there shouting their defiance beside the young, and intellectuals and workers mingling in a common cause.

But mere rebellion, however widespread, and even the overthrow of authority are not enough, as anarchists have always argued. If new authoritarian structures are not to be imposed, the people must set about creating their own voluntary networks of mutual aid, and above all — as Kropotkin stressed in *The Conquest of Bread* — they must ensure that the revolution is fed by putting under the direct control of the people the production and distribution of food and other consumer goods.

So far as is evident up the day I write, the leaders and the spokesmen of the largely ad hoc groups that have coalesced out of the popular revolt in the Communist countries have ignored these truths, even if they are aware of them. Instead of abolishing governmental authority, they are seeking to participate in it, even to share power with the discredited communist parties themselves. There is as yet no move towards creating decentralized workers' and peasants' and students' groups and bringing them together in free federations to run economic affairs, which political action has so notably failed to do. Even Solidarity, which has been so long in existence, has made no serious attempt to develop a system of production and distribution based on the initiative of the producers themselves working in conjunction with communal and co-operative distribution services.

It is all very well to preach, which is what I am starting to do. Anarchists have always tended to do that, shielded as they have been by the fact that anarchism is the one major political theory that has never been proved ineffective because it has never been tried out on any conclusively large scale. But one can ask where anarchists stood and what they have really done in the rebel decades of this century, and speculate on what they might do now.

In the series of Russian events that led up to the Bolshevik coup d'état in 1917 and the civil war that followed it, the anarchists played a scanty role, for though the two most famous anarchist theoreticians — Bakunin and Kropotkin — were Russians, the movement flourished mainly in exile and in Russia was eclipsed early on both by the Social Democrats (Bolsheviks and Mensheviks alike) and even more by the populist Social Revolutionaries with their strong peasant base. It was only in the special circumstances of the civil war in the Ukraine that Nestor Makhno and his rebel army sustained for a few years a considerable area of libertarian communes, defending it against both the White and the Red Armies; by 1921 Makhno had been forced out of the country, the peasant communes had been destroyed, and anarchism had been stamped out in Russia by the Cheka and its successors; it has not visibly re-emerged there by 1990.

By the 1930s it had been pretty thoroughly repressed as well in Italy, where it had once been so active, and also in Germany, while in France it had lost ground to the communists, who had converted enough of the militant syndicalists from their anarchist allegiance to take control of the major labor union organization, the Confédération Générale du Travail. In Spain, however, the syndicalists had remained faithful to their libertarian traditions, and the CNT, the most numerous labor organization, was still controlled by the anarchist militants of the FAI. During the early stages of the civil war in Spain, Catalonia and large areas of Andalusia were mainly controlled by the anarchists, and during this brief period the factories and public services of Barcelona and the other large Catalan towns were operated by the workers' syndicates, while in Andalusia and Velancia many villages turned themselves into agrarian free communes which a great deal of evidence suggests were successful within their limited areas. It was perhaps too brief an experiment to be called a complete success; on the other hand, it did not fail from the inner defects of the system of free communism, since the village communes flourished until they were overwhelmed by Franco's advancing troops in Andalusia and elsewhere by the Communist columns behind Republican lines, which were equipped by arms sent from Russia and denied to all non-Stalinist groups. The industries and services communalized by the anarcho-syndicalists continued to flourish until Franco's forces entered Barcelona; then the anarchist groups, like everyone else, seemed more intent on fleeing into France than on resisting (and who can blame them in such a hopeless moment?); and in their downfall and the Nazi surge to the Pyrenees a short while afterwards anarchism as a recognizable movement virtually ceased to exist on the continent of Europe, and survived mostly in small groups — consisting mainly of intellectuals — in Britain and the United States.

During the 1960s the role of anarchism was markedly different from what it had been in the late nineteenth and the early twentieth centuries. Vestigial groups indeed remained — or revived in countries like Italy and France — that claimed to be the heirs of older movements, and quite impressive international conferences were held in places like Carrara and Venice, but in Spain itself, even after the dictatorship ended, no mass movement developed with the power and membership of the CNT in the past; a small, divided CNT did emerge, but appears to have spent far more time on internal disputes than on renewed industrial militancy.

But while the anarchist *movement* walked again into the middle of the present century as a tenuous ghost of its past — deprived of its mass following but still often clinging to the old mythology of dramatic revolutionary action — it was the *idea* of anarchism that re-emerged most notably and claimed attention. Bakunin appeared beside the "young Marx" in the confused debates of the New Left, which — perhaps fortunately — never developed its own consistent ideology. Anarchist groups as such may not have made a great showing among the *groupucules* of Paris 1968, but the whole student movement at that time was permeated with libertarian ideas, and the black flag at the Sorbonne had as legitimate a place as the red flag in other parts of the city. It was a spontaneous uprising in which professional revolutionaries were mainly disregarded, and in some ways it prefigured the insurrections that have recently taken place in eastern European cities. Kropotkin would have greeted it with excitement, though I doubt if Marx would have seen much that suited his authoritarian ends, for the Communist leaders at the time gave it only slow and grudging approval so that they would not lose control over their own trade union followers in the CGT.

In every way the anarchist *idea* was disseminated during the 1960s and the 1970s. The first real histories of anarchism appeared, and serious biographies and other studies of important anarchist thinkers were published. The theoretical writings of Kropotkin, Bakunin, and Proudhon were reprinted, and no longer by groups of militants with scanty funds, but by publishers who distributed them widely. Anarchism became for the first time a serious subject of academic study, and anarchist viewpoints gained a more serious hearing than they had ever done before.

All this might be dismissed as a matter of academic fashion — which it partly was — if it had not been accompanied by some important shifts in the attitude of anarchist thinkers, a kind of neo-Kropotkinist movement in which some of the more fertile insights of *Mutual Aid* and Kropotkin's other works were re-examined in a way that is still relevant in the 1990s. This involves an acceptance — which Kropotkin himself never entirely achieved — of the fact that nineteenth-century anarchists (with the possible exception of shrewd old Proudhon) had been beguiled, though to a lesser degree than their socialist and communist rivals, by two contemporary illusions. One of these was the bourgeois myth of the inevitability and necessary desirability of material progress. The other was the transfer from Judeo-Christian-Islamic religion to utopian and neo-utopian movements of the eschatology first developed by Zoroaster; the concept of a continuing struggle between the forces of good and evil in which — at the end — good is destined to triumph. Secularized, this prospect terminated not in the kingdom of God but in the perfect earthly society of utopia. All progress would now be ended, since nothing better could be expected. Life, once the dictatorship of the proletariat had loosened its grip, would be benign, if not anything so positive as joyful.

The classic anarchists tended to be ambivalent about this prospect; with the echoes of the era of barricades still ringing in their ears, they rather looked forward to the period of struggle, though they regarded the utopian future with proper distrust, since they recognized the end of change as death, moral if not physical, and thus we find Kropotkin thinking in terms of an insurrection that will bring about a complete social transformation, and thinking also of the means to safeguard it, but refusing — as he does in *The Conquest of Bread* — to do more than sketch out the possible lines on which the people in the liberated future will shape their communal lives.

I have always believed that this reluctance on the part of Kropotkin — and of most other anarchists — to think in terms of a planned and laid-down structure is connected with his desire to find in society the natural tendencies that will guide man, once he is liberated, to develop — without the direction of revolutionary planners — a free and fulfilling way of life based on cooperation rather than coercion. This emerges both in Kropotkin's search for libertarian ancestors, so elaborately developed in *Modern Science and Anarchism*, and also in the resolute enquiry, in *Mutual Aid, Fields, Factories and Workshops*, and other writings, into the buried roots of free institutions within existing society.

The implication of those searches is really that anarchism is not a revolutionary doctrine in the millenarian sense of offering, like Christianity, a New Heaven and a New Earth. It is rather a restorative doctrine, telling us that the means by which we can create a free society are already there in the manifestations of mutual aid existing in the world around us. Before governments existed men cooperated, and below all the structures of power that have since been developed, the processes by which society as a community of people actually survives have always been the voluntary ones, those of people acting on their own account or in various mutual aid relationships which come into existence whether governments are in

position or not. Kropotkin is telling us what Wordsworth put in
another way:

> Not in Utopia, — subterrean fields, —
> Or some secreted island, Heaven knows where!
> But in this very world, which is the world
> Of all of us, — the place where, in the end,
> We find our happiness, or not at all!

Kropotkin was saying that what happiness we have in society at present is not owed to the state but to the natural relationships we freely
develop, and he was further saying that on such relationships, not on
any professional revolutionary's handbook or politician's plan, a
future free society must be built.

    This, it seems to me, is Kropotkin's great message for the 1990s,
and it was developed already in the 1960s and early 1970s by some of
the best new anarchist thinkers, notably Colin Ward in *Anarchy in
Action* (1973) and Paul Goodman in a whole series of books of the
1960s like *People or Personnel, Growing Up Absurd,* and *New
Reformation.* What Goodman and Ward and others at the same time
told us was that there was no need to wait for the great day of revolution, the apocalyptic moment; in fact, if we waited we might be
caught unawares. What we should do was to recognize how far in
society anarchistic relationships actually exist, and to begin now to
build on those relationships, nourishing and encouraging voluntary
initiatives based on mutual aid as distinct from official initiatives in
welfare and other directions — based on paternalism and leading to
dependence.

    These arguments, I think, have a very great bearing on the
1990s and the extraordinary events with which the decade begins:
popular movements — undirected by authoritarian parties or any
parties — which destroyed autocratic governments that for more
than forty years had been thought impregnable. With surprisingly
little violence — almost all on the side of the panic-stricken oppressors

— the people of the eastern European countries have shaken themselves free. In some ways they would seem to be in an astonishingly favorable position, since the old so-called revolutionary elite, in the shape of the various Communist parties, is at present in total disarray and discredit, and — except for Poland where Solidarity has long proclaimed itself a party rather than a movement — the triumphant opposition is not yet well-organized in a political way. The eagerness with which the defeated Communist leaders in these countries seem to be accepting the idea of multi-party systems clearly reflects their idea that a return to conventionally "democratic" political forms gives them their best guarantee of keeping some of their power and winning more of it back. How far the insurrectionary people in the various countries are aware of these dangers, how far they are creating their own alternative forms of administration, their safeguards against deceit and exploitation, we do not know yet. And that will always remain dependent on the vigilance and the initiative of workers, peasants, and intellectuals in the various countries. If they do not decide to help themselves, there is not a great deal outsiders can do to help them, except to try and make sure they get the food and raw materials they will need to start again.

But there is a great deal we ourselves can learn from observing the situations in eastern Europe, and the insurrectionary situation that is sure to mature very shortly in China. We can learn that when a whole people crowds the streets in anger, the powers of even the most ruthless government are immediately weakened and with continued resolution can be swept away with no more than accidental violence. We can also learn how watchful the people must be, in the hour of triumph which joy can turn into weakness, to prevent another herd of power seekers starting the evil process of government going all over again. And to develop that theme will require someone to write another *Conquest of Bread*, adapted for the 1990s.

1990

ESSAYS ON ANARCHISM

1

Pierre-Joseph Proudhon: An Appreciation

The extent to which Pierre-Joseph Proudhon's contributions to radical thought are overlooked even among radicals was impressed upon me by an article in *Dissent* in which Lewis Coser and Irving Howe discussed the differences between Marx and his utopian socialist contemporaries in a way which suggested that they considered Marx and Engels to be alone in their anti-utopianism. As if laying extended claims for Marxian originality, they talked of "the importance of Marx's idea that socialism is to be brought about, in the first instance, by the activities of a major segment of the population, the workers"; they added that "Marx found the sources of revolt within the self-expanding and self-destroying rhythms of the economy itself," and that he "gave new power to the revolt against history, by locating it, 'scientifically,' with history." In fact, not only was Proudhon as persistent and pertinent a critic of utopian tendencies as either of the German socialists but he also anticipated the very insights for which Coser and Howe appear to regard Marx-Engels as originally responsible. What is perhaps more important for our own day is that he developed them in a way that enabled him to foresee and to warn against some of the more disastrous tendencies (e.g. towards centralism and bureaucratization) that have become frozen into many areas of socialist practice.

Proudhon was an *aficionado* of irony and paradox, and it was therefore appropriate that his introduction to socialism should have come through the utopians he later rejected. As a young printer in Besançon, he supervised the production of Fourier's *Le Nouveau Monde Industrial et Sociétaire* and was fascinated by its author's strange combination of insight and eccentricity. At the same time he was strongly critical of the more fantastic aspects of Fourier's work, and a little later, in 1832, when the Fourierists invited him to edit a paper, he showed an independence that anticipated his later development as a critical, un-utopian social thinker. "You asked me yesterday," he wrote to them, "whether I would write in a public sheet opinions which I profess and which we hold in common, and you added: 'Undoubtedly not' ... Why should we not invite the population to make themselves capable of managing their own affairs and of preparing the way for a confederation of peoples? Let them see, through instruction, science, moral health and patriotism, how to dispense with all ministerial hierarchy, while in the meantime profiting from the little good it will do them."

This is the first existing document in which Proudhon assumes an emphatic attitude, and it already incorporates some of the salient elements of his later views — the distrust of authority as such and of centralized authority in particular; the desire to see the working people learn to manage their own affairs with a minimum of intervention (already a sharp divergence from the utopian preoccupation with societies planned from above); the fear of Jacobin nationalism implied in the hope for a "confederation of peoples."

During the formative, autodidactic years of the 1830s, Proudhon's sense of the needs and potentialities of the working class, to which he declared himself to belong "today and for ever, by nature, by habit and above all by the community of interests and wishes," led him through the devious courses of philology and Biblical scholarship, and by way of such curious speculations as whether the Mosaic command, *Lo thignob,* meant "Thou shalt not steal" or "Thou shalt not lay anything aside for thyself," to a consideration of the economic bases of socialism and, in particular, of property relationships. The scattered apprentice essays of this period, on such subjects as the origin of languages and the utility of Sunday observance, are studded with ideas which intimate the independent development of a social attitude.

By 1840 these hints had been integrated into his first influential work, *What Is Property?* which Marx hailed five years later as "truly the first decisive, vigorous and scientific examination" of property, as "a great scientific progress, which revolutionizes political economy and for the first time permits one to make a true science of it." In the present essay it is impossible to examine every aspect of this provocative book, which created one of the great political catchwords of the nineteenth century ("Property is theft") and made one of its historic definitions by applying the name "anarchism" to that trend in socialism which regards the elimination of government as of primary importance. But a number of points demand consideration for the light they throw upon the general Proudhonian attitude.

Proudhon, we should emphasize, does not set himself up as a communist, even in the sense of the 1840s. In emphasizing as a goal equality of condition, he still defends possession. What he attacks is the property by which a man exploits the labor of others, the property associated with interest, rent, the wage system. But a man's right to control the house he inhabits and the land and tools he needs to work and live, so long as he uses them for these purposes alone, Proudhon regards as a keystone of liberty. Control of production should lie at the point of production, and the social function of distribution should grow upward and outward from that point. At the same time, as becomes evident in his later works, Proudhon was not exclusively — as some of his critics have suggested — an advocate of the individual worker. For large-scale industry and transport he envisaged cooperative operation, but his attitude towards such matters was strictly functional, and he held that the invocation of association as a principle would tend towards social rigidity and the destruction of freedom. It was particularly their tendency to erect hypothetical systems which had little relationship to the actual needs of individual men and women that he held against the utopians. His criticism of the Phalansterian and Icarian communists of his time has an extremely topical interest in its anticipation of the situation that has tended to develop in the countries which today claim to be communist and, indeed, everywhere that socialism has taken a centralist, bureaucratized form:

> The members of a community, it is true, have no private property, but the community is proprietor, and proprietor not only of goods, but also of persons and wills. In consequence of this principle of absolute property labor — which should only be a condition imposed on man by nature — becomes in all communities a human commandment and therefore odious. Passive obedience, irreconcilable with a reflecting will, is strictly enforced. Fidelity to regulations, which are always defective, however wise they may be thought, allows of no complaint. Life, talent, and all the human faculties are the property of the State, which has the right to use them as it pleases for the common good. Private associations are sternly prohibited, in spite of the likes and dislikes of different natures, because to tolerate them would be to introduce small communities within the large ones . . . Communism is oppression and slavery. Man . . . wishes to dispose of his own time, to be governed only by necessity, to choose his friendships, his recreation and his discipline; to act from judgment, not by command; to sacrifice himself through unselfishness, not through servile obligation. Communism is essentially opposed to the free exercise of our faculties, to our noblest desires, to our deepest feelings.

At the same time, while attacking the utopians for a doctrinaire desire to freeze human lives within a static society, Proudhon was not an individualist in the manner of contemporaries like Stirner. The essentially sociological aspect of his outlook appears when he discusses the question of property in relation to work. Labor alone, he contends, is the basis of value, but it does not confer a right to property, since labor does not create the means out of which the product is made. And this means does not consist only of the raw material provided by nature, but also of the vast heritage of installations built by our forerunners, the accumulated techniques and traditions of civilization, and, perhaps most important, the element of cooperation in labor that makes each man's work so much more effective than it would be if he acted in solitude. It is evident why Marx should have regarded *What Is Property?* as a seminal work in the development of political economy; it is also evident that Marx's own conception of socialist economics owed a great deal more to Proudhon than Marxists admit.

Yet despite its many important insights, one is impressed by the relatively undeveloped form of Proudhon's thought in *What Is Property?* As Theodore Royssen remarked, there is a "static quality" about it; "history in the real sense of the word occupies hardly any place." This fact cannot be dissociated from the sharply limited nature of Proudhon's experience at this time. What he is discussing is property as seen by the peasant, and his solution is an agrarian one. But if little attention is paid here to industries that cannot be run by independent artisan "possessors," we should remember that up to 1840 Proudhon had slight contact with the industrial revolution that was developing during the July monarchy in France. The railway, pioneer of industrialism, had not reached his native Franche-Comté, and the Latin Quarter of Paris, with which he was familiar, has remained to this day a stronghold of small workshops. It was in later works, after he had come into contact with the movement of history through his observation of the industrial proletariat in Lyons and his participation in the Revolution of 1848, that Proudhon's social views took on movement and perspective.

Another reason for the "static" quality in *What Is Property?* is to be found in a lingering utopian influence that made Proudhon desire, even though he declared emphatically "I build no system," to envisage at least the possibility of a permanent social stabilization. *What Is Property?* is more influenced by Hegelianism than any of his other books, and in the acceptance of a stabilizing synthesis (the reign of "Liberty," product of the marriage of property and communism), there enters a chiliastic element similar to that which brings Marxian history to a halt in the final stasis of eternalized and generalized quasi-utopia.

Such a solution was both unsatisfactory in terms of social reality and unsympathetic to Proudhon's critical temperament, and later, in such works as *The Philosophy of Poverty* (1846) and its successors, he abandoned the Hegelian formulae and adopted a method of antinomical argument that fitted more closely, not only his own passion for exploring each side of every argument, but also the pattern of mutually warring contradictions which he perceived within society. This elaborate exploration of contradictions is the cause of much of the confusion that has arisen over Proudhon's ideas, but it also gave rise to a more acceptable view of the progress of society, not towards an ideal and a historical construction, but towards a dynamic and developing equilibrium of varied forces. Proudhon was not a cyclical thinker; he shared the nineteenth-century belief in progress, but he did not trade in teleological speculations, and anything in the nature of a perfect society he came to regard as not merely impossible, but also undesirable. Imperfection and conflict were the attributes of life as he saw it, and when he considered the nature of war (in *War and Peace*, 1861), he saw the end of military struggle only as a transition to an intensification of productive struggle in industry and culture. In his view, society moved, and would always move, by an organic rhythm of constant growth, and even his favorite concept of Justice was not an idealist absolute, but a quasi-anthropological entity that grew with man's development and in a measure shared his limitations. "We are born perfectible; we shall never be perfect. Perfection, immobility, would be death."

It was in the decade between the publication of *What Is Property?* and the accession of Louis Napoleon to the Presidency of the Second Republic in 1849 that Proudhon gathered the experiences that were basic to his later and most important books. An insight into the role of the working class which led him in 1842 to declare, "Workers, laborers, men of the people, the initiative of reform is yours," was confirmed and strengthened when he went to Lyons in the following year and encountered the Mutualists, a proletarian secret society which had abandoned Jacobin ideas of political conspiracy in favor of industrial association. His contact with these men strengthened Proudhon's faith in the workers ("The people are better judges than all their critics") and increased his apolitical bias. "The new socialist movement will begin by . . . the war of the workshop," he wrote in his diary, and added another thought that echoed through the history of Latin Syndicalism down to the Spanish Civil War when he noted: "The social revolution is seriously compromised if it comes through a political revolution."

The Revolution of 1848 proved the most important single event in Proudhon's life, as in the lives of a whole generation of European radicals. He was one of the few active participants, in France or elsewhere, who immediately recognized the social character of the Revolution and detected the emergence of the working class as an autonomous force. But he was appalled by the ineptitude of the Jacobins and liberals at the head of the Second Republic, whose minds were full of the democratic political ideals of 1789 and 1793, but who had no conception of the problems that had gained urgency from the rapid impetus of the industrial revolution. "They have made a revolution without ideas," he lamented on the day of the Republic's foundation, and a few weeks later he denounced the palliative measures of the government, such as the herding of the unemployed into the National Workshops, as "the organization of poverty."

As a delegate to the National Assembly, and in his efforts to found a credit bank for the workers, he strove to give some positive social content to the revolution, but it was as a journalistic critic that he was effective. His first paper, *Le Répresentant du Peuple*, appeared under the motto: "What is the Producer? Nothing. What should he be? Everything." From the beginning he maintained that the inadequacy of political liberalism in a time of social revolution forced the workers to find their own economic solution. "The proletariat must emancipate itself without the help of the government," he remarked before the revolution was two months old, and after the rising of the faubourgs in June he recognized immediately that "the first and determining cause of the insurrection was the social question, the social crisis, work, ideas." It was in the month after the rising, in introducing to the National Assembly a proposal for a moratorium on rents and debts to alleviate public distress, that he defined most boldly the class struggle that had become dramatically evident in French life.

Having stated his ultimate aim as the liquidation of property, and called upon the proprietors to accept voluntarily the first step in that direction, he added: "In the case of refusal we ourselves shall proceed to the liquidation without you." "Whom do you mean by *you*?" shouted his audience. "When I employed these two pronouns, *you* and *we*," said Proudhon, "it is evident that in that moment I was identifying *myself* with the *proletariat*, and that I was identifying *you* with the *bourgeois class.*" "*It is the social war,*" his rivals shouted. "Capital is afraid," Proudhon replied, "and its instinct is not wrong: the eye of socialism is upon it."

The *Communist Manifesto* had expressed very similar sentiments to a restricted audience a few months before, but it was Proudhon in this debate who first drew to the attention of the wider public of Europe the fact that socialism would henceforward become identified, not with the plans of utopian dreamers, but with the concrete and daily struggle of the working class. His comparative loneliness in this recognition was illustrated by the fact that, when the Assembly came to a vote, only one man, an old Lyons Mutualist, voted with him, while the utopian socialists demonstrated their failure to recognize the social realities of the time by abstaining.

Proudhon's defiance of the increasingly reactionary tendencies that emerged in France during the latter part of 1848 led him eventually to a three-year prison sentence for having the foresight to accuse Louis Bonaparte of monarchical ambitions. Prison, he wryly declared, was "just like Icaria," but it was remarkably lenient by present-day standards, and, after the frantic activity of the revolutionary year, he made use of his enforced leisure to work out the constructive elements of his social outlook. His brief and dramatic interval as a man of action was ended, and it is in the books of the period after his entry into prison that we encounter the development and refinement of his contributions to socialist thought.

Crammed with a baroque abundance of scholarship and written in a classic prose that was admired by Sainte-Beuve, Baudelaire, and Flaubert, these later books, from *Confessions of a Revolutionary* (1849) down to the posthumously published *Political Capacity of the Working Class*, cover a vast range of miscellaneous topics, from theories of taxation to studies of the social relevance of art, from literary copyright to Biblical exegesis. Contradictions and ambiguities abound, and in this fertile jungle of argument it has not been difficult for the disingenuous to find texts which, wrenched from their contexts, make Proudhon appear as the advocate of reactionary doctrines that are plainly contrary to the general direction of his thought. Yet in fact the main themes of Proudhon's political philosophy, the themes that have most relevance for the modern student, remain surprisingly constant. They can be divided into three categories: 1. His criticism of the Jacobin idea of political revolution and centralized government, and his substitution of a view of social revolution based on a decentralized mutualist economy. 2. His theory of federalism as a solution to the problems of national administration and international relationships. 3. His theory of the political function of the working class as an autonomous revolutionary force moving towards its own liberation. .

At no time during his career could Proudhon be regarded as

favorable to the Jacobin attitude, but it was the experience of 1848 that revealed to him in full the hollowness of a political revolution unsupported by a revolution in economic relationships. Universal suffrage was the great watchword of the Jacobins of 1848, and they saw little beyond, but for Proudhon this reform was pointless outside the context of a social transformation. "How could universal suffrage reveal the thought, the real thought of the people," he argued in *Confessions of a Revolutionary*, "when the people is divided by inequality of fortune into classes subordinate one to the other and voting either through servility or through hate; when this same people, held in restraint by authority, is incapable notwithstanding its sovereignty of expressing its ideas on anything; and when the exercise of its rights is limited to choosing, every three or four years, its chiefs and its imposters?"

In Jacobinism, Proudhon saw, not a genuine movement towards liberation, but a "hypocrisy of progress," which, in dreaming of liberty without social vision, merely produced dictatorship. The real struggle was between the extremes of absolutism and socialism, and for Proudhon socialism was not the rigid doctrine of the Icarians, who take "their hypotheses for reality and their utopias for institutions," but a dynamic and realistic viewpoint based on the observation of society, not as one would like to make it, but as it is, with its inherent contradictions and conflicts. It was in this way, as "a phenomenon of our collective life," that he assessed political institutions. "The best form of government, like the most perfect of religions," he concluded, "is a contradictory idea. The problem is not to know how we shall be best governed, but how we shall be most free. Liberty adequate and compatible with order, that is all the reality which is contained in power and politics." And thus he saw the development of society as a progress from the authoritarian concept of centralized power. Proudhon was no millenarian; he did not believe that liberty could be achieved in a single leap, in a sudden Bakuninist overturning of the edifices of power. On the contrary, he often declared that anarchy — the society of free contracts — might take centuries to mature, and that it was likely to come through a long process of equilibration. "Equality comes to us by a succession of tyrannies and governments, in which liberty is continually at grips with absolutism like Israel and Jehovah."

What remains most important in Proudhon's criticism of the Jacobins is the shift of viewpoint from politics as a self-subsistent entity to politics as a changing and dispensable social phenomenon, the shift of objective from the seizure of power over men to the achievement of economic organization between men. This attitude is closely linked to a view of revolution as a spontaneous social force, not created politically, but rising from the needs of the people and irresistible in its eventual triumph. Social revolution had become inevitable, Proudhon believed, because of the limitations of the men of 1789, who had ignored the economic revolution called for by the abolition of feudalism. "The Republic should have established Society; it thought only of establishing Government . . . Therefore, while the problem propounded in '89 seemed to be officially solved, fundamentally there was a change only in governmental metaphysics — what Napoleon called *ideology . . .*"

The suggestions for social reform which Proudhon puts forward in such works as *The General Ideal of the Revolution* (1851) are in fact not so strictly apolitical as those of later anarchists like Kropotkin. They take rather the form of a pluralist socialism, in which the political is subordinated to the social. In opposition to the centralized nationalism of Jacobin democracy, Proudhon's vision is characterized by the utmost degree of administrative decentralization:

> Unless democracy is a fraud, and the sovereignty of the people a jest, it must be admitted that each citizen in the sphere of his industry, each municipal, district or provincial council within its own territory, is the only natural and legitimate representative of the sovereign (people), and that therefore each locality should act directly and by itself in administering the interests which it includes and should exercise full sovereignty

in relation to them. The people are nothing but the organic
ᴧ union of individually free wills, which can and should work
voluntarily together, but never abdicate their freedom. Such a
union must be sought in the harmony of their interests, not in
an artificial centralization, which, far from expressing the collective will, expresses only the antagonism of individual wills.

Where necessary — but only where necessary — the individual
control of work and the direct contact between man and man are
replaced by associational bodies. One such body is the commune,
organ of local administration, which should have full independence,
unsupervised by any centralized authority, in the conduct of public
works and local affairs, even in the making of laws. Other undertak-
ings, like railways, factories, and harbors, would be administered by
associations of workers, and parents and teachers would come
together to conduct a form of education integrated to industrial and
professional apprenticeship. Litigation would be replaced by the
arbitration of *ad hoc* juries of neighbors, and courts, those beach-
heads of autocracy, from which Proudhon himself had suffered,
must be eliminated as the first act of the revolution.

Such generalized suggestions are as near as Proudhon ever gets
to the blueprinting of an ideal society. In his reaction from utopia he
was as disinclined as Marx to plan in detail for other men, and at
times he seems to have retreated into unnecessary vagueness. His
positive suggestions are indeed considerably less impressive than his
exposures of the Jacobin political fixations, and this is not entirely
due either to the fact that he himself was personally better fitted for
the role of critic or to that lack of precise detail and rigid structure
which is inevitable in a libertarian social vision. Beyond these factors, there is a naively optimistic tendency to see reason as over-
powerful, a faith in man's propensity to detect his own good that is
not wholly borne out by experience. It is true that the solution of
social ills rests by definition on a social level, and can only be
attained when political centralization has been replaced by a much

more basic administration of economic affairs than existed in Proudhon's time or exists today. The arguments for workers' control of industry, for regional and local autonomy as an antidote to bureaucratic centralism, are convincing, but only the hardy idealist would suggest today that the solution can be quite so simple a matter of contractual adjustment as, in his more optimist flights, Proudhon suggested. Nor, indeed, did Proudhon consistently hold this view; there were times when he stressed less the peaceful agreement than the fruitful conflict of a free society, while the very fact that he still envisaged the presence of local "laws" suggests that he felt the need for sanctions of a moral and possibly even a physical character.

It is necessary to distinguish between what Proudhon meant by federation and what is meant by those who nowadays think in terms of a kind of super-centralized government to administer Europe or the world. Such a parody of federation would mean an intensification of the very centralism which Proudhon dreaded, the creation of an authority all the more dangerous because of its concentration of power. He was in fact so opposed to centralized power that he envisaged federation, not as a means of establishing authority over existing states, but as a way of dissolving them. A union between these states would suffer from the inequality between them, and hence he stressed "the interior distribution of sovereignty and government," the breakdown of that national unity — which in history has always been productive of war without and exploitation within — into smaller units where "there is nothing for the bourgeoisie to profit from" and the vigilance of the people can be most actively promoted.

Confederation, like the revolution, should begin with the people; it should build upwards from the most primary levels. The basic administration should be local and as near the direct control of the workers as possible. Hence, while safety demanded a strict limitation on the largeness of units, social necessity need set no limits on their smallness. "Any agglomeration of men, comprised within a clearly circumscribed territory and able to live an independent life in that spot, is meant for autonomy." In this way the smallest regional or racial enclave could enjoy its independence and participate in federal cooperation with its neighbors of differing outlooks without sacrificing its own way of living. Above the primary level of small autonomous units, confederal organization should become progressively less a matter of administration than of cooperation between the "natural groups." A series of delegations would bring together the common economic interests of the various units, and in each region would coalesce in a central committee whose function would be confined to the coordination of interests in accordance with the general will. Its complete sensitiveness would be assured by the perpetual revocability of any delegation as soon as it ceased to act in harmony with the group it represented. Since the "natural groups" which formed the confederation would in their turn be based on the working units — the cooperative associations and productive exchanges — within society, the nature of the state would change from political to economic, and Saint-Simon's vision of the government of men being replaced by the administration of things would be finally achieved.

If anywhere, it is in this plan of the federal society that, by the happy process of paradox, we find the utopia of the great anti-utopian, a utopia in negative, with casual agreement replacing minute regulation as its basic pattern. Proudhon, moreover, differed from most of the utopians in realizing the need to face the immediate problems of a society yet unripe for revolutionary change. Total federalism might be sketched as a destination, but the way there had to be traced through the jungle of nineteenth-century international politics, and often Proudhon was faced with decisions which could not be postponed. Always, he stood out against the proliferation of new and aggressive national states and sought to encourage any kind of decentralist tendency that might set the tide of events running in the direction of an international outlook.

Nor did he restrict his hopes of internationalism to the political field. In the background he saw the anonymous power of the working class, a latent force that would soon play its independent part in the determination of history. To make that class conscious of its role and its potentialities was the final task to which he turned his attention. The international identity of the workers' interests had long preoccupied him; even before 1848 he had dreamed of a mutualist association that would spread over the whole world; and after the disillusionments of the Revolution his faith was renewed in the revival of French working-class activity during the early 1860s, a revival in which he played a considerable role. The Jacobins had been discredited among the more militant workers for their ineptitude during 1848; the utopians had declined into minor cults which suffered from the failure of their attempts to create socialist communities in the New World; Marx and his doctrines were as yet almost unknown. Proudhon alone stood as a symbol of plebeian resistance, and his anti-political campaign of 1863, when he called for abstention from voting as a means of undermining the Empire, appealed to a working class that was tired of the existing political situation. It was to these reawakened workers that he addressed his last book, *The Political Capacity of the Working Classes.*

In his book Proudhon celebrates the arrival of the urban proletariat as a new social force. Like all other historically significant classes, it has become conscious of its collective identity, and the idea which it pursues as a result of this dawning self-consciousness is that of mutuality. The possession and development in real terms of this idea distinguishes the working class (including the peasants) from the bourgeoisie, and gives it a progressive character. The *laissez faire* bourgeois ideology eschews mutuality, and consequently the bulk of the middle class declines into a subordinate stratum at the mercy of the monopolists whose viewpoint it still accepts. But the workers, by developing their sense of mutuality, can at last bring justice into the economic life of society by organizing its functions on an egalitarian basis.

Proudhon believes that against the *grande bourgeoisie*, the real capitalists, the struggle must be pursued without hope of reconciliation. But he does not exclude that larger section of the middle class whose independence is threatened with extinction; their alliance should be sought so that the whole community may move towards liberation without that violence of civil war which Proudhon always regarded as inimical to progress.

Thus, while regarding the proletariat as a progressive class which would spread the leaven of mutuality, he did not, like the Blanquists and the Marxists, envisage it as an élite, destined to assume power and govern by class dictatorship, either delegated or direct. "Federalism is the alpha and omega of my policy," he insisted, "and to be realized that solution requires the participation of the whole people."

It is not possible here to investigate the wide influence of Proudhon's theories in the First International and the Paris Commune, in European revolutionary syndicalism and Mexican agrarianism, in such movements of the English-speaking countries as Guild Socialism and the I.W.W. What is more to our immediate point is the fact that the split between the social democrats and Proudhon's disciples, which was given finality (over the protesting voices of such socialist pioneers as William Morris, Keir Hardie, and Robert Blatchford) in the expulsion of the libertarian delegates from the International Socialist Congress of 1896, deprived the socialist movement of the very points of view that might have helped to correct the more harmful errors of twentieth-century socialism. The failure to foster industrial control by the workers led to that doctrinaire reliance on state control and bureaucratic administration which marred the attempt to achieve socialism in Britain. The lack of a strong federalist policy left socialist parties everywhere helpless in the face of the temptations of nationalism and the threats of war. The tendency to concentrate on the industrial worker to the exclusion of other classes resulted in socialist ineptitude when faced by agrarian problems or by situations, like those in the United States and Canada, where large sections of the workers begin to move culturally and economically into the middle class. Finally, a preoccupation with political activity, with the mechanics of elections, parliamentary maneuvers, and governmental machinery has produced the very Jacobin error which Proudhon castigated — the tendency to seek a speciously easy way out through legislation and regulation instead of concentrating on the basic functional changes in social activity on which, in the end, freedom and security alike depend.

Much of Proudhon's work is outdated, and he would have expected nothing else, for he claimed to erect no foolproof system, he eschewed the idea of establishing a party doctrine, and, having lived through 1848, he was well aware how much events can prove a political thinker wrong. "I mistrust an author who pretends to be consistent with himself after twenty-five years," he once said, and he would have viewed with ironic contempt any latter-day admirer who tried to establish a faultless canon from his works. But the general themes that run consistently through his writings still have a great relevance, and those who are puzzled by the unresolved problems of modern socialism may gain from considering some of the aspects of that libertarian point of view which he represented and which was banished from the orthodox socialist movement in this century.

1955

2

Michael Bakunin: The Destructive Urge

O n a rainy night of June 1840, the future anarchist Michael Bakunin departed for the first time from Russia. Only Alexander Herzen had come to see him off on his journey — appropriately, perhaps, since Herzen, that unofficial banker for so many European revolutionaries of the mid-nineteenth century, had provided the funds that made Bakunin's departure possible. "I expect from this journey a rebirth and a spiritual baptism," Bakunin had written when he asked for the loan. "I feel within myself so many great and deep possibilities, and I have realized so little."

Bakunin was at this time a student of philosophy, twenty-six years old and unknown beyond a tiny circle of Moscow intellectuals. Eleven years later he was to return to his country, via the barricades of Paris and Prague and Dresden and the fortress prisons of Saxony and Bohemia; at the frontier the Austrian guards knocked the chains from his legs so that the heavier Russian manacles could be fitted in their place. Another decade later, in 1861, Bakunin made his second and last departure from Russia. It was one of the most sensational escapes from Siberia, and it took him to Japan and over the Pacific to America and Europe, there to play out the last years of his life as the great rival of Marx and the founder of organized anarchism.

Western Europe was the stage on which Bakunin acted the heroic and often farcical drama of his life; it was also the school where he developed the possibilities he felt within himself in those impatient days of 1840. In comparison, Russia was the land that imprisoned him in manhood and frustrated him in youth; only in the romantically remembered childhood on his father's estate in the province of Tver — long ago in the halcyon days of Alexander I — had it ever brought him happiness, and it had never given him the possibility of action, the chance to use and spend his untiring vitality.

Yet in the West, where he is barely remembered, and in Russia, where he is officially forgotten, Bakunin wielded an influence whose effects have even now not died away, and the ideas he strove so incessantly to turn into action were derived in equal measure from both. Other Russians of his time — those at least who took sides — can usually be classed as either Westerners or Slavophils, lovers of French rationality or Russian irrationality; in Bakunin Westerner and Slavophil, reason and instinct, met in dynamic union, and even the particular type of anarchism that he made his own combined the blind fury of Russian peasant uprisings with a nineteenth-century faith in the inevitable progress of man towards the heights. Stenka Razin and Herbert Spencer seemed often to meet incongruously in the gigantic body and the fertile, chaotic mind of Michael Bakunin. He could see with joy an apocalyptic vision of "the star of revolution rising high and free above Moscow from a sea of blood and fire," but he could also dream of the light of humanity that would rescue man from his animal self, "the only light that can warm and enlighten us, the only thing that can emancipate us, and give us dignity, freedom and happiness, that can make us realize our fraternity."

The course that led Bakunin to seek, through universal destruction, the goal of human brotherhood began in the quiet depths of the Russian countryside two years after Napoleon gave up his disastrous attempt to conquer its hostile vastnesses. Alexander Bakunin, Michael's father, was an amateur poet who ruled benevolently over five hundred serfs and brought his children up according to the precepts of Rousseau. He was a liberal who had been in Paris during the Revolution, and his wife, Varvara, belonged to the great Muraviev clan which was closely involved in the constitutionalist movement of early nineteenth-century Russia. Three of her cousins took part, when Michael Bakunin was a boy, in the Decembrist rising of 1825.

But the tradition of rebellion that hung over the Bakunin home had been diluted as Alexander grew more cautious with age and with the advent of Nicholas I's harsh rule; and, when Michael Bakunin himself began to revolt against his world, it was many years before his resistance took on a political form. He led the defiance of parental authority by his younger brothers and sisters. He rebelled against the discipline of the Artillery School where he was sent to follow the military career expected of a nobleman's eldest son, and later against the dullness of the Polish villages where he served on garrison duty. He malingered well, got himself dismissed from the service through influential connections of the Bakunins in St. Petersburg, and set off to Moscow in search of learning.

The intellectual circles of Moscow were then, in the 1830s, feeling the full impact of influences from Western Europe. Romantic poetry, Gothic novels, German metaphysics, French socialist tracts, were all finding their converts among the *literati*. Those who inclined towards social rebellion gathered around Alexander Herzen and studied Fourier and Saint-Simon and Proudhon. Bakunin was not among them; he came under the influence of Nicholas Stankevich, that genius whose premature death in 1840 robbed nineteenth-century Russia of one of its purest spirits and its seminal minds. With Stankevich and Belinsky, Bakunin ran the gamut of the German philosophers — Schelling, Fichte, and, inevitably, Hegel — but, while Belinsky's studies led him towards radicalism, Bakunin showed, right up to his departure in 1840, a singular indifference to social questions and revolutionary ideas. It was a sense of spiritual claustrophobia rather than any political passion that led him to long for the outside world where he could tap the true sources of philosophic inspiration.

Even after his arrival in Germany, where he haunted the lecture rooms of the philosophy professors and the salons of aristocratic Bohemia, it was still some time before any real change became evident in Bakunin. Ivan Turgenev, who was his constant companion during his early months in Berlin, later used him as the model for the hero of his first novel, *Rudin*, and something of Bakunin's well-meaning aimlessness at this period emerges from that tragic portrait of the superfluous man of Tsarist Russia, the man whose great capabilities find no room for expression in his own land.

Gradually, however, Bakunin began to become restlessly conscious that the West had not yet given him what he expected; Berlin had become irksome and the teachers of philosophy had been disappointing. Yet at the same time Bakunin could not bear to exchange the relative mental freedom of Europe for the intellectual stultification of Russia. It was in this mood, receptive to any new influence, that he traveled to Dresden and encountered Arnold Ruge, a rather pompous polemicist who played minor parts in the lives of Marx, Engels, Proudhon, and many other socialist thinkers of the age.

In Bakunin's life Ruge's role was a major one, for he introduced him to the writings of the Young Hegelians, who at this time were turning Hegel's doctrines upside down by demonstrating that the dialectic could be used to prove that all is flux and movement and revolution is therefore the true reality. Bakunin was shaken by the arguments of the Young Hegelians; he was really converted by Lorenz von Stein's *Socialism and Communism in Contemporary France*. The doctrines of Fourier and Proudhon, which had meant nothing to him in Moscow, suddenly appeared to offer "a new world into which I plunged with all the ardor of a delirious thirst." At this point, the future course of his life was set; his vague rebelliousness had at last found the channel in which it was to run to the end of his life.

Bakunin's conversion was marked by the almost immediate writing of an essay that has remained among the best of his works. It was called *Reaction in Germany*, and appeared under the names of

"Jules Elysard" in Ruge's *Deutsche Fahrbucher* (1842). The central thoughts of *Reaction in Germany* are characteristic of Bakunin; they represent an aspect of his philosophy that, once formed in the ardor of conversion, never substantially changed. In some respects his arguments are typically Young Hegelian; they seek to trim the conservative elements in the Master's doctrine so that it may appear as a justification for revolution. It is the peculiar tone of exaltation and the passionate emphasis on destruction as a prelude to creation that really mark the essay as Bakunin's own work. In present society, he asserts, revolution is necessarily negative, but at the moment of triumph it will transform itself and become positive. Then "there will be a qualitative transformation, a new, living, life-giving revelation, a new heaven and a new earth, a young and mighty world in which all our present dissonances will be resolved into a harmonious whole." Yet clearly Bakunin is drawn as much towards the thought of destroying the old world as towards that of building the new, and he ends with the peroration that has become the one familiar Bakunin quotation: "Let us put our trust in the eternal spirit which destroys and annihilates only because it is the unsearchable and eternally creative source of all life. The urge to destroy is also a creative urge."

Barely a year after publishing *Reaction in Germany*, Bakunin met the man who began his transformation from a theoretical into a practical revolutionary, the German socialist Wilhelm Weitling, a self-taught sailor who wandered over Europe propagating his doctrines, and who, when Bakunin encountered him, was busy forming secret societies of Swiss artisans devoted to violent rebellion in the name of a "perfect society" with "no government, but only an administration, no laws, but only obligations, no punishments, but means of correction." Weitling's anarchistic ideas, and his emphasis on destruction as a way to a free society came close to Bakunin's own new ideas, while the German tailor's activities aroused what was to become a lifelong passion for conspiracy. How far Bakunin became involved in Weitling's plots is hard to tell, but he was mentioned in a Zurich police report and shortly afterwards was summoned to St. Petersburg to explain his conduct. Instead, he set off for Paris, still — despite Louis Philippe — the Rome of all European revolutionaries.

There Bakunin met Marx for the first time, and George Sand, but the most important of his new acquaintances was Pierre-Joseph Proudhon, the blunt printer from the Jura who in 1840 had been the first man to claim with pride the name of "anarchist." Bakunin and Proudhon had similarly baroque minds, delighting in paradox and extremity, and in their long conversations during 1844 in Latin Quarter hotel rooms, Bakunin's formless revolutionism received its first shaping. He did not at once become an anarchist; but Proudhon's federalism and his rejection of the state were firmly lodged in the mind of his Russian pupil from this time onward.

Yet it was a wind from the Slav world that stirred Bakunin into his first action. In 1846 there were risings in Austrian Poland, and their suppression led him to make common cause with the Poles in exile. In November 1847, he made his first public speech, at a banquet attended by fifteen hundred Polish refugees. Speaking of an alliance of "free Poland" and "free Russia," Bakunin not only openly challenged the Tsarist autocracy, but also launched the Pan-Slavist dream that was to dominate the first period of his revolutionary life. And beyond the liberation of the Slavs he saw the spread of revolution through the western world. "The reconciliation of Russia and Poland is a great cause. It means the liberation of sixty million souls, the liberation of all the Slav peoples who groan under a foreign yoke. It means, in a word, the fall, the irretrievable fall, of despotism in Europe."

This speech led to Bakunin's immediate deportation from France. A few weeks later, as Louis Philippe himself went off to exile, he returned on the wave of the February Revolution, and arrived in time to take part in its later stages. "I breathed through all my senses and through all my pores," he recollected years later, "the intoxication of the revolutionary atmosphere. It was a holiday without beginning and without end." He preached the indefinite extension of the revolution, socially and geographically, until even the revolutionaries grew tired of him. "The first day of the revolution he is a perfect treasure, but on the next day he should be shot," said Caussidière, according to one of the legends of 1848; whether Caussidière actually said this or not, many people felt it, and the Provisional Government gladly subsidized Bakunin with 2,000 francs when he proposed an expedition to foment insurrection in Poland.

Bakunin set off for Posen, but the Prussian police intercepted him in Berlin and, obligingly giving him two fake passports, diverted him to Breslau. There he could do nothing, since the Tsarist agents were spreading among the Poles a story — which was unjustly to follow him for many years — that he was one of their own spies. He gained new confidence, however, when he heard that a Slav Congress had been called in Prague by the Czech National Committee, and he set off immediately for the Bohemian capital.

The Congress itself was disappointing. Bakunin had hopes to establish a revolutionary alliance of the oppressed Slav peoples, but he found very few supporters for his plans; the Serbs and Bulgars looked to Russia to save them from the Turks, and the Czechs and Croats hoped to make their peace with the Hapsburgs at the expense of the Austrians. But Bakunin's peculiar talents were unexpectedly aroused when, on the last day of the Congress, an insurrection began in the streets of Prague. There are dubious accounts that credit Bakunin with actually starting the uprising by shooting at Austrian soldiers from the windows of the Blue Star hotel. He was certainly in the thick of the fighting once it began, showing that extraordinary energy which quickly made him a legendary figure among European revolutionaries; he drew upon his own military training to advise the insurgents, and took his place at the barricades among the Prague students and workers. After five days, the Austrian troops quelled the rebellion, but Bakunin slipped through their ranks and took refuge in the Duchy of Anhalt, where he wrote in *Appeal to the Slavs*, calling for a great national rising linked with a social revolution.

Yet it was not the struggle for Slav liberation that initiated the most epic passage of Bakunin's early manhood; it was, ironically, the defence of the German democrats whom he despised for their moderation. By March 1849, his wanderings had taken him to Dresden, which he decided to use as a base for agitation in Bohemia. In that month the people of Dresden rose in support of a democratic constitution rejected by the Saxon king. Bakunin had no sympathy for their aims; he was never a constitutionalist. But he was unable to resist the appeal of a revolution, and eventually he became so involved in the defence of Dresden that, when most of the democrats had prudently dispersed, he remained to be arrested by the advancing Prussians.

This was the beginning of a long pilgrimage through some of the worst prisons of Europe. The Saxons kept him for a year, sentenced him to death, reprieved him, and then passed him on to the Austrians, who claimed him for his part in the Prague rebellion. The process was repeated — imprisonment, court martial, death sentence, reprieve — and then he was handed over to the final claimant, Russia. The Tsarist government had long condemned him; he disappeared immediately into the silence of the Peter-and-Paul Fortress.

For six years he remained there, and in the even worse prison of Schlusselberg. His health was destroyed, and solitude ate into his spirit. Yet, in spite of a curious half-deferential and half-defiant *Confession* which he wrote at the request of the Tsar, he retained his ideals undiminished. A letter smuggled to one of his sisters told of the despair that often came upon him at the thought of lifelong imprisonment; yet in the same letter he said: "Prison . . . has changed none of my old sentiments; on the contrary, it has made them more ardent, more absolute than ever, and henceforward all that remains to me of life can be summed up in one word: liberty."

Often the will of a dedicated individual survives the obstinacy of the most absolute government. In 1857 Bakunin was finally released from prison and sent to Siberian exile. For a while he played with the idea of creating a revolutionary Slav alliance under the dictatorship of his cousin Muraviev-Amurski, then Governor of Siberia; he had not yet made the final shift to anarchism. But Muraviev

departed, and Bakunin fled down the Amur to the Pacific and over
the two oceans to the house in Orsett Terrace from which Alexander
Herzen, by means of his illegal periodical *The Bell*, was now wield-
ing a great liberalizing influence on Russian educated opinion.

Now, at the beginning of the last phase of his career, Bakunin
was a shambling bear of a man, toothless from scurvy, his good looks
destroyed by the rigors of prison, with an inordinate appetite for
food, for cigars, for strong spirits, for talk, for everything but — significantly — women. Yet his personality remained fascinating and
magnetic. He had retained his aristocratic charm, and he could win
working men by making them feel equal to him, not on their level —
for he was no democrat — but on his own. He returned to the world
he had left twelve years before with an amazing freshness of mind.
Prison and exile had enabled him to live in a mental state of suspended animation. The disillusionments other men had suffered were not
part of his experience. "The European reaction did not exist for
Bakunin," Herzen commented. "The bitter years from 1848 to 1858
did not exist for him either; of them he had but a brief, far-away,
faint knowledge. . . . The events of 1848, on the contrary, were all
about him, near to his heart; . . . they were still ringing in his ears and
hovering before his eyes."

Even when Bakunin turned to action, it was still the old dreams
of Polish liberation and Slav federation that haunted him; and, after
an ineffective attempt to collaborate with Herzen, he was inspired by
the Polish insurrection of 1863 to join an attempt to invade
Lithuania by a party of Poles who had evidently been inspired by
Garibaldi's recent exploits in Sicily. Two hundred of them chartered
a British boat, the *Ward Jackson*, to take them from Stockholm with
a cargo of arms; after landing, they hoped to rouse the peasants and
carry out a flank attack on the Russian army engaged in Poland
proper. But Bakunin and the Polish leaders were both so indiscreet
that the destination of the *Ward Jackson* was known publicly even
before it set sail; the legionnaires quarreled between themselves from
the moment of leaving Stockholm; and the British captain, fearful of

Russian warships, turned in mid-Baltic and took the legion back to Sweden, where it dispersed in mutual recriminations. Bakunin was cured of his admiration for Polish nationalists, and his pan-Slavist aims rapidly faded.

With their fading, the final, internationalist phase of his career began; and it first took shape in Italy, where he went in the winter of 1863. He found the country, the climate and the people congenial, and he slipped easily into the atmosphere of conspiracy that had been fostered since the days of the Carbonari. He also found an unexpected response to his own brand of revolutionism. Not only the Savoy monarchy, but also the nationalism of Mazzini, had become too conservative for the more revolutionary republicans; and Bakunin quickly gathered around him in Florence a circle of Italians and Slav expatriates out of whom he formed a secret Brotherhood.

Little is known of the Florentine Brotherhood; and it was not until late in 1865, when Bakunin moved to Naples, that his activities seemed to take definite form in what appears to have been a new organization, the International Brotherhood. Bakunin founded a central committee in Naples; several branches were formed in southern Italy and Sicily; and some foreigners were recruited, including the French geographer Elisée Reclus and César de Paepe, later one of the founders of Belgian socialism. Bakunin optimistically assured Herzen that the Mazzinian organizations and the peasants of the Mezzogiorno were flocking to him *en masse*; but there is no evidence that at this time he attracted more than a scanty following of intellectuals.

What, in fact, makes the International Brotherhood significant is not its actual strength or influence, both of which were obviously slight, but its position in political history. There had already been anarchist theoreticians — Godwin, Stirner, Proudhon and such lesser figures as Coeurderoy, Bellegarrique, and Déjacque — but there had been no organized anarchist movement. With the International Brotherhood, such a movement began. Its peculiar form of dual organization — with a secret core of tried militants (the International

Family) and a larger following of the half-initiated (the National Families) — actually survived in Spain until 1939 in the parallel organizations of the exclusive FAI and the mass CNT. Moreover, the *Revolutionary Catechism*, which Bakunin composed for the International Brotherhood, indicated clearly that he and his immediate followers were now taking the final step towards anarchism. The Brotherhood opposed the state and organized religion; it advocated federalism and communal autonomy in the manner of Proudhon, and departed from that philosopher in declaring that the social revolution could not be achieved by peaceful means. Socialism was accepted because labor "must be the sole base of human right and economic organization"; and an equivocal bow was made in the direction of unconverted Mazzinians by an acceptance of "libertarian nationalism," with the rider that nationality must quickly be replaced by "the comprehensive principle of liberty."

Clearly, by the mid-1860s the main outlines of Bakuninist anarchism had been formed, and the first prototype of its organization had been created. But the International Brotherhood was still limited to a few dozen adherents; and in August 1867, in the hope of widening his following, Bakunin left Naples for Geneva to take part in the Congress for Peace and Freedom, a heterogeneous gathering of liberals, pacifists, and socialists from many nations who were concerned over the threat of war created by the growing rivalry of France and Prussia. Bakunin was at first welcomed enthusiastically by the six thousand delegates, who rose spontaneously to applaud this legendary veteran of barricades and prisons, as Garibaldi came forward to embrace him on the platform. Bakunin was even elected to the central committee of the League for Peace and Freedom founded by the Congress; and during the following year he so far dominated this group by his personal dynamism that it submitted to the 1868 Congress of the League a report recommending the replacement of centralized states by federations of autonomous provinces and communes, the universal disestablishment of religious bodies, and the "equitable division of wealth, labor, leisure and education." The recommendation was rejected by the liberal majority; and Bakunin, with seventeen other delegates, walked out of the Congress.

He gained more than he lost by this defeat. He had used the League as a sounding board; he had gained a wider international following; he had made the transfer from the conspiratorial activity of his past to the public activity of his final years. Now the men who had followed him out of the League for Peace and Freedom became the nucleus for a new and larger Bakuninist organization. This was the International Alliance of Social Democracy. For the first time, "international" was not a misnomer. Bakunin's followers moved rapidly into those Mediterranean regions where socialism was only beginning to awaken. Branches of the Alliance were founded in Geneva, where the central bureau was located, in Lyons and Marseilles, Naples and Sicily, Barcelona and Madrid. The strength of the Alliance in fact lay in those very regions which, in later decades, became the strongholds of European anarchism — Italy and Spain, the South of France and French-speaking Switzerland.

But Bakunin was not content with the Alliance alone: it was to be the springboard for wider conquests in the European labor movement. A short while before founding it, he had joined, as an individual member, the International Working Men's Association, formed in 1864; and now he wished to lead his Alliance into it as a special corps of "propagandists, apostles and, finally, organizers." At this time, the International had already survived one vital struggle, between the Mutualist followers of Proudhon and Marx's adherents who — in alliance with the Blanquist exiles in London — controlled the General Council of the organization. At the Brussels congress of 1868, the Mutualists were finally defeated by the acceptance of collectivization of property as the International's principle for economic organization; and Marx, who had now reached the peak of his influence in the General Council, was not anxious to see Bakunin's followers admitted as a semi-autonomous group with special privileges — for the Alliance asked to retain its own central bureau and to hold congresses parallel to those of the International.

The General Council rejected the Alliance's application, but agreed eventually to admit the individual branches provided the organization as a whole were dissolved. Bakunin accepted; he had nothing to lose, since his Italian and Spanish followers did not change their attitudes with the titles of their branches; and, on entering the International, he actually increased his strength by gaining the support of the celebrated Jura Federation, composed of the independent watchmakers of French-speaking Switzerland.

As the conflict within the International shaped up, it was clearly not entirely a clash of personalities, though it is hard to imagine any organization having room for two such autocratic yet mutually incompatible individuals as Bakunin and Marx. It was not even wholly a struggle between authoritarian and libertarian types of socialism, between the Marxist desire to seize control of the state and the Bakuninist desire to destroy it. Just as important as the personal and ideological elements was the regional difference of outlooks. The more industrial northern countries, with the temporary exception of Belgium, tended to accept centralized organization, while the Mediterranean and Alpine countries favored the loose organization of the Bakuninists, which was now evolving into the network of autonomous groups that — except in Spain — would later constitute the customary form of anarchist organization.

The regional differences of outlook, and a widespread resentment of the oligarchical tendencies of the General Council, assured Bakunin his following in the International; and the conflict assumed an open form when, at the Basel Congress of 1869, he effectively marshalled the malcontents and inflicted a crushing defeat on the General Council over the abolition of the right of inheritance, whose inclusion in the platform of the International the Marxists somewhat inconsistently opposed.

Marx had no intention of accepting a Bakuninist ascendancy within the International; but the renewal of the struggle, at least openly, was postponed by the Franco-Prussian War and the Paris Commune. Not until 1871 was anything approaching a plenary

gathering of the International brought together; and, in the meantime, Bakunin, whose influence remained secure in his Spanish,
Italian, and Jura strongholds, became involved in two rather unfortunate adventures.

In 1869 Serghei Nechaev — the terrorist who became the original for Dostoevsky's Peter Verkhovensky — arrived in Switzerland,
and immediately established a surprising influence over the much
older Bakunin. Not only did he use Bakunin's name to obtain funds
for his own activities, but he also involved him in the publication of a
series of anonymous terrorist pamphlets. "We recognize no other
activity but the work of extermination," says one of them, entitled
Principles of Revolution, "but we admit that the forms of this activity
may be extremely varied — poison, the knife, the rope, etc." That
Bakunin wrote these lines is by no means certain; he thought of
destruction in cataclysmic terms, and the methods suggested here
smack far more of Nechaev's narrow and cruel mind. But his enemies at the time certainly blamed him for them.

Nechaev finally disappeared, extradited from Switzerland to a
living death in the Peter-and-Paul Fortress. In the meantime, Bakunin
became closely interested in the Franco-Prussian War. In one of his
most coherent pamphlets, *Letters to a Frenchman*, he called loudly on
the people of France to embark on "an elemental, mighty, passionately energetic, anarchistic, destructive, unrestrained uprising" that
would at the same time overthrow their own government, drive the
Prussians from their soil, and start the European revolution on its
way. After Sedan, he decided that the moment for such a rising had
come, and set off to Lyons, where he had a small following. The situation in Lyons, where the republic had been declared, was still fluid;
and Bakunin immediately set up an anarchist Committee for the
Salvation of France, which aimed at abolishing the state, establishing
"popular justice" and suspending taxes and mortgages. A workers'
riot, which the Committee did not actually organize, placed its members in unexpected control of the Hotel de Ville, where they reigned
for a few hours until the bourgeois National Guard dispersed them

and arrested Bakunin. He was later rescued by his followers and fled via Marseilles to Genoa.

"Goodbye to all our dreams of approaching liberation," Bakunin lamented at the end of this fiasco. But he still entered enthusiastically into the last fight within the International, in which he was now supported by a group of energetic disciples who were to shape the anarchist movement of later years — Carlo Cafiero, Andrea Costa, and Enrico Malatesta in Italy, James Guillaume in Switzerland, Farga Pellicer in Spain. (Peter Kropotkin was only to become active in Western Europe in the year of Bakunin's death.)

The split became definite when the General Council called a special Conference in London during 1871 and, on technical grounds, failed to invite the Jura Federation, now Bakunin's most faithful followers; the Conference also passed several resolutions directed against the anarchists, including one affirming the need for working-class political activity and another, aimed particularly at Bakunin, publicly disavowing the activities of Nechaev. The Jura Federation in turn called a conference of Swiss and of French Communard delegates at Sonvillier; it issued the famous Sonvillier Circular, denouncing centralism in the General Council and calling for the reconstruction of the International as a "free federation of autonomous groups."

The final battle came in the last Congress of the united International, held at the Hague in 1872. The Italians boycotted this gathering, which gave the Marxists a secure majority; they proceeded to expel Bakunin and his friend James Guillaume for allegedly maintaining the Alliance as a secret organization; and they also — on Marx's insistence — shifted the General Council to New York, well away from corrupting influences. But Marx had won a Pyrrhic victory. The Bakuninists immediately held their own Congress at St. Imier in the Jura, and set up a rival "true" International, to which a majority of the old International eventually adhered, including not only the Federations of the Latin countries, but also those of Belgium, Holland and even, for a time, Britain. The Marxist rump died quickly of inactivity in New York. The St. Imier International survived until 1877; and by then the anarchist movements, founded under its influence in various European and Latin American countries, were able to develop on their own in the congenial world of the *fin de siècle*.

But, long before that time, Bakunin had withdrawn from the public struggle. The years of prison and the impoverished wanderings of his later years had aged him terribly; and in 1872, at fifty-eight, he felt physically worn out and mentally dispirited. In the following year, he actually made a public announcement of retirement in a Geneva newspaper. "I feel neither the strength nor, perhaps, the confidence that is needed to go on rolling Sisyphus's stone against the triumphant forces of reaction." But Sisyphus could not leave his stone, nor could Bakunin renounce his revolutionary past. He became involved in a plan to buy a house in Ticino with money belonging to a rich Italian anarchist; the house would be a center for conspiratorial work in Italy; but Bakunin could also spend his last years there with the Polish wife he had married in Siberia. He behaved with extraordinary irresponsibility, squandering the funds like a Chekhovian aristocrat, until even his disciples disowned him. Then he dragged his massive, ailing body down to Italy to purge his misdeeds in the Bologna insurrection of August 1874. It was his last expedition, and he hoped to die gloriously on the barricades. But the rising was abortive; the insurgent columns never even got inside the walls of Bologna, where Bakunin was waiting to take part in the storming of the arsenal; and he fled back to Switzerland, disguised as a village priest with blue glasses.

It was his last venture as an anarchist. The remaining fragment of his life was an unhappy tale of declining health, nagging poverty, failing friendships. He died in July 1876, and was buried in the curiously alien atmosphere of the cemetery at Berne.

After his death, the anarchist movement he had founded grew rapidly; and for a while it became the kind of terror to rulers that would have delighted his violent and generous mind. Sixty years after his death, it was fighting its last battles for freedom in the streets of Barcelona and the hills of Andalusia and Aragon. But Bakunin stands in history as a kind of Janus figure, one face turned towards liberty and the other towards its antithesis. For the unanarchistic ideas of his earlier decades — the messianic dream of a world saved by Slavdom and the vision of revolution through a disciplined party of conspirators and an iron dictatorship — did not die; they lived on to permeate the whole Russian underground movement of the late nineteenth century, and reached their ironic end in the Bolsheviks, who have always shown a most suspect fervor in their denunciations of Bakunin.

1961

3

Alexander Herzen: Ancestor in Defeat

"The whole bourgeois world blown up by gunpowder, when the smoke disperses and reveals the ruins, will start again with different variations — *another bourgeois world*." It was these words of Alexander Herzen that occurred to me when I finished reading Ilya Ehrenburg's *The Thaw*, that tenth-rate echo of Arnold Bennett. In Ehrenburg's petty world of essentially middle-class relationships, of intrigues and ambitions and half-hearted rebellions hardly distinguishable from those of Levitown and Tooting, Herzen would certainly have detected the new bourgeois world which he prophesied as the result of a revolution misconceived and misapplied; he would have seen here, as he saw in Western Europe during the mid-nineteenth century, facile materialism spreading like "a syphilitic growth infecting the blood and bone of society."

My first impulse, on comparing the shallow and timid perception which Ehrenburg directed upon his environment with the penetrating irony that characterized Herzen's criticisms of the nineteenth-century world, was to draw the comparison between the vigor of the generation of Russian intellectuals that arose in defiance of Nicholas I, and the melancholy flutters of quasi-independence on the part of present-day Russian writers, to which western liberals are inclined to attach such exaggerated importance. The comparison is instructive, but it merely deepens what we already know in general terms: that the autocrats of the nineteenth century were not so acutely conscious as modern totalitarians of the need to prevent the emergence of any kind of genuine intellectual liberty. The climate of free thought in the Russian universities that bred Herzen and Belinsky and Bakunin has long been extinct, and even if in some way a critical mentality like theirs were to emerge it would find no vehicle of expression in the controlled Russian press. Ehrenburg is tolerated precisely because his meager shows of rebellion are harmless to the existing regime and have their uses as external propaganda.

But having realized that a direct comparison between Ehrenburg and any nineteenth-century Russian writer was perhaps superfluous, I was brought back to the ironic figure of Herzen himself, that ancestor in disillusioned radicalism, and to the realization that, as a critic of revolutionary attitudes and as an observer of the nineteenth-century world, Herzen has an interest for us today which could hardly be brought out of a routine comparison with a contemporary Stalinist hack. And so this essay has become rather a re-examination of Herzen in his own right, with the original point of comparison fading into an initial and discarded excuse.

Herzen is perhaps best known in the English-speaking world through E. H. Carr's study of him and his circle, *The Romantic Exiles;* and Carr's thesis that Herzen was primarily a romantic among romantics has colored most recent judgments of him. It presents, however, an incomplete and distorted view of a complex and often contradictory personality.

Like his literary contemporaries, Herzen was at first influenced by the Romantic movement which flowered belatedly in Russia during the 1830s. In some aspects of his life and thought, in the curiously morbid sentimentality that ruled his personal relationships, in the quasi-mystical elements that sometimes emerged in his political attitudes, the influence was enduring. His attachment to France before

1848 was transferred to Russia, so that, throughout the most active part of his career, Herzen's outlook on his homeland was consistently ambivalent, combining with hatred of autocracy a strong feeling that Russia had regenerative powers that might yet give it a positive role in European affairs.

But even in his youth elements of resistance to this influence were present; his father had been a Voltairean, and Herzen inherited his eighteenth-century intellectual irony. When most of his friends, following the romantic trend, became enamoured of German philosophy, he avoided that crepuscular labyrinth, and turned instead to the clearer thought of France, of socialists like Saint-Simon and Fourier, whose extravagances he rejected, but whose essential insights he took as a basis for his own social views. While his friend Bakunin, an unregenerate romantic to the end, went through a period of fanatical Hegelianism, Herzen realized fully the amibiguities of the German philosopher's dialectic; faced with the celebrated phrase, "whatever is real is rational," he objected, early in the 1840s: "But once any existing social order is justified by reason, so can the struggle against that order, if the struggle *exists,* be equally justified."

He was a romantic in whom the antibodies of intellectual scepticism grew steadily stronger, until, on most questions, he developed an ironic detachment such as was attained by few of his contemporaries. He liked to compare himself with Byron, and the comparison is not inapt, for in both of these radical aristocrats one sees the romantic and the Voltairean passions in perpetual conflict, the emotional vision being constantly undermined by eroding doubt, yet never completely disintegrating. It was this sustained duality within Herzen's outlook that made him that rare bird indeed, the radical who is always disillusioned and yet who is renewed by a recurrent hope that makes action seem ever important, even in a cause that the sceptical self regards with pessimism.

For Herzen, as for his friend Proudhon and for many other radicals of the mid-nineteenth century, 1848 was the Great Divide, the line that marked off the relatively facile optimism of youth from the conflict between idealism and despair that dominated the years of maturity. But in Herzen's early life there had already been another catastrophic event of almost traumatic intensity: the revolt of the Russian officers in December, 1825, and its ferociously brutal suppression by Nicholas I. Herzen was then a boy of thirteen, and he tells in his memoirs — *My Past and Thoughts* — how he and his friend Ogarev went into the Sparrow Hills outside Moscow and there swore that they would devote their lives to fulfilling the ideals of the Decembrists. Both of them kept their oaths to the best of their ability, and Herzen's radical ideas undoubtedly took their original form from the Decembrist programs. In particular, he was indebted to Pavel Ivanovich Pestel. Pestel, who was executed in 1826 at the age of thirty-three, demanded the emancipation of and the granting of land to the serfs, a progressive agricultural program, universal manhood suffrage and a democratic republic. All these demands were later developed by Herzen, and the only major point on which he seems to have disagreed with Pestel is to be found in his rejection of the latter's desire that the state be centralized; Herzen, though never an anarchist in any doctrinaire sense, distrusted the State (this was part of a natural reaction against the elaborate bureaucracy set up by Nicholas I) and advocated a thorough policy of administrative decentralization.

Herzen's Decembrism, reinforced by French socialist ideas, led him into the circles of student discussion which sprang up in the universities during the 1830s; as a result of the vaguely liberal ideas which he propounded, he was banished in 1835 to the Urals, whence, in Byronic spirit, he emerged secretly to marry his cousin and whisk her off to his place of exile. A few years late he returned to Moscow, but a mild criticism of the inefficiency of the Tsarist police in preventing murders was enough to bring him a second term of exile, this time in Novgorod. It is from the time of this last experience that the characteristic tone of bitterness, the tendency towards habitual disillusionment, became evident in Herzen's attitude. Seeing no chance of any improvement in Russia while Nicholas I was still autocrat, Herzen resolved to leave the country as soon as he could; the death of his father, a wealthy landowner, gave him the means to travel, and in 1847 he crossed the frontier into Western Europe.

From this time onward Herzen was to remain an exile, never establishing a permanent home or becoming assimilated into any of the countries that gave him passing hospitality. After 1848, he knew that he was never likely to return to Russia, yet he did not attempt in any real way to sever the emotional links that tied him to his past in that country. Even the pattern of his daily life remained in many respects, despite his acceptance of the title of socialist, that of a Russian feudal landowner. He arrived in Europe with two carriages full of relatives and retainers, and, wherever he lived, he maintained the lavish feudal manner, surrounding himself with dependents, handing out largesse to those exiles who were less fortunate than himself, and not only financing his own periodicals, but also playing patron to that of Proudhon, *La Voix du Peuple.* Ironically, all this was made possible by the intervention of the financier Rothschild, who forced the Tsarist authorities to liberate Herzen's funds within Russia by threatening to sabotage a frontier into Western Europe.

In his more general attitudes, too, Herzen remained the Russian and the aristocrat. His love of Western Europe was a short-lived phenomenon which did not survive the storms of reality. In 1847, he entered Paris "with reverence, as men used to enter Jerusalem and Rome." But the ineptitudes of most of the revolutionaries in 1848 and the horror of the repression that followed the June insurrection of that year precipitated a reaction of feelings. Herzen began to see the West as degenerate and without hope of revival from within, and he found in the materialism of the bourgeoisie — who in 1848 turned from revolution to reaction — a reason for this degeneracy. He came to hate the middle class of Western Europe with a detestation that never waned, and, though his sympathies were aroused by the French workers who fought behind the June barricades and by such individualistic radicals as Proudhon and Orsini, he did not feel that they had the power to halt the decline of the West. More and more he began to turn towards Russia, the land which had not undergone the corrupting process of mercantilism and industrialism the land where the peasants were still a vast inarticulate potential force.

In this he established a pattern that was followed by all the Russian aristocratic revolutionaries—Bakunin, Kropotkin, Tolstoy, Lavrov, Cherkesov, and so on. All of them retained and incorporated into their political philosophies the contempt for the shopkeeper which is shared by most aristocrats, and all of them showed the former landowner's tendency to see virtue in the country and the former proprietor's guilty inclination to elevate the peasant above the town classses of bourgeois and proletariat. But the aristocratic revolutionary cannot entirely be dismissed in negative terms of this kind. For, in general, it was these former noblemen, with their more liberal educations, who were the least liable of the nineteenth-century radicals to become bogged down in parochial and doctrinaire political attitudes, and at at the same time the most open to fresh and invigorating ideas.

It was the feeling, after 1848, of the bankruptcy of the west that led Herzen to concentrate more and more of his energy on the task of initiating propaganda in Russia, and in this role he became the great pioneer of all the Russian liberal and radical movements of the later nineteenth century. It was typical of his situation as an exiled nobleman that his first attempts in this direction, involving the printing and the despatch by secret means to Russia of one or two pamphlets criticizing the Tsarist regime, should have arisen as much out of the bored need for action of a leisured and moneyed expatriate as it did from any hope that his actions would bear fruit. The foundation of the Free Russian Press was indeed very largely a sentimental gesture in the direction of his ancient ideals, of his oath to the Decembrists, and nobody was more delightedly astonished than he when the first fugitive publications of the press aroused great attention in Russia. Herzen had in fact initiated someting totally new in Russian history — the publication of direct criticisms of the Tsar, and to those who read them in the fear-ridden atmosphere of Nicholas's Russia his writings seemed audacious and stimulating in the extreme. On the strength of these slight publications Herzen not only became recognized by the liberals within Russia as a kind of intellectual mentor — a position which he held for more than a decade while he published his expatriate periodicals, *The Northern Star* and *The Bell* — but also assumed, as if by acknowledged right, the position of unofficial ambassador in Western Europe of the dissident forces within Russia. Once, at least, this last fact had a consequence that appears more ironical to us than it can have done to anybody in Herzen's day. A mass gathering was held in London in February, 1855, to commemorate the revolutions of 1848; Victor Hugo, Arnold Ruge, Kossuth, and Mazzini represented their own countries, and Herzen was chosen as the Russian speaker, upon which Marx, who had also been invited, refused to have anything to do with the meeting. "I will nowhere and at no time appear on the same platform as Herzen," he explained to Engels, "since I am not of the opinion that 'old Europe' can be rejuvenated by Russian blood."

Herzen's role in preparing the end of Tsarism in Russia belongs to history; he showed the Russians that it was possible to criticize the regime, but, once they had learned this from him, the radical groups which sprang up during the 1860s soon abandoned the gradualism that underlay his policy and the limited program of reforms with which he expressed it in *The Bell*. Towards the terrorism of the Narodnaya Volya, towards violent anarchism, towards Marxism, the young generation rapidly moved away from Herzen, and, except in a general way as an innovator who started the wave of intellectual rebellion in the 1850s, he did not have a great direct influence on his successors. Bakunin, Pisarev, Chernyshevsky, even Nechaev, all contributed more to the tactics and programs of later movements than Herzen did. Indeed, in some respects he was actually nearer to the liberal wing of the Slavophiles, with their rejection of autocracy and their sense of the destiny of Russia, than to any of the wide array of revolutionary groups that took part in the first Russian revolution of 1905.

This fact needs to be stressed in view of the Communist attempts to claim Herzen as an ancestor. Herzen, in fact, was in no way a proto-Communist; once, it is true, he published under the aegis of the Free Russian Press a translation of *The Communist Manifest* (ironically, this first Russian version was the work of Bakunin!), but he did so in the spirit of making available to Russians the most interesting publications of contemporary radicalism, and his own view is expressed more exactly in his remark that "Communism is Russian autocracy turned upside down." Lenin, in his anxiety to prepare a family tree for the Bolshevik regime, went to the extent of claiming that Herzen was "the first to raise the standard of battle by turning to the masses with the free Russian word," and other writers have seen in Herzen the precursor of the Narodniks, with their creed of "going to the people." But Herzen never even attempted to produce a propaganda that would reach the Russian peasants (the only "masses" that existed in his time), and his writings and the publications which he sent into Russia were all calculated to appeal to the intelligentsia and to the liberal minority in the official class and among the aristocracy. Again, while he anticipated the Narodniks in their theory of a society based on a modification of the primitive peasant commune, he did not evolve any plan of direct work among the peasants comparable of the movement which led the Narodnik intellectuals to leave the cities and work in the villages in the hope of turning the peasants into the vanguard of the revolution.

Essentially, Herzen was neither a propagandist nor a conspiratorial organizer (1848 cured him of that), but a revolutionary intellectual, and it is for this reason, more than any other, that, while the Narodnik movement and its tacticians have been rendered obsolete by events, Herzen is still interesting to us today. His ideas have been somewhat obscured by his record as a publicist and by that romantic element in his personal life which so appealed to Professor Carr, but when one comes to consider them, they still have a provocative relevance both to Russian problems and also to certain perennial problems of socialism. The emphases change, the degrees of enthusiasm vary, but the essential attitudes remain.

Herzen was always a socialist, but in the Proudhonian sense, rejecting governmental socialism in favor of a conception based on modificatons of the peasant *mir* and the cooperative *artel* of workmen. He remained always anti-bourgeois, and he looked with distrust on western forms of democracy which, like de Tocqueville, he feared might end in the universal reign of mediocrity. He rejected industrialism as he saw it developing in England and other Western countries, but he did not reject the idea of applying science to production, provided this application were based on "the relation of man to the soil," which he regarded as "a primordial fact, a *natural* fact." He believed that socialism could only be justified if it enriched rather than impoverished life, and for this reason he rejected its more ascetic forms. "We can make of our world neither a Sparta nor a Benedictine convent," he said. "The coming revolution must reconcile all the elements of social life for the general good, as the Fourierists dreamed of doing: we must not stifle some elements for the advantage of others." He regarded governmental or administrative centralization as inimical to freedom, but, though he was influenced to this extent by anarchist conceptions, he saw the complete elimination of the state as an almost infinitely receding possibility.

Finally, Herzen's concern with Russia, his sense of an immense potential energy underlying the hard crust of autocratic rule, never vanished. Like Marx, most of the radicals of Western Europe refused to share his belief in the destiny of Russia, and they were right in rejecting the mystical elements that entered into his point of view. At the same time, Herzen's arguments were not entirely governed by sentiment. As an exile, he was able to look on Russia with more detachment than anyone within the country, and on Western Europe with more detachment than most of the radicals who had spent their lives in its liberal and revolutionary movements. And, as the events of our century have tended to show, there was perhaps more truth in his idea that social initiative was passing out of the hands of Western Europeans than in the thoughts of those who believed that Paris was the permanent capital of the revolution or that Germany would lead the new uprising of the proletariat. Behind all the writings of Herzen's later years there hovers the vision — how prophetic one is too uneasily aware — of Russia and America facing each other over a dispirited Europe.

A last — and not least — reason for Herzen's enduring relevance is to be found in the elaborate documentation of the nineteenth-century revolutionary personality that appears in his memoirs. Herzen, the ironical radical aristocrat, was the nearest thing the nineteenth century produced to Orwell and Silone. Like them, even in disillusionment he could not destroy the rebellious inner urge that bound him to the movements of his time. Intellectually critical of the prejudices and follies of the men of 1848, he was still fascinated by their personalities and compassionate of their misfortunes. During his years in Switzerland and England he continued to live among political exiles, and from among them he chose most of his friends. He watched them with irony and perceptiveness, and in *My Past and Thoughts* he left a series of portraits of revolutionary leaders and followers and of comments on the psychological quirks of the professional rebel which, even today, might be made into a handbook that radicals themselves could read with profit.

To anyone who has known the boredom and exasperation of most radical group activity, Herzen's description of what he calls "the chorus of the revolution" ("Immovable conservatives in everything connected with the revolution, they stop short at some program and never advance beyond it") and the revolutionary bureaucracy, which "dissolves things into words and forms just as our official bureaucracy does," will seem apt and perennial, while those who have moved in contemporary circles of political exiles in Paris or London or Mexico City will recognize the melancholy truth of these remarks on the mentality which is developed by all but the most exceptional expatriates:

> Exile, not undertaken with any definite object, but forced upon men by the triumph of the opposing party, checks

into the domain of fantasy. Leaving their native land with concealed anger, with the continual thought of going back to it on the morrow, men make no advance, but are continually thrown back upon the past; hope hinders them from settling down and undertaking any permanent work; irritations and trivial but exasperated disputes prevent their escaping from the familiar circle of questions, thoughts and memories which make up an oppressive binding tradition.

In the last resort, Herzen can be fitted into no category in the history of radicalism. He represents, more than almost any other man of his age, the kind of disillusioned yet committed intellectual, the revolutionary *malgré lui,* with whom we have become familiar in the twentieth century. For him, as for the best of his type today, the rejection of methods, the loss of facile optimism, the development of a realistic view of persons, did not mean the abandonment of an ideal, the rejection of a moral standpoint. The kind of betrayal of inner experience, the masochistic self-degradation which one encounters in men like Chambers and Koestler, and which in Herzen's day formed the less pleasant side of Dostoevsky's mental history, would have seemed too undignified and — perhaps most important — too absurd for him even to consider. Herzen had his faults in plenty — his aristocratic habits and prejudices, his semi-romantic lapses from realistic thinking, his considerable vanity, his comparative ignorance of economic trends — but, even when these are taken into account, he belongs to a breed of men whose therapeutic irony and psychological penetration make them indispensable to any movement of thought that is to avoid its own conservatism, its own ossification into orthodoxy. For, if the radical intellectual has a second purpose beyond that of thinking creatively about the world in which he lives, it is surely that of preventing the radical mind from becoming so armored with complacency that it loses all power of adaptability and growth.

1960

4

Peter Kropotkin: A Libertarian Life

"**K**ropotkin," said Bernard Shaw, "might have been a shepherd from the Delectable Mountains." Oscar Wilde revered him, in somewhat incongruous company with Paul Verlaine, as a man of Christlike life. Among geographers he was regarded as one of the great Asian explorers, and biologists paused with respect to hear his reflections on the factors in evolution. The English aristocrats never quite forgot that he was a prince of the line of Rurik, and the English working men remembered that it was in their ranks he had marched to Trafalgar Square in the great demonstrations of the 1880s. The ubiquitous Frank Harris maliciously represents him hurrying out to the kitchen of his Bromley cottage to tell his wife Sophie to add water to the soup as more and more guests arrive. For his suburban home, with its well-trimmed and productive garden, was for decades a place of pilgrimage for writers and geographers, for socialists, anarchists, and trades union leaders, who would listen to Kropotkin's amiable and illuminating talk and occasionally be allowed to hear him playing the piano; the latter, G.D.H. Cole recalled from boyhood, was atrocious. Peter Kropotkin was one of the notable institutions of late Victorian England, with enough all-round talents to excite the admiration of Britons, and enough of a past to allow them to dwell on their own broad-mindedness in giving his asylum.

Apart from the position of revered exile which he fulfilled so adequately for his thirty-odd years in England, Kropotkin was one of the four great figures of the anarchist tradition, the equal of Godwin, Proudhon, and Bakunin; he was also a prolific writer whose influence spread far beyond the confines of the anarchist movement, influencing socialism in its more libertarian aspects, helping to form the social philosophy of Gandhi, and contributing, through Patrick Geddes and Lewis Mumford, to modern discussions on the interpretation of urban and rural life and on the balance between academic and vocational training.

In his *Memoirs of a Revolutionary*, one of the more admirable Russian autobiographies, Kropotkin tells of his youth in a feudal household in the days before the emancipation of the serfs. He was born in 1842; his father was a general, one of the military martinets beloved of the Tsar Nicholas I, and Peter Kropotkin found companionship among the serfs in the servants' hall, with the French tutor who talked of the Great Revolution, as Kropotkin always afterwards called it, and with the Russian tutor who introduced him to the poems of Pushkin and the radical journalism of Chernyshevsky.

Meanwhile, as a hereditary prince and the son of a high-ranking officer, Kropotkin was expected to make his career in the Emperor's service. He was chosen for the Corps of Pages, and became the personal page to Alexander II. When his time came to enter military service, he relinquished his page's privilege to serve in the Guards and chose instead the Mounted Cossacks of the Amur; he felt that in Siberia he would have an opportunity to fulfil his scientific interests. There he investigated the prison system, but found his recommendations of reforms falling on deaf ears. In disillusionment, he accepted a commission to explore the eastern regions of Siberia; he traveled 50,000 miles through this region and elaborated a theory on the structure of the East Asian mountain ranges which revolutionized current conceptions of Eurasian geography. At the same time he began to experience one of those crises of conscience common among Russian noblemen in the nineteenth century. A political exile introduced him to the writings of Proudhon, and the execution of a group of Polish convicts who had escaped from Lake Baikal completed his conversion. He resigned his commission, and returned to St. Petersburg, where he enrolled as a student, renouncing his wealth and living by casual work for the Russian Geographical Society.

The most important turning point in Kropotkin's life came in 1871, when he was offered the secretaryship of the Russian Geographical Society, and had to choose between the life of a scientist and that of a revolutionary. He picked the latter, and set out for Switzerland to learn about the socialist movement in western Europe. There, meeting the watchmakers of Jura, who were Bakunin's most devoted followers in the First International, he became a lifelong convert to anarchism, which throughout his life he regarded as a form — the best form — of socialism.

Returning to Russia in 1872, he joined the Chaikovsky Circle, and used his geographical studies as a cover for propaganda in the working-class districts of St. Petersburg. At this time he advocated producers' cooperatives which might eventually lead to workingmen's associations to take over the land and the factories. He was arrested in 1874, and spent two years in the Peter-and-Paul Fortress, until his health broke down and he was transferred to a military hospital, from which, in 1876, he made his escape to England. In 1877 he was organizing anarchist groups in Paris, and in 1878, in Switzerland, he founded the famous anarchist paper, *La Révolté*. After taking part in the International Anarchist Congress in London in 1881, he was expelled from Switzerland and settled in France. There he was arrested in 1882 on a nebulous charge of belonging to the International, by now defunct, and in 1883 was sentenced to five years' imprisonment. The case aroused international protests, and in 1886 Kropotkin was pardoned. He made his way to England, which remained his home until, after the March revolution of 1917, he returned to Russia.

Kropotkin's life as an explorer and an active revolutionary propagandist was ended. His imprisonments had left him delicate in health, and in England he slowly adapted himself to the different conditions of political life in a country where the working-class movement has always favored undogmatic and rather libertarian forms of socialism. He and his friend William Morris certainly influenced each other greatly, and Kropotkin's ideas played their part in shaping the theories of the Guild Socialists. But he remained an anarchist, founding *Freedom* in London in 1887, and continuing as an influential figure in the International Movement until, in 1914, he supported the Allied side in the First World War and lost the confidence of the anti-militarist majority of his former comrades. Most of all, he devoted his thirty years in England to writing such books as *Memoirs of a Revolutionist*, *Mutual Aid*, *Fields, Factories and Workshops*, and *The Great French Revolution*.

The book which most clearly summarises his vision is *The Conquest of Bread*, compiled mainly from articles written before he reached England. In it Kropotkin elaborated the doctrine with which his name is particularly associated, anarchist communism. Kropotkin did not actually originate the theory of anarchist communism, which was first sketched out in 1876 by a Geneva artisan, François Dumartheray, but he developed it and became its best-known exponent. Like other forms of anarchism, it rejected the state and other forms of coercive organization, and envisaged a society of self-governing communes and workingmen's associations, regulating all municipal and industrial matters by mutual consent, and united in regional and ultimately world federations. The distinguishing feature of anarchist communism was the idea — already put forward by Sir Thomas More in the sixteenth century — that distribution should not be related, by wages or labor checks, to actual work performed, but should be based on need, since the collective character of the human heritage makes it impossible to determine each man's contribution.

Kropotkin's later works tended to elaborate and bring scientific support to this central theory. *Mutual Aid*, studying the presence of cooperation in animal and human societies, aimed to prove that government was both unnecessary and against nature. *Fields, Factories and Workshops* supported Kropotkin's ideas of administrative decentralization with a reasoned plea for industrial decentralization. *The Great French Revolution* sought to establish a historical tradition for anarchism, and *Memoirs of a Revolutionist* was the eloquent apologia for an anarchist's life. Except in Spain, where he had little influence, Kropotkin was the most important libertarian teacher of his time.

His last years formed a rather melancholy finale. Returning to Russia after forty years, he found himself out of touch with the revolutionary movements. But in spite of his isolation, he continued to work on a last book, *Ethics*, and, while opposing firmly the intervention of the Western powers, he protested courageously against the Bolshevik restrictions on liberty and the excesses of the Cheka. He died on the 8th of February, 1921, and a procession five miles long, bearing anarchist and socialist flags, wound its way through Moscow to the cemetery in the suburbs. It was the last great public demonstration of left-wing opposition to Bolshevism.

c. 1975

5

Henry David Thoreau's Anarchism

"How big a stone was needed to slay Goliath?" is the kind of question one begins asking when one looks after a long interval at Henry David Thoreau's *On the Duty of Civil Disobedience*. It is a short essay, less than forty modest pages, and brief even in comparison with Marx's and Engels's deliberately condensed *Communist Manifesto* (written in the same year of 1848), yet it manages its score or so of inspiring aphorisms and anecdotes and images so easily that one never feels one is reading within bounds.

On the Duty of Civil Disobedience is not even a particularly original or innovative work, except insofar as it projects Thoreau's personal idiosyncrasies. Introducing a recent edition, Gene Sharp claimed that before Thoreau, "There is little or no thought given to civil disobedience for producing social and political change." This is just not true; Thoreau comes relatively late in a long tradition, as anyone who studies the history of the civil war period in seventeenth-century England will quickly find. In the 1630s John Hampden refused to pay a tax called "ship money" which King Charles I arbitrarily imposed. Even when the courts decided against him, Hampden still refused to pay and stayed in jail until he was released under writs of *habeus corpus*. As I remark in my book called

Civil Disobedience, in doing this Hampden followed "a pattern of Civil Disobedience similar to that advocated by Thoreau in his essay."

Only a few years after Hampden, on a much more plebeian level, Gerrard Winstanley and the Diggers declared that the solution of the social problem lay in the return of the land by non-violent direct action to the people. Winstanley proclaimed: "True religion and undefiled is this, to make restitution of the earth that hath been taken and held from the common people, by the power of Conquests formerly, and so set the oppressed free." In April 1649 Winstanley and the Diggers went out to till by hand the common land on some hills overlooking the Thames, and though they suffered great persecutions from local landowners and clergy, they kept up their civil disobedience for a whole year, to such effect that General Fairfax was unwilling to use his own soldiers against the Diggers lest they become corrupted by non-violent example.

The tradition of civil disobedience, and of the constructive non-violent action which is its positive aspect, continued strongly in England. When William Godwin published in 1793 the first great exposition of anarchism, *Political Justice*, the plan he essentially offered was that of rational men withdrawing their support from government, on the assumption that in the end no regime could endure without it. (He still had much to learn about the ingenuities of tyranny.) Later, when Godwinian teachings reached the British working classes in the 1830s, filtered through the cooperativism and trade unionism of his disciple Robert Owen, one of the great myths of civil disobedience appeared in the idea of the General Strike, the great universal folding of arms that would bring down the old order and usher in the millennium.

In 1832 one of the most remarkable pamphlets in the history of civil disobedience appeared under the title of *The Grand National Holiday and Congress of the Productive Classes*; it was written by William Benbow, proprietor of a London coffeehouse. In launching the idea of the General Strike, which did not cease echoing until

Spanish anarcho-syndicalism expired in 1938, Benbow assumed that since the whole of society rests on the toil of the workers, a month of "grand holiday" on their part would bring the ruling order to the verge of collapse: production would be paralyzed, the government would be immobilized, the armed forces would be lost in the vast sea of patient idleness, and at the end, as Benbow rhapsodized, the strike would usher in the reign of "equal rights, equal respect, equal share of production." It is impossible not to be touched by the naive nobility of this vision of a vast collective act of civil disobedience bringing to an end, in one great swoop, all the inequalities and injustices that had accumulated over the long collective history of humankind.

Even in the United States, the abolitionist movement had already, by the time *Civil Disobedience* was written, thrown up widespread manifestations of active civil disobedience in operations like the Underground Railroad, designed to transport fugitive slaves to Canada, while among Thoreau's New England associates the State was regarded with constant mistrust, and even the cautious and conservative Emerson declared, "Good men must not obey the laws too well."

All this, it seems to me, in no way diminishes Thoreau; rather, it places him at the heart of one of those movements of consciousness through which a new idea comes into the world, and which, as Peter Kropotkin noted in his *Memoirs of a Revolutionist*, speaks often through many voices. Thoreau was not one of those who defied the *zeitgeist*; he gave it his own voice, and his uniqueness really lies in how he spoke rather than in what he said.

It is not always easy to fix in our minds Thoreau's voice as a writer. He stubbornly and slyly resists grandeur, and mocks us when we confer it on him. I think everyone, in the early stage of reading Thoreau, has gone through the phase of seeing him as a great pretender.

There is, to begin with, the retreat from the world that made Walden Pond the very symbol of the rejection of civilization through immersion in the wilderness. But then we realize that Concord was just a little walk away, and that when solitude got too intense

Thoreau could always escape cabin-fever by strolling in for a long conversation or an evening of music with his friends.

And then there is the famous imprisonment. Kropotkin and Bakunin went through months and years incarcerated in the terrible Peter-and-Paul Fortress. Gandhi was for long periods the guest of Their Britannic Majesties in South Africa and India. Today, every month the *Bulletin of Amnesty International* brings accounts of men and women losing years of their lives in prison, often for the very "crime" that Thoreau advocated in this essay. Then we look at Thoreau's experience. He spends a night in the old town jail, and is let out next morning because one of his neighbors has paid the tax. "That night in prison was novel and interesting enough," he remarks, and we say to ourselves: "What a sly fellow to make so much out of so little!"

In fact, of course, Thoreau did not "make much" of his imprisonment any more than he did of his experience at Walden. He stated exactly what happened and the legend grew out of the simplicity of his statement and the largeness of our hopes. Out of the legend grew the strange pervasive influence that Thoreau and his plea for civil disobedience have wielded in many places over the past century and a quarter.

Thoreau was seen by his New England neighbors as a failure. He made no attempt to succeed in any of the formal ways, the two books he published during his lifetime were failures, and his ardent abolitionism was that of the early unsuccessful days. In fact, the failure at Harpers Ferry in 1859, and John Brown's hanging, seem to have precipitated his early death in 1862 at the age of forty-five. Even *On the Duty of Civil Disobedience* was ignored when it appeared in 1849 in Elizabeth Peabody's *Aesthetic Papers*, and only began to command attention after it was included in his own posthumous group of essays, *A Yankee in Canada with Anti-Slavery and Reform Papers* (1866).

Gandhi's discovery of *On the Duty of Civil Disobedience* in 1907 — appropriately enough in the library of a South African prison where he was incarcerated for practicing civil disobedience —

marks the period when the influence of Thoreau, channeled mainly through this single brief essay, was spreading rapidly. It spread largely in reaction to the confrontations between right and left in the United States during the 1880s, which culminated in the Haymarket tragedy, and which led many to seek forms of action that would be effective on an individual or collective level without leading into the morass of violence and retaliation in which modern terrorists involve themselves.

A great advantage of *On the Duty of Civil Disobedience* is that it formulates an attitude that can be applied to a wide variety of circumstances. An individual can use it to formulate a protest against evil laws; it can be used by small groups, as it often is by environmentalists today, to achieve local objectives; and finally — imaginatively adapted by a Gandhi — it can help direct the disciplined action of masses of people.

One can, indeed, exaggerate the influence Thoreau actually wielded posthumously over Gandhi's non-violent thought and action. Gandhi had already in 1906 formulated both the philosophy and the practice of *Satyagraha* (which translates as "Truth-force," and means the development of a moral strength that can be expressed in passive resistance without hatred of the opponent.) This was one of the reasons why in the next year he would find himself in a Johannesburg prison reading Thoreau. Much as he was drawn to Thoreau, and often as he utilized his essay as a text, the American writer is not among the men Gandhi listed many years later as having most influenced his life, though Tolstoy and Ruskin are. Having forged the philosophy and the militant technique of *Satyagraha*, which in the end were to make him the greatest and the most successful of all civil disobeyers, Gandhi embraced Thoreau as a brother and fellow thinker rather than as a teacher, and went on to his work for sustenance rather than illumination, which he had already gained from Tolstoy and Ruskin as he moved towards the creation of *Satyagraha*.

I think there are many of us for whom Thoreau and *Civil Disobedience* have come as a sustenance rather than as illumination. Thoreau sharpens and strengthens our own illuminations. We reach our anarchist or pacifist or Wobbly standpoints — often hardly sharp enough to be called beliefs — through the attempt to give form to the sense of rebellion we feel towards the state-dominated world in which we find ourselves. And then we discover this pamphlet in which shape and reason are given to our hardly-more-than-felt beliefs in a language that has remained clear and direct for a century and a half.

On the Duty of Civil Disobedience achieves the unusual combination of a clear-eyed humanism with a tough existentialism — recognizing the world as it is — and this, it seems to me, explains why it was so often found in the packs of wandering Wobblies and in the pockets of conscientious objectors on the run.

Man might not be, for Thoreau, the measure of all things, but he was certainly the measure of right action, which springs from the inner judgment. "The only obligation which I have a right to assume, is to do at any time what I think right." And near the very end of his essay, he adds: "There will never be a really free and enlightened State, until the State comes to recognize the individual as a higher and independent power, from which all its power and authority are derived, and treats him accordingly."

Here we have Thoreau's irony in full play, for he knows as well as we do that there cannot be such a State. We realize to the full the point he has been making throughout the essay, without declaring himself openly an anarchist, without closing off his options with a label, that the State can never in fact meet the needs of individual morality. At one point he talks of "That government which governs not at all," but then, a little farther on, his true conviction of the incapacity of the State emerges, when he remarks:

> As for adopting the ways which the State has provided for remedying the evil, I know of no such ways. They take too much time and, a man's life will be gone.

Civil Disobedience is full of such splendid aphorisms, such self-evident statements that need no support from argument, that speak to and fill the rebel's heart with certainty:

> When the subject has refused allegiance, and the officer has resigned his office, then the revolution is accomplished.

> Under a government which imprisons any unjustly, the true place for a just man is also a prison.

> Any man more right than his neighbors constitutes a majority of one already.

> It costs me less in every sense to incur the penalty of disobedience to the State, than it would to obey. I should feel as if I were worth less in that case.

"How does it become a man to behave toward this American government today?" Thoreau asked himself in 1849. "I answer that he cannot without disgrace be associated with it." Would his answer be any different in today? And can the answers be different for anyone who lives in any of the world's states today with an eye as open as Thoreau's?

That is why *On the Duty of Civil Disobedience* is as timely today as it was on first writing.

1989

6

Herbert Read:
The Philosopher of Freedom

"I have never been an active politician, merely a sympathizing intellectual," said Herbert Read in 1940, and the statement is generally true of his whole career as a social and political philosopher. Yet I do not think the title "philosophic anarchist," which has so often been applied to him, is really justified. It suggests the detached thinker who conceives an ideal ungoverned commonwealth, but does not concern himself with the means by which that society might come into being. Read, as I shall show, was deeply concerned with the means by which, through art and education, men could be made receptive to the great political and social changes needed to create a libertarian world. He was also, on occasion, willing to take other action. But he certainly did not become involved in the day-to-day business of politics — even anarchist politics. This was mainly because he held strongly the anarchist idea that the struggle for freedom must be initiated by the worker within his own occupational group, and Read's vocation was that of poet and critic of art and literature. He believed the freedom of the arts was linked intimately with general freedom; he believed also that the artist had a function as mediator between the individual and society; these were the paths he mainly followed when he

approached political terms. To stand as a representative of the workers, or even a preacher to them, would have seemed to him pre-
sumptuous. "Intellectuals writing for proletarians will not do," he
wrote to me in 1949. "It is merely another form of *la trahaison des
clercs*."

I knew Read for the last quarter of a century of his life, and during the 1940s, until I came to Canada at the end of the decade, I saw
him often. As a publisher he brought out two of my books, one of
verse and the other a biography of the anarchist Pierre-Joseph
Proudhon. That combination marked the areas of our common
interests in those days — literature and anarchism; not until a decade
later did I also begin to write on the visual arts. But it was anarchism
rather than literature that first brought us together, and, when I look
over the letters Read wrote to me, I realize that it remained the subject we discussed more than any other until our last contact late in
1966. During the 1940s I observed directly the voluntary limitations
of Read's engagement in anarchism, and his inclination to remain
aloof, even among anarchists, from anything that resembled political
organization. He did not aspire to be a leader. "Power corrupts even
the intellect," he once said. But he had no intention, either, of being
caught in the net of group orthodoxy.

I first met Read in 1942. I was then publishing in Cambridge a
little magazine, *Now*, and, having come through pacifism to what
still seems to me its logical end of non-violent anarchism, I asked
Read for a contribution. He sent me "The Paradox of Anarchism,"
and a few weeks later he came to Cambridge. We met in a chintzy
café on King's Parade, Read in the black pork-pie hat and bow-tie
which in those years were almost a customary uniform, and I
remember my slight bewilderment when I talked to him of the anarchist group which then ran Freedom Press and published *War
Commentary*, and he replied vaguely. I thought then that he was an
initiate being politic with a stranger; within a couple of months,
when I myself had made contact with the movement in London, and
became active in it, I realized that his vagueness was, on the contrary,

due to his own very loose connection with the militants.

At that time the militant anarchists in Britain had a double organization. The Freedom Press group was a circle of intellectuals, some of them personal friends of Read, who operated openly and were concerned mainly with publication. It was part of a larger, secret organization, The Anarchist Federation of Great Britain, which balanced the grandiosity of its title by the thinness of its ranks. I was admitted to both groups, but Read did not belong to either, partly from his own choice, but partly also because, like Kropotkin before him, he supported Britain's participation in World War II, which the other British anarchists, except for a small Jewish group in the East End of London, opposed.

In 1943 or 1944 — I cannot now remember the exact date — the Anarchist Federation decided to come into the open, and, with the pressure of secrecy removed, immediately broke apart, the anarcho-syndicalist faction (which included a few real workers) retaining the title, a hollow victory, since the intellectuals retained the printing press, the stocks of literature, the paper license (vital in war-time), and the Freedom Press bookshop. A new organization of "pure" anarchists led by the intellectuals was formed in 1945, with a London Group and a Federation of Anarchist Groups, and Read took a close interest in the developments. He attended at least one of the organizational meetings, and in August he wrote to me from a summer villa at Braemar ("a Victorian house with all its period equipment — amusing but exhausting, a relic of the slave age"): "I am glad to hear that the London Group is taking shape. I would like to see a copy of the programme." I think he hoped it would be a true guild of anarchist intellectuals, which he could have joined, but the old pseudo-proletarian line prevailed, and he held aloof, as did Alex Comfort. I joined for a while, and withdrew in 1948; my reasons, discussed elsewhere, have no place in this essay.

If Read evaded involvement, he did not avoid action. As he wrote in one of his poems of this period:

But even as you wait
like Arjuna in his chariot
the ancient wisdom whispers:
Live in action.

He wrote pamphlets to be published by Freedom Press (*The Philosophy of Anarchism* and *Marxism, Existentialism and Anarchism*); he wrote occasionally for *Freedom*, the propagandist sheet that followed *War Commentary*, and more often for *Now*; he spoke at meetings commemorating the Spanish Civil War. When four members of the Freedom Press group were arrested in 1945 on charges under a wartime press law, he spent a great deal of time and energy in their defence. I remember drafting with him a letter which we persuaded a group of writers to sign, denouncing the arbitrariness of the government's action. Spender, Eliot, and Forster were among them. Spender was censured by the Foreign Office, for which he was then working, and refused to sign any more protests. Forster insisted on altering a few words in the letter after Eliot had signed it. Eliot was angry that we had allowed Forster to change anything he had signed, but stood by the protest, a fact which I am always happy to quote against those who describe him as a reactionary. Read also became chairman of the committee which was set up to conduct the defence of the four anarchists, made speeches, wrote articles, raised money.

Later this committee was continued as a semi-permanent organization, the Freedom Defence Committee, to take up the cases of people arrested under the more oppressive wartime regulations, and to protest against police violations of civil rights. Read remained its chairman until the committee came to an end in 1949. Orwell was vice-chairman, Julian Symons a member of the working committee, and I the secretary. Read and Orwell, libertarians of different shades who shared the inability to live happily with organized political groups, were closer than their differing life styles and ways of writing may suggest. "His personality, which remains so vivid after all these years, often rises like some ghost to admonish me," Read wrote to me of Orwell in 1966. "I suppose I have felt nearer to him than to any other English writer of our time, and though there were some aspects of his character that irritated me — his proletarian pose in dress, &c., his insensitivity to his physical environment, his comparatively narrow range of interests — yet who was, in general, nearer in ideals & even in eccentricities?"

To me, when I met Read in 1942, anarchism was new and dazzling. To Read, who held it as almost a life-time faith, it was already a familiar doctrine to which he had been converted in his own youth almost thirty years before. "Actually," he tells us in *The Contrary Experience*, "there was an unfailing continuity in my political interests and political opinions. I would not like to claim that they show an unfailing consistency, but the general principles which I found congenial as a young man are the basic principles of the only political philosophy I still find congenial."

The continuity was not quite as unbroken as Read suggests, for as a teenage bank clerk he followed the traditions of his class of Yorkshire farmers by becoming a fanatical Tory: "I worshipped my King with a blind emotional devotion, and even managed to make a hero out of Lord Salisbury." He also read all of Disraeli's novels, and these — with their doctrine of the two nations — appear to have disturbed rather than confirmed his conservatism, for as soon as he entered Leeds University, he began to read socialist writings, discovered Nietzsche and Sorel, and remained true to his ancestry by finding the opposing pole of peasant politics to Toryism — anarchism.

As he wrote in *Poetry and Anarchism*:

In spite of my intellectual pretensions, I am by birth and tradition a peasant. I remain essentially a peasant. I despise this foul industrial epoch — not only the plutocracy which it has raised to power, but also the industrial proletariat which it has drained from the land and proliferated in hovels of indifferent brick. The class in the community for which I feel a

natural sympathy is the agricultural class, including the genuine remnants of a landed aristocracy. This perhaps explains
my early attraction to Bakunin, Kropotkin and Tolstoy, who
were also of the land, aristocrats and peasants.

"Proudhon, Tolstoy and Kropotkin were the predilections of my
youth," Read remarks elsewhere; add William Morris, Edward
Carpenter and Sorel, and one has the central political influences over
Read in the years of his early twenties after the Tory enthusiasm
passed. Add Nietzsche on the individualist periphery, and Marx on
the collectivist, and the pattern of shaping influences is complete. It
was a pattern not unusual at the time among the literary young;
Joyce in Dublin and Kafka in Prague were studying roughly the
same writers at the same period. But Read remained permanently
and profoundly under their influence; the others did not.

In his early thoughts, Marxist and Anarchist attitudes were
intermingled, and he still believed — as he did not in later years —
that nationalization of the means of production might be the prelude
to the dissolution of the state. In a note written in 1914, and quoted
in *The Contrary Experience*, he says:

For the present, both Collectivism and Syndicalism have their
respective duties. The role of Collectivism is the expropriation
of Capital. This is to be brought about by the nationalization
of industry. But Collectivists are wrong in regarding nationalization as an end in itself: it is only a means. For whilst the
Collectivist state is evolving, Syndicalism will be playing its
role — i.e. it will be developing the economic, industrial and
educational functions of the Trade Unions. Trade Unions are, I
am convinced, the units upon which the future society will be
built. They must be organized and extended so as to be powerful enough to demand, and fit enough to undertake, the control
of industry when it has been nationalized by the state. . . . By a
devolution of power, a decentralization of control, and, above

all, by a development in the social conscience of the nation, the ideals of today will become the realities of tomorrow.

Read was always to respect the doctrines of anarcho-syndicalism, and to regard the natural organization of society as one based on workers' control of industry; it was his trust in the state as a mechanism for achieving any social good that rapidly dissolved under the impact of his wartime experiences.

Read had been — as most socialists and anarchists were in 1914 — a theoretical pacifist, but at the same time he was a member of the O.T.C. at Leeds University. When he found himself thrust incontinently into the war, and realized that the international working class was unprepared to halt the militarists by a universal general strike, he made the Nietzschean best of a bad job, and set out to meet what he saw as a challenge. As late as May 1917, when he had reached the front but had not yet experienced war's full horrors, he could still write to a woman friend in England:

> I've no doubt about my position. If I were free today, I'm almost sure I should be compelled by every impulse within me to join this adventure. For I regard it as an adventure, and it is as an adventure that it appeals to me. I'll fight for Socialism when the day comes, and fight all the better for being an 'old soldier' (*The Contrary Experience*).

Eight months later he had again become a pacifist, and this time with the conviction of experience. He remarked that "the means of war had become more portentous than the aim" and that among the soldiers there had been "an immense growth of pacifist opinion." And during 1917 and 1918, while he was writing articles for the *New Age* supporting both Syndicalism and Guild Socialism (variants of the doctrine of the control of production by producers), he was experiencing a cumulative revulsion against static social orders and the state in particular. In January 1917, he wrote to the same friend:

I've a theory that all the evil things in the world are static, passive and possessive; and that all good things are dynamic, creative. Life is dynamic: death is static. And as life is dynamic, passive remedies of society are false. Hence the folly of having cut and dried Utopias as ultimate aims: by the time you get to them, life has left them behind. Hence the folly of basing society on possessive institutions (such as property and marriage, as a rule). Our institutions should appeal to our creative impulses: what a man *does* and not what he *has*.

In April 1918:

I don't think I'm ready to discuss the change that is taking place in my 'political sentiment'. It is a revolt of the individual against the association which involves him in activities which do not interest him: a jumping to the ultimate anarchy which I have always seen as the ideal of all who value beauty and intensity of life. 'A beautiful anarchy' — that is my cry.

In May 1918:

But simply because we are united with a callous inhuman association called a State and because a State is ruled by politicians whose aim (and under the circumstances their duty) is to support the life and sovereignty of this monster, life and hope are denied and sacrificed.

In a positive as well as a negative way, Read's anarchist tendencies were intensified during the war, for he found — like Orwell during the Spanish Civil War — a comradeship in the trenches of a kind he had never before known, "a feeling of unanimity aroused by common stresses, common dangers," and so, in this unlikely setting, his convictions of the validity of the anarchist doctrine of mutual aid seemed justified.

Looking back in 1962 over the period after 1918, Read felt that "the no-man's-years between the wars" had been "largely futile, spent unprofitably by me and my kind," largely, he felt, because of forces outside their power to change — "blind forces of economic drift and political ineptitude with the walls of faith and reason turning to air behind us." At the same time, he adds that "in spite of a disillusion at once personal and universal, I persisted in a simple faith in the natural goodness of man," and it was towards the end of the inter-war period that he began to develop his theories of the inter-relationship of art and anarchism, and to write the series of essays and books that contain his socio-political arguments.

From 1919 to 1931 were in these respects years of enforced silence. There are points in Read's career when he surprises the observer — as he surprised many of his friends — by acting with an inconsistency that seems to exceed even the licence to impulsiveness which he allowed himself as a proclaimed romantic. A pacifist, he fought in World War I. After declaring in *Poetry and Anarchism* (1938) that "anarchism naturally implies pacifism," he came out in 1939 in support of Britain's participation in World War II. In 1953 he bent the knee to receive a knighthood, and set off an international storm among anarchists in which — so far as I remember — Augustus John and I were alone among his comrades in defending the right of a libertarian to make his own choices — even in his relations with the state. 1919 was another such time; after considering such strange careers for a professed anarchist as a permanent commission in the army and professional politics, Read finally elected for the civil service, in which he felt he would have more time and energy to devote to literature. He served for several years in the Treasury, where he acquired a lifelong loathing for bureaucrats, and then moved to the Victoria and Albert Museum, where he gathered the knowledge on which he was to base his career as an art critic. In 1931 he was liberated when the University of Edinburgh offered him its Professorship of Fine Arts. For twelve years the rules of the civil service had prevented him from publishing anything expressing his political views, and even when he was set free, it was some years before, in 1938, he expounded his complete libertarian views in *Poetry and Anarchism.*

In the meantime, however, *The Green Child* (1935) was written with at least an oblique political intent. Read tells us that in this novel he "described symbolically" how "the realization of a rational blue-print leads to the death of a society." And if we look at *The Green Child* we see this process happening on two levels.

Olivero, the hero, became the ruler of Roncador, a mountain-bound South American Republic — a minute, self-supporting, agrarian land. After establishing a democratic constitution based on the best theories of the Enlightenment, he discovers that the simple people of Roncador are willing to accept the good government he gives them, and he finds himself — with no effort of his own — established as a kind of philosopher-king, able to apply the "sense of order" which he regards as "the principle of government as well as of art." He constructs a self-contained world in which his people enjoy sufficiency, security, and freedom from oppression. But it is almost an axiom of Read's political doctrines that the only healthy political order is a natural order, sustained by tensions between the individual and society. Olivero's imposed order merely produces stagnation: "In the absence of conflicts, of contending interests, of anguish and agitation, I had introduced into my environment a moral flaccidity, a fatness of living, an ease and a torpor which had now produced in me an inevitable ferment."

Olivero arranges his own fake assassination, to free Roncador from his good-intentioned but deadly rationalism, but he does not free himself; instead he enters the underground world of the green people, who have lost sense of time and space, who regard living flesh and the life-breath with disgust, and whose vision is bounded by the contemplation of crystaline forms and the mathematical structures of music, in preparation for death, when the green people themselves are turned into rational shapes of crystals in a world growing even more narrow because of the encroaching multitude of the petrified dead who fill its caves. It is a narrative told in deceptively attractive prose;

it must nevertheless be read, the author makes clear, as a minatory parable as well as a poetic fantasy.

The hopes generated by the Russian Revolution died hard and slowly during the 1930s even among many who were in no way orthodox Marxists. As Read confesses in *Poetry and Anarchism*:

> From 1917 onwards and for as long as I could preserve the illusion communism as established in Russia seemed to promise the social liberty of my ideals. So long as Lenin and Stalin promised a definitive "withering away of the State," I was prepared to stifle my doubts and prolong my faith. But when, five, ten, fifteen, and then twenty years passed, with the liberty of the individual receding at every stage, a break became inevitable.

The suicide in 1930 of the poet Mayakovsky, hounded by the Stalinist bureaucrats, began to stir Read's doubts, and in the Introduction to *Surrealism* (1936) he complained that "even Communism, the creed of liberty and fraternity, has made the exigencies of a transitional epoch the excuse for an unnecessary and stupid form of aesthetic intolerance." Two more or less simultaneous events in 1936 left Read with the conviction that he had no alternative but to break openly with Marxist communism and declare just as openly for anarchism. These were the Moscow Trials, and the outbreak of the Civil War in Spain, where anarchism emerged from the shadows Marxist had cast over it and attempted, in a land at conflict, to lay the foundations of a libertarian society.

Read wrote for *Spain and the World*, the anarchist paper of the time, addressed meetings, and wrote two of the best poems about the civil war, the compassionate and angry "Bombing Casualties in Spain" and "Song for the Spanish Anarchists," in which is condensed his whole vision of the organic strength of a free and natural society where the individual is defined by what he *does*, and where men *have* in common.

The golden lemon is not made
    but grows on a green tree:
A strong man and his crystal eyes
    is a man born free.

The oxen pass under the yoke
    and the blind are led at will:
But a man born free has a path of his own
    and a house on the hill.

And men are men who till the land
    and women are women who weave:
Fifty men own the lemon grove
    and no man is a slave.

Read's socio-political writings, with minor exceptions, appeared between 1938 and 1954, and the most important had seen first publication by the end of 1943; one can perhaps fairly assume that Read's impulse to write on anarchism began to fail as the sense of glory associated with the early days of the Spanish Civil War faded in his mind. There is a great deal of confusion in the publication history of these writings because of the various combinations in which Read issued and re-issued them. *Poetry and Anarchism* (1938), *The Philosophy of Anarchism* (1940), and *Existentialism, Marxism and Anarchism* (1950) all appeared first as separate volumes, or at least pamphlets, while "The Paradox of Anarchism," printed first in *Now* (1942) was later collected in *A Coat of Many Colours* (1945). All these eventually came together, with a new introductory essay, "Revolution and Reason," in *Anarchy and Order* (1954). "Chains of Freedom" appeared first in *Now* (1947), in an expanded version in *Existentialism, Marxism and Anarchism*, and in an even more expanded version in *Anarchy and Order*. *To Hell with Culture* appeared separately as a small pamphlet in 1941, and in 1943 was included as a chapter in *The Politics of the Unpolitical*, but a new volume in 1963, comprising most of *The Politics of the*

Unpolitical, plus a few essays mainly concerning problems of the arts, was entitled *To Hell with Culture*. As I go on to discuss the leading themes of Read's socio-political philosophy, I shall do my best to avoid confusion by giving each book or pamphlet the title under which it was originally published.

The opening lines of "Song for the Spanish Anarchists" contain the image which most concisely expresses Read's view of the nature of a free society:

> The golden lemon is not made
>   but grows on a green tree . . .

Free society cannot be developed according to a plan; it must grow according to nature; it is not Utopian, but organic.

The laws that govern its development may be according to reason, but they are not in the narrow sense rational, and perhaps it is from this distinction that one can begin the examination of Read's attitudes towards society and its political development. He calls himself a materialist; he declares that we must "admit the universalism of truth and submit our life to the rule of reason." The life of the reason he sees as "a practical ideal, extending to wider and wider circles of humanity, and promising an earthly paradise never to be attained only because each stage towards its realization creates its superior level" (*The Politics of the Unpolitical*). But he says also in *Reason and Romanticism* that reason is much more than rationality or mechanistic logic: "Reason should rather connote the widest evidence of the senses, and of all processes and instincts developed in the long history of man. It is the sum total of awareness, ordained and ordered to some specific end or object of attention." In Read's view, a society that tried to exist on a purely rational basis "would probably die of a kind of communal accidie." We are involved inevitably in "certain intangible and imponderable elements which we call emotion and instinct," and while himself adhering to no religion, Read grants that "a religion is a necessary element in any organic society" and that a new religion might even develop out of anarchism (*The Philosophy of Anarchism*). For "if . . . religion is the life of contemplation, the fruit of pure meditation, spiritual joy, then it cannot help but prosper in a society free from poverty, pride and envy" (*Poetry and Anarchism*).

Freedom and anarchism are synonymous, but anarchism is not nihilism, and freedom is not license. It is, on the contrary, Read insists, part of natural law, and intimately linked with the phenomenon of evolution. "Freedom is not an essence only available to the sensibility of men; it is germinatively at work in all living beings as spontaneity and autoplasticity" (*Anarchy and Order*). But just as society gains life from its dialectical opposition to the individual, so freedom is made real by its dialectical opposition to existence:

> And so with the individual and the community: complete freedom means inevitable decadence. The mind must feel an opposition — must be tamped with hard realities if it is to have any blasting power (*Politics of the Unpolitical*).

Thus Max Stirner's egoism is rejected by Read in favor of the libertarianism of Kropotkin:

> In all that concerns the planning of economic life, the building up of a rational mode of living in a social community, there can be no question of absolute liberty. For, so long as we live in a community, in all practical affairs the greatest good of the greatest number is also the greatest good of the individual (*Poetry and Anarchism*).

The "duty to create a world of freedom" is far removed from the "freedom to do as you like," which is the characteristic excuse of the capitalist and the imperialist. In opposition to such anti-social concepts of freedom Read is even willing to use that word shunned by most anarchists — *government* — though he quickly makes clear

that he means some form of control quite different from the processes of State we know:

> Government — that is to say, control of the individual in
> the interests of the community, is inevitable if two or more
> men combine for a common purpose; government is the
> embodiment of that purpose. But government in this sense
> is far removed from the conception of an autonomous state
> (*Poetry and Anarchism*).

In choosing his political reforms, Read rejects both authoritari-
anism (including communist as well as fascist totalitarianism) and
democracy as history has known it. A single passage of dismissal is
enough to express his rejection of the authoritarians:

> The authoritarian believes in discipline as a means; the libertari-
> an in discipline as an end, as a state of mind. The authoritarian
> issues instructions; the libertarian encourages self-education.
> The one tolerates a subjective anarchy below the smooth sur-
> face of his rule; the other has no need of rule because he has
> achieved a subjective harmony reflected in personal integrity
> and social unity (*Anarchy and Order*).

There is of course no essential difference between ideal democracy and anarchy, since neither has in fact been tried. The democracy that has been tried has failed because it was tied to the notions of
universal suffrage and majority rule. The theory of majority rule and
the concentration of power in central parliaments have between
them imposed on democracy the tendency to seek continually "some
form of centralized control," and hence to increase the power of the
state. As for universal suffrage, Read condemns it as emphatically as
Proudhon did: "It is a myth, a quite illusory delegation of power . . .
a fiction of consent where in fact no liberty of choice exists" (*Poetry
and Anarchism*).

It is the myth of universal suffrage that allows even communists and fascists to claim that they are democrats: "They all obtain popular consent by the manipulation of mass psychology." What else, Read implies, do parliamentary politicians do?

The ideal democracy is another matter, and, as one sees by the three conditions which Read lays down for its fulfilment, it is, in his mind, not different essentially from anarchism:

> The first condition is that *all production is for use, and not for profit.*

> The second condition is that *each should give according to his ability and each receive according to his needs.*

> The third condition is that *the workers in each industry should collectively own and control that industry* (*Politics of the Unpolitical*).

These conditions represent Read's view of necessary organization as functional and economic rather than political and social, and of equality as dependent on community:

> For the essential is not to make all incomes equal — the ideal of the average democratic socialist — but to abolish all incomes and *hold all things in common* . . .

> It is essential to stress the radical nature of the distinction between equal partition, and community ownership. It is the distinction between false communism and true communism, between the totalitarian conception of the State as a controlled herd, and the libertarian conception of society as a brotherhood. Once this conception is fully realized, the ambiguities of the doctrine of equality disappear: the concept of equality is dissolved in the concept of community (*Anarchy and Order*).

This, of course, brings us to the classic anarchist position: the denunciation of the state, the proclamation that societies must be built, like houses, from the ground up. For a culture "grows out of the soil, out of the people, out of their daily life and work. It is a spontaneous expression of their joy in life, of their joy in work, and if this joy does not exist, the culture will not exist" (*Politics for the Unpolitical*).

Like all anarchists, Read is reluctant to create elaborate plans for the ideal society. Warnings against such presumptuousness are scattered through his writings. "The Utopia fades the moment we try to actualize it." Anarchism is planless, "a point on the horizon" towards which we progress. "It is foolish to indulge in anything but relatively short-term policies for the human race." "It is always a mistake to build *a priori* constitutions. The main thing is to establish your principles — the principles of equality, of individual freedom, of workers' control."

Decentralization and arbitration instead of normal legal procedures are the main additions that Read makes to these simple requirements on the rare occasions when he draws a sketch plan for the future, as in the early 1940s he did in *The Politics of the Unpolitical*. He listed as follows the features of his plan for a "natural society":

I   The liberty of the person.

II   The integrity of the family.

III   The reward of qualifications.

IV   The self-government of the guilds.

V   The abolition of parliament and
       centralized government.

VI   The institution of arbitrament.

VII   The delegation of authority.

VIII The humanization of industry.

Read differs from most anarchists other than Proudhon in the stress he laid on the family as the basic natural social unit. It is "the integral unit," "the most effective unit" because it is the smallest, and it is the basis on which can be built the next unit upwards, the parish, "the local association of men in contiguous dwellings": "Such local associations may form their courts, and these courts are sufficient to administer a common law based on common sense" (*A Coat of Many Colours*).

Next in importance comes the guild, which anarchists with a different background from Read's early connection with *The New Age* might call the syndicate — "the association of men and women according to their calling or practical function." With "political power" distributed among families and parishes ("human tangible units"), with economic power vested in the guilds and workshops, with financial power "altogether excluded from society," with "productive labour" recognized as "the basic reality and honoured as such," the organizational shell of Read's vision of the free society is complete.

So far it is little different from other anarchist sketches of the future. One finds the same ideas more forcefully expressed by Proudhon and more elaborately by Kropotkin. What most distinguishes Read's anarchism from the anarchism of past theoreticians, and brings it closer to the socialism of William Morris, is the stress he places on the role of the arts — on the artist as mediator, and on art itself as the vehicle of a revolutionary form of education. In my view this particular emphasis is much more important than the other novel feature of Read's anarchism, the wide introduction of psychoanalytical concepts and terminology, which mainly serve to replace the somewhat outdated scientism of Kropotkin and Reclus, who used evolutionary concepts in much the same way as Read uses psychoanalytical ones, to prove that anarchism was given support — and hence credibility — by the most contemporary scientific developments. I have always found Read's borrowings from Freud, Jung, *et al* the least convincing features of his literary and artistic criticism, and I doubt if such borrowings have greatly strengthened his case for anarchism, though he has drawn out of them a few entertaining aphorisms; for example, "I would define the anarchist as the man who, in his manhood, dares to resist the authority of the father" (a definition I am inclined to dispute, since I have known many anarchists with gentle fathers and domineering, hated mothers).

The place of art in Read's ideal society becomes clear as soon as we move away from his plans for its organizational functioning, and sense the kind of life he would like to see lived in that future. It is, needless to say, the rural world of a self-proclaimed peasant, rather like that of *News from Nowhere* without its earnest laboriousness, for Read, while at times he denounces the factory system, realizes that "industrialism must be endured," and goes beyond that to search for means by which the machine can not merely perform the unpleasant tasks, which Morris eventually allowed, but can also produce beautiful objects, which Morris would never admit. At the same time, Read is aware that no civilization or people can lose touch with things, can abandon organic processes, can forget the feel of wood and clay and metal worked with the hands, and still remain healthy. Therefore he wishes to use machinery to simplify existence, to bring more leisure, to end pointless labors, so that when men leave the cities they will find "a world of electric power and mechanical plenty where man can once more return to the land, not as a peasant, but as a lord."

In such a world play will resume its true place in human life:

> It was *play* rather than work which enabled men to evolve his higher faculties — everything we mean by the word 'culture' . . . Play is freedom, is disinterestedness, and it is only by virtue of disinterested free activity that man has created his cultural values. Perhaps it is this theory of all work and no play that has made the Marxist such a very dull boy (*Anarchy and Order*).

Of play, of course, art is the highest form, and Read sees for the artist a high role in the free society, for he is "the man who mediates between our individual consciousness and the collective unconsciousness, and thus ensures social re-integration. It is only in the degree that this mediation is successful that a true democracy is possible" (*Poetry and Anarchism*).

Read wrote almost all his works on anarchism from the viewpoint of the artist or poet; in this he resembled and may have been influenced by Oscar Wilde, whose *Soul of Man Under Socialism* also envisaged a libertarian society as the best environment for the arts to flourish. But Read did not express an élitist point of view. He might intend artists to be, in Shelley's phrase which he quotes approvingly, "the unacknowledged legislators of the world," but he does not see them in this role as a minority, since what he hopes for, following on the development of a free society, is the universalization of art, in the sense that its standards will be applied to all human work (factory-made or hand-made) and that by this token all men will become artists. As the aim of work changes from profit to use, so will the life-view of the workers change: "The worker has as much latent sensibility as any human being, but that sensibility can only be awakened when meaning is restored to his daily work and he is allowed to create his own culture" (*Politics of the Unpolitical*). Then we shall realize that "every man is a special kind of artist," for "art is skill: a man does something so well that he is entitled to be called an artist." So art is brought down from the isolation to which bourgeois cultures have condemned it, and becomes a matter of everyday activity. This does not mean that art itself has progressed, for it is impossible to see any pattern of qualitative evolution from the painters of prehistoric Lascaux to those of the School of Paris. But it does mean that civilization has progressed because it has admitted artistic impulses into its life and its relationships.

What applies to the man also applies to the child, who is a potential artist from the beginning, and in whom a system of education through art can induce — in Read's view — inner harmonies which will make him better prepared for social initiation. Undoubtedly Read saw such a system of education as a potent agent for social liberation, but he also held, for long periods, to more orthodox views of change by physical means.

In a general sense Read regarded revolt as an inevitable and regenerative element in any human society. "Freedom is not a state of rest, of least resistance. It is a state of action, of projection, of self-realization." But this natural and spontaneous revolt was different from the specific kind of rebellion which Read deemed necessary in the unregenerate present. Poverty must be abolished, the classless society brought to an end, at the very least the more monstrous injustices of the social order must be ended, "and if we do not revolt . . . we are either morally insensitive or criminally selfish" (*Anarchy and Order*).

During the late 1930s Read envisaged revolt in activist terms. "Naturally the abolition of poverty and the consequent establishment of a classless society is not going to be accomplished without a struggle," he said in *Poetry and Anarchism* (1938). "Certain people have to be dispossessed of their autocratic power and of their illegitimate profits." And two years later, in *The Philosophy of Anarchism*, he declared that "an insurrection is necessary for the simple reason that when it comes to the point, even your man of good will, if he is on the top, will not sacrifice his personal advantages to the general good."

Read did not, however, think in terms of violent action. He insisted that anarchist rebellion must be non-violent, that the example of Gandhi must be followed, and the only insurrectionary strategy he discussed at any length was the general strike, which he believed had never been used to its full effect. And, though he saw himself as a rebel, he did not admit to being, at least in the political sense, a revolutionary. As early as 1940 he accepted the validity of Max Stirner's distinction between *revolution* and *insurrection*, and later, when Camus made in *The Rebel* his even sharper distinction between *revolution* (a totalitarian act) and *rebellion* (a libertarian act),

Read adopted it:

> Revolutions, as has often been remarked, change nothing; or
> rather, they merely substitute one set of masters for another
> set. Social groups acquire new names, but retain their former
> inequality of status.

> Rebellions or insurrections, on the other hand, being guided
> by instinct rather than reason, being passionate and sponta-
> neous rather than cool and calculated, do act like shock thera-
> py on the body of society, and there is a chance that they may
> change the chemical composition of the societal crystal . . .
> [Rebellion] eludes the world of power — that is the point, for
> it is always power that crystallizes into a structure of injustice.

It was, ironically, not until long after the period of his anarchist
writings, not until the early 1960s (his own late sixties) that Read
eventually moved into practical activism, and became involved in the
passive resistance tactics of the Campaign for Nuclear Disarmament
and the Committee of 100, sitting down in Whitehall not to usher in
anarchy but to protest, with more conviction than hope, against the
destructive aspects of the existing unfree society.

Read's later years were marked by a steady loss of hope of seeing
a better world in his time or foreseeing one for his children. He
seized comfort where he could, and sometimes in unlikely places, for
I find a letter written in November 1959, with a postscript on his
recent trip to China: "China — very exciting! The communes as near
to our kind of anarchism as anything that is likely to happen." But
soon he realized that even here his optimism had been misplaced,
and it was with a flickering confidence in the world that he performed in 1962 the symbolic act of putting his autobiographical
writings together in the final form of *The Contrary Experience*:

Nihilism — nothingness, despair, and the nervous hilarity that goes with them — remains the universal state of mind [he wrote then]. From such an abyss the soul of man does not rise in a decade or two. If a human world survives the atomic holocaust — and it is now difficult to see how such a holocaust is to be avoided — it will only be because man has first overcome his Nihilism. A few prophets have already pointed the way — Gandhi, Buber, Simone Weil, C. G. Jung — but the people are also few who pay heed to them. Spiritually the world is now one desert, and prophets are not honoured in it. But physically it still has a beautiful face, and if we could once more learn to live with nature, if we could return like prodigal children to the contemplation of its beauty, there might be an end to our alienation and fear, a return to those virtues of delight which Blake called Mercy, Pity, Peace and Love.

Resignation, with a little hope: a melancholy but not an unusual end for an anarchist. One cannot help contrasting the mood of this passage with that in which *The Philosophy of Anarchism* was brought to an end twenty-two years before:

Faith in the fundamental goodness of man; humility in the presence of natural law; reason and mutual aid — these are the qualities that can save us. But they must be unified and vitalized by an insurrectionary passion, a flame in which all virtues are tempered and clarified, and brought to their most effective strength.

It is such words that evoke for me the Read I knew. Though in many ways his life was curiously bourgeois, his anarchism had fostered — or perhaps merely refined — a limpidity of nature and outlook such as I have always imagined Kropotkin possessed. His periodical relapses into the Tory conformity of his youth one had to balance against the occasions when he took public stands, particularly in the defence of other people, that cost him a great deal materially and in terms of his career. One blamed at times his inconsistency, but never doubted his sincerity. I still do not know what romantic aberration leaping from a Yorkshire childhood induced him to become Sir Herbert, but I do know that Queen Elizabeth II never dubbed a gentler knight.

When one tries to sum up his achievements as a social and political writer, if one leaves out *The Green Child* and the poems of war and anarchism, they seem perhaps less than those in his other fields. He gave a new and attractive expression, a luminous clarification, to the few and simple truths that make up the anarchist doctrine. He investigated more thoroughly than any of his predecessors the relationship between freedom, art, and the artist. He was largely responsible for the libertarian attitudes which dominated much English and American poetry during the 1940s. But one cannot say that in any of these fields — except in his work on education through art — he was a great originator. I believe his anarchist beliefs and writings attract and give most light when they are seen in the context of his entire achievement, in relation to his poetry, to his writings on education and revolutionary art, on industry and romantic poetry, for then one sees his world view complete, with the love of freedom its moving spirit.

1969

7

Noam Chomsky's Anarchism

H aving lived though the 1940s and 1950s and most of the 1960s as a politically conscious being, when anarchism was a doctrine to be derided by such socialists as did not by some strange mental alchemy identify it as "objectively" reactionary, I cannot help a feeling of churlishness in criticizing the essay which Noam Chomsky wrote to introduce the American edition of Danial Guérin's *Anarchism (1970)*, since Chomsky's effort to understand not only the proposals of the anarchists, but also the libertarian criticism of state socialism (even as defended by Marx and Lenin), is patently sincere. Yet those who sympathize from the outside with a philosophy of living and seek to discover a means of utilizing it to support their own somewhat different doctrines, often in the process diminish the scope and potentialities of that philosophy, and likewise of the practice ensuing from it, by seeking to approximate it to their point of view. This Chomsky has done, and so has Guérin in the book Chomsky introduces, and thus they draw our attention once again to a danger which anarchists have been articulately aware at least since the International Congress of 1907, when Enrico Malatesta argued the case of the "complete" anarchist against the economically orientated viewpoint represented on that occasion by the anarcho-syndicalist, Pierre Monatte.

I am doing neither Chomsky nor Guérin an injustice in stating that neither is an anarchist by any known criterion; they are both left-wing Marxists. Yet their awareness of the perils of any attempt to equate workers' control of the means of production with a state taken over by the proletariat — as Marx and Engels conceived it — is genuine, and in exploring the possibilities of finding a way out of this essentially Marxist dilemma they are ready to examine once again the possibility that the anarchists may have been right on the question of the "conquest or destruction of state power" which, Chomsky contends, "is what Bakunin regarded as the primary issue dividing him from Marx."

At this point begins my dissent from Chomsky and Guérin. Perhaps the matter of the "conquest or destruction of state power" was the "primary issue" that divided Bakunin from Marx, but there were other issues of almost equal importance, which Bakunin had inherited from Marx's original anarchist opponent, Proudhon; among them were the theory of the utmost decentralization of control in a completely federalist structure, basic to any vision of a society not governed from above by the state, and the complementary view that society is multifarious in its manifestations, and that voluntary organization must extend in many directions other than the economic.

It is on this issue of the protean character of the anarchist approach to social change that Chomsky's argument, I suggest, most clearly fails. He portrays anarchism as in practice a way of struggle on the economic level; more precisely, on an obsolescent nineteenth-century industrial level. It is true that he pays homage to Bakunin's all-dominating passion for freedom; that he begins by echoing Guérin's praise of anarchism as being the opposite of a "fixed, self-enclosed system." Yet the way he argues the anarchist case does in fact enclose it within the very limits of narrow anarcho-syndicalism from which Malatesta sought to keep anarchist aims free more than sixty years ago.

It is of course not with the aim of deliberate distortion, but because of his Marxist orientation, that Chomsky relies — apart from Bakunin — mainly on the syndicalist spokesmen in defining anarchism, but distortion is the result. It is impossible to give any feeling of the richness and variety and depth of anarchist thought when we have copious quotations from syndicalist spokesmen like Rudolf Locker, Diego Adad de Santillan, and Augustin Souchy, as well as from left Marxists like Anton Pannekoek and William Paul, but nothing at all from those who establish the theoretical basics of anarchism. There is no reference to Kropotkin or Malatesta, none to Herbert Read or Paul Goodman, none to the determined exploration of the application of anarchist ideas to community organization, to education, to local administration, to the problems of an automated society, to cultural questions, which was pursued by a numerous and often extemely clear-sighted group of writers in the journal *Anarchy* during the 1960s. Proudhon is mentioned only once, and then in a way which shows that Chomnsky does not begin to understand, any more than Marx did, the complexities of what Proudhon meant by "property."

The exclusions in Chomsky's approach are shown not merely in the theoretical company he chooses. They mark also his discussion of the practical achievements of anarchists and of others who have sought to change society by direct action. When he talks of Spain, and the libertarian achievements of the early part of the Civil War, he is thinking — in his own words — of "specifically, industrial Barcelona," and he goes on to talk of industrial proletarians, not of the land workers who were the real masses supporting Spanish anarchism. There is not a word about what was probably the most striking manifestation of anarchist activity in Spain between 1936 and 1938 — the thousands of agrarian communes in which whole villages would not merely take over the land and work it in common, sharing the produce, but would also set themselves up as communes dedicated to what Malatesta, in his denunciation of the narrowness of anarcho-sydicalist aims, defined as "the complete liberation of all humanity, at present enslaved, from the triple ecomonic, political, and moral point of view."

It is, I would suggest, not merely the anarchist emphasis on workers' control that explains the vastly renewed speed of anarchism during the past decade, for the response to libertarian teachings in any articulate way has in fact been least strong among those who fall into the classic category of the industrial proletariat, in any case a class that will continue to diminish both in numbers and in strength if present technological trends continue (and will change into an artisanate if they do not). The response to anarchism has come rather from those people of all classes who seek a society where the potentialities of existence are varied and liberated, a society to be approached by lifestyle rebellion *as well* as by economic struggle, a society to be integrated — as Malatesta would put it — "from the triple economic, political, and moral point of view" in a way that Marxists, even the most open-minded of them, seem quite unable to conceive. As Malatesta also pointed out in 1907, to equate the anarchist struggle with a single class, as the anarchists followed the Marxists in attempting, is to abdicate the true anarchist ideal of a revolution seeking "the complete liberation of all humanity at present enslaved."

I find it especially significant that there should be no reference at all in Chomsky's essay to education, in view of the attention which anarchists have paid to this vital aspect of social life and social struggle ever since Herbert Read wrote that classic treatise on non-violent struggle, *Education through Art*, and especially in view of the importance of student rebels — some at least convinced anarchists, even if others may have been badly disguised authoritarians — in the radical movements of the 1960s. At least as important in any stategy of social transformation during the rest of the present century as the struggle for workers' control is the remaking of the system of education, and especially the breaking down of the academic hierarchy not in the direction of students seizing control of existing campuses — already an obsolete concept — but of what we now call "higher education" being diffused in the community so that it is not only physically decentralized and organizationally democratized, but also reorganized in such a way that it becomes a lifelong process and work and life are both endlessly enriched by it, eliminating the boundaries between a man's work life and the rest of his existence. Is not, after all, the continuance of the use of the word "worker" in the special connotation used in socialist discussions an oblique admission that Marxists have not yet been able to conceive imaginatively a society in which a "worker" is anything more? Certainly he has not become anything more in any self-styled Marxist society that has yet existed; under Stalin and Brezhnev, and equally under Mao and Castro, his alienation has been undiminished.

The mental imprisonment in nineteenth-century categories appears to affect most modern neo-Marxists, and to give their writings a curiously arid doctrinaire quality. I was impressed by this recently on reading a newly published collection of essays, *The Politics of Literature*, written by American university teachers of "radical" inclinations, of whom all but one called themselves Marxist. What they were concerned with was the publicized exploitation of literature in a partisan way, rather than the role it might take in our processes of education that would make it part of the work of beginning to change society *now*, a question to which anarchist writers like Read and the Goodmans have given copious and constructive thought.

I do not suggest that Chomsky is as obtuse as these callow disciples of Christopher Caudwell; obviously he plays a much suppler mind over his subject. Yet when he quotes Guérin as saying that "the constructive idea of anarchism" can "contribute by enriching Marxism," he appears to be reflecting his own outlook which, by regarding Marxism as *primary, selects* from anarchism those elements that may serve to diminish the contradictions in Marxist doctrines; thus, both Chomsky and Guérin in fact impoverish the anarchism they portray by abandoning its essential extremities.

1974

8

Paul Goodman: The Anarchist as Conservator

narchism has sometimes been described, especially by the
Marxists, as a regressive doctrine, and insofar as anarchists have
never accepted the necessary desirability of progress, the criticism is justified, though to admit it does not mean admitting that
anarchism is ahistorical. It means that the anarchist moves through
history in a different way from the liberal or the socialist, who is
always inclined to assume that the future necessarily promises the
greater good. It means that, where the Marxist — for example —
seems destined to carry to a further degree of efficiency the rationalization of human control over the material world which capitalism
and the Nation-State achieved, the anarchist stands aside in criticism
of the very concepts of efficiency and rationalization when they are
derived only from a consideration of economic factors. Anarchism
recognizes the perilous importance of the psychological element at
work in the development of human institutions, the element whose
dangers were best defined by that acute observer of political societies,
Lord Acton, in his famous aphorism: "Power tends to corrupt, and
absolute power corrupts absolutely." The anarchists have always seen
the tragic flaw in social democracy as its assumption that by the use
of power transferred from one élite to another, coercive institutions

can be melted away — the State, as Engels once claimed, can paradoxically wither under the dictatorship of one class within it, the proletariat. The anarchists have recognized — and the history of socialist countries seem to have proved them right — that the use of power merely feeds the desire for power.

It is because the anarchists have never been able to accept the power-dominated politics of the world in which they live that they have so often — from Gerrard Winstanley down to Paul Goodman — seemed to assume a posture rather like the legendary position of Mahomet's coffin, suspended between its two lodestones in sacred Mecca. It is very easy to see the anarchist lodestones as an idealized future towards which they yearn without great hope and an ideal past to which they look back with frustrated longing.

In fact, the situation is somewhat less simple than that, since what the more perceptive anarchists actually believe is not that we have to yearn towards future or past, but that in any society there are really two kinds of presents between which we have to make our choice. One is the institutional present, that of the authoritarian structures under which we live and which atomize society and alienate individuals by weakening the sense of social responsibility that is innate in all people. For, as I have said elsewhere in *Anarchism*:

> All anarchists, I think, would accept the proposition that man naturally contains within him all the attributes that make him capable of living in freedom and social concord. They may not believe that man is naturally good, but they may believe very fervently that man is naturally social. . . . Not merely is man naturally social, the anarchists contend, but the tendency to live in society emerged with him as he evolved out of the animal world. Society existed before man, and a society living and growing freely would in fact be a natural society.

Here we come to the second anarchist present. For, as thoughtful anarchists from Kropotkin onward have always argued, the institutions of power have never completely eliminated man's natural inclination to cooperate; if they did, George Orwell's nightmare of *1984* would indeed be fulfilled. In fact, it is because men carry on their benign way of free and natural cooperation parallel to the malign and coercive way of the State that society continues to exist as an endurable human environment. As Colin Ward put it in *Anarchy in Action*, one of the most important theoretical works on the subject, "An anarchist society, a society which organizes itself without authority, is always in existence, like a seed beneath the snow, buried under the weight of the state and its bureaucracy, capitalism and its waste, privilege and its injustices, nationalism and its suicidal loyalties, religious differences and their superstitious separatism."

What the anarchist seeks to do, according to this viewpoint, is not to destroy the present political order so that it may be replaced by a better system of organizing; that is the Marxist fallacy which produced the tragic history of post-Tsarist Russia. Rather, anarchism proposes to clear the existing structure of coercive institutions so that the natural society which has survived in a largely subterranean way from earlier, freer, and more originative periods can be liberated to flower again in a different future. The anarchists have never been nihilists, wishing to destroy present society entirely and replace it by something new, precisely because they have never been neophiliacs either, who see virtue only in what is novel. The anarchists have always valued the endurance of natural social impulses and of the voluntary institutions they create, and it is to liberating the great network of human cooperation that even now spreads through all levels of our lives rather than to creating or even imagining brave new world that they have bent their efforts. That is why there are so few utopian writings among the anarchists; they have always believed that human social instincts, once set free, could be trusted to adapt society in desirable and practical ways without plans — which are always constructive — being made beforehand.

To declare that the capacity to live a free life — and the rudimentary institutions for it — exists among us and needs to be liberated and encouraged, is at once revolutionary and conservative: revolutionary in the sense that the destruction or at least the erosion of a whole structure of power is contemplated; and conservative in the sense that the successful outcome of the revolution is seen in terms of the preservation and renewal of something that already exists. For the fact that authoritarian institutions are dismissed by anarchists as transient aberrations which, as Godwin put it, "reverses the genuine propensities of mind," does not lessen the conservative element within the divided heart of anarchism, since all conservatives regard what they condemn as transient and aberrant. And in this sense anarchism is not merely conservative.

In terms of popular ideas of progress, anarchism is indeed regressive. Its proponents have always seen liberation in terms of simplification rather than complication. Where the price of affluence is the progressive loss of freedom to develop — to use Paul Goodman's terminology — as 'people' rather than 'personnel,' they have always, from Proudhon onwards, praised the virtues of poverty (as distinct from pauperism) and where possible (as in peasant collectives in the Spanish Civil War) sought to achieve them in austere practice. They have always favored decentralization (being the true originators of the idea that 'small is beautiful', and in the organizational sense decentralism means devolution, however much its defenders may see it as favorable to the creative and spiritual evolution of humanity.

It is not, therefore, entirely accidental that a conservative like Lord Acton, a Catholic who saw the declaration of Papal Infallibility in 1869 as an insufferable imposition on his own spiritual freedom, should in his remarks on power have given the most eloquent expression to one of the central anarchist beliefs. Nor is it a matter of caprice that a latter-day anarchist like Paul Goodman, one of the most painstakingly honest intellectuals of his time, should say, and be right in saying: "I am anarchist and agitational, and I am conservative and traditional" (*Creator Spirit, Come*), and, not long before his death and in a book he sub-titled *Notes of a Neolithic Conservative*: "I am not a 'romantic': what puts my liberal and radical critics off is that I am a conservative, a conservationist. I do use the past: the question is how."

What I propose in the rest of this essay is to examine, in an appropriately desultory manner, how Goodman does in fact use the past, and how in doing so he continues and extends one of the vital currents in anarchist thought — the current which, to use terms that seem at variance with most commonly held views of anarchism, is both traditional and aristocratic. For a viewpoint that treasures the past (as Kropotkin and Herbert Read as well as Goodman did) for the social virtues that have been destroyed or are threatened by authority obviously does not seek to level people down to the common denominator of the proletarian (the alienated of the industrial revolution). Rather, it is a matter of being raised to a cultural level once enjoyed only by the rich and powerful, for, as I once suggested:

> In reality the ideal of anarchism, far from being democracy carried to a logical end, is much nearer to aristocracy universalized and purified. The spiral of history here has been turned full circle, and where aristocracy — at its highest point in the Rabelaisian vision of the Abbey of Thelème — called for the freedom of noble men, anarchism has always declared the nobility of free men (*Anarchism*).

It is an aristocracy purged of privilege, whose demand on the material world is no more than "the sufficiency that will allow men to be free" (*Anarchism*), or what Goodman repeatedly called "decent poverty"; it is, as Goodman further defined it, "aristocratic equality."

Within this pattern Goodman saw himself — in the words of the editor of his essays, Taylor Stoehr — as "the poor scholar, ragged but learned, able to philosophize with newsboys as well as clerics," the equivalent of the Greek philosopher who — as Goodman remarked more than once in his books on education — turned unpromising boys into men of true culture by wandering through the streets with them and mingling his discourses with the observation of actual daily life in all its forms.

As for the tradition to which Goodman saw himself belonging — and the past he used — Goodman defined it in a passage that is worth quoting at length because it defines and differentiates so well both the sources of his knowledge and the framework within which his insights emerge:

> The culture I want to teach — I am myself trapped in it and cannot think or strive apart from it — is our Western tradition: the values of Greece, the Bible, Christianity, Chivalry, the Free Cities of the Twelfth Century, the Renaissance, the heroic age of Science, the Enlightenment, the French Revolution, early nineteenth-century Utilitarianism, late nineteenth-century Naturalism.
>
> To indicate what I mean, let me mention a typical proposition about each of them. The Greeks sometimes aspire to a civil excellence in which mere individual success would be shameful. The Bible teaches that there is a created world and history in which we move as creatures. Christians have a spirit of crazy commitment because we are always in the last times. Chivalry is personal honor and loyalty, in love or war. Free cities have invented social corporations with juridical rights. The Renaissance affirms the imperious right of gifted individuals to immortality. Scientists carry on a disinterested dialogue with nature, regardless of dogma or consequence. The Enlightenment had decided that there is a common sensibility of mankind. The Revolution has made equality and fraternity necessary to liberty. Utilitarian economy is for tangible satisfactions, not busy work, money or power. Naturalism urges us to an honest ethics, intrinsic in animal and social conditions.
>
> Needless to say, these familiar propositions are often in practical and theoretical contradiction with one another; but

that conflict too is part of the Western tradition. And certainly they are only ideals — they never did exist on land or sea — but they are the inventions of the holy spirit and the human spirit that constitute the university, which also is an ideal.

Naturally, as a teacher, I rarely mention such things; I take them for granted as assumed by everybody. But I am rudely disillusioned when I find that both my students and my younger colleagues take quite different things for granted (*Compulsory Miseducation*).

This passage, from a book first published in 1962 and revised in 1964, not only helps us define Goodman's position as a humanist scholar in relation to the academic situation in the early 1960s. It also provides a starting point for assessing his position within the tradition of anarchism.

Goodman saw himself as a humanist rather than as an academic, and as a writer rather than as a professor, in which role — despite the excellence of his teaching — he turned out somewhat too eccentric in behavior for the academic community to assimilate easily. Nevertheless, the universities were for him one aspect of the culture he valued, even if he felt that he stood outside them:

When I consider the long lineage: Paris manned Oxford, and Oxford manned Cambridge, and Cambridge Harvard, and Harvard Yale, and Yale Chicago, etc., I realize that I am not a scholastic nor a university man though I ceremonially defend them. I am a humanist, that kind of Renaissance free-lance. At present I seem to be seeking a different lineage: Charcot to Freud, Freud to Reich, and so forth; but I am significantly unable to belong to it. In fact, I was born fatherless (*Nature Heals*).

It is here, in this context of the universities and of education in general, that we see Goodman taking some of his great steps into the past. Constantly, he urges on the universities that their duty was to conserve the Western tradition which he believed had shaped him. He takes up what he defines as "a very old-fashioned topic of educational theory, how to transmit Culture with a big C, the greatness of man" (*New Reformation*). He upbraids the universities for their acceptance of army subsidies, which he denounces as "the end of free research and liberal education, for he who pays the piper calls the tune." And he calls for a revivification of the humanities within the academies, since it is only if we understand and use language clearly and expansively, and not merely as a "code to render information narrowly," that we shall be able to understand and "manage the exploding scientific technology and the collectivism which are the conditions of the foreseeable future. . . . Just now the method of literature is indispensable: to find and say the humanities in new science, the morality in technology, and the community and individualism in collectivism" (*New Reformation*).

Such views resemble in many ways those of educational conservatives with the difference that Goodman embodies them in a generally libertarian theory of education. Education in the humanities is essential to the health of society, but this does not mean that all people are adapted mentally to absorb in academic form what their culture has to offer.

And of course, while most educational conservatives seek the rigidities of past systems of teaching and educational organization which were little better than what we have, Goodman sought a decentralization and diversification and deinstitutionalization of education that is entirely in keeping with his anarchism. *Growing Up Absurd* (1960) showed how 'problem children' were held in that role because their 'problems' were institutionalized in the kind of schools that purported to 'treat' them. *The Community of Scholars* revealed Goodman as an advocate of free and highly experimental forms of education, though he was by no means a single-minded advocate of the progressive school movement, which he recognized developed its own rigidities. Yet when he wrote of the universities in this book and elsewhere, it was clear that he in no way aspired to destroy the tradition of education as transmitted by the academies, or the high tradition of Western culture which at its best he felt it expressed and transmitted. What he attacked was the physical gigantism and the bureaucratic inhumanity of the multiversities. In its place he suggested a return to the medieval kind of college in which bands of teachers and students came together to teach and learn, with a recognition that those who know most must in the field of learning — but there alone — be regarded as the masters.

Goodman was always hoping to find this kind of community of scholars. He hoped he might encounter it at Black Mountain College, whose informal structure attracted him, but, quite apart from the vestigial moralism of the place, which led to his being eased out for his frank expression of homosexual desires, Goodman found a "feebleness" in the presentation of traditional humanities there and insisted on teaching more scholastically than his fellows. Going to Berkeley at the height of the Free Speech movement in February 1965 to report on it for *Dissent*, he found

. . . an uncanny re-emergence of the primitive medieval University, with its fat-cat professors lecturing in the central halls, a ragged student community living in its own neighborhood, and, astoundingly, a new student leadership by the graduates and teaching-assistants, the very Masters of Arts who used to cause all the trouble in 1200! One would have expected, in the era of the Organization Man, that precisely the bright graduate-students, the junior-executives, would be the most conformist, to protect their status and advancement; yet we see at Berkeley that the teaching-assistants provided leaders and almost unanimously went on strike.

Yet he had to admit wryly that when he said all this to the students, they were not entirely responsive:

> To my surprise, the students did not dig what I was saying; they do not have much memory of the tradition of the West. They know what freedom is, yes, they do — but they don't really know what a University is.

And, indeed, it was not long after 1965 that Goodman began to realize that, for all the anarchistic elements in the student revolt of the early 1960s, many of the activists did not know enough about politics or history to prevent their sliding into authoritarian, neo-Leninist political stances, while the rest of the students revealed themselves as — in his view — virtual philistines because of their unawareness of the tradition he treasured and in which he had grown up. By 1969 he was talking like this:

> When I speak at a college, I pepper the discussion with references to Spinoza, Beethoven and Milton, hoping that the students will learn that former great men were real human beings, but the poignant effect is that they regard me wistfully because I seem to have a past, and they are more forlorn than ever. If I try to analyze a text in its own terms, to find a human spirit coping with its particulars and *therefore* relevant to us, it is taken as an irrelevant exercise in order to avoid present gut issues. Naturally, inability to read a book is cumulative. Since there is no belief in the tradition or habituation in its ways, it becomes a chore to read the sentences, and why bother? (*New Reformation*).

But, as we realize from reading Goodman's essays on education, and particularly those collected in *Compulsory Miseducation*, he is not blaming the students who react in this way so much as the system that has taken them out of a natural social situation and put wrong demands on them. For instead of being oriented towards creating a human being capable at the earliest possible stage of playing a productive and therefore satisfying role in his world, contemporary education — in Goodman's view — has become a holding operation by which millions of young people are kept out of mischief and out of the labor market until they have reached their early twenties and by any normal standards are well into adulthood. In this system, whether education benefits the students emotionally or intellectually has become irrelevant.

Thus we see Goodman advocating, time and again, that it might be a good idea if we were to step backward mentally in time, reconsider our thoughts on education and perhaps start off again from scratch. So, at the same time as he suggests that the universities should devolve from vast expansive multiversities (where overheads cost three times as much as the actual teaching) into something small and intimate like the medieval universities, Goodman is also pointing out that even in our present century enormous numbers of people did very well for themselves and enriched society with only a fraction of the time in school (as distinct from real education) that their descendants endure:

> When there was academic instruction for many for a short time, or for a few for a longer time, it is possible that some academic education occurred. To be sure, most education for most people happened by means other than schools. Society functioned very well and many people became very expert and learned without going to school — in 1900, 6 per cent graduated from high school and less than half of 1 per cent went to college. Now, however, 100 per cent are forced to go to high school and last year 75 per cent graduated. On this scale, it is my observation as a reporter, very little education is occurring. For academic purposes, we might do just as well if we closed all the schools, though of course they serve for baby sitting, policing and so forth. We could surely provide

all the academic instruction that is achieved by far simpler and cheaper methods (*Compulsory Miseducation*).

George Orwell made a very similar point when he remarked in *The Road to Wigan Pier* on the irrelevance of academic education to the life of the workers, pointing out that the normal English working-class boy of the 1930s longed for the day he would leave school and be "doing real work," as a result of which at eighteen he was a man with adult responsibilities, while a middle-class boy of the same age attending a public school was little more than a baby. Goodman's ultimate position is not far from Orwell's, since he concludes that real education is not what goes on in the school:

> It is a natural community function and occurs inevitably, since the young grow up on the old, towards their activities, and into (or against) their institutions; and the old foster, teach, train, exploit and abuse the young. Even neglect of the young, except physical neglect, has an educational effect — not the worst possible (*Compulsory Miseducation*).

What Goodman really proposes is that education should once again be an extension of activities that normally take place in a healthy society outside the schoolroom, and therefore, for the majority of children (those with no aptitude for scholarship or the arts) of learning by experiencing and doing, which means being an apprentice more than a student in the academic sense, and in the case of town children, learning the processes of cultivation and growth by living and working for long periods on renovated marginal farms. The desystematization of education, the breaking up of the learning process into a multitude of improvized responses to particular situations, would allow such a flexible approach.

An implication of such a concept of education is that the function of the scholar and the artist are detached from the role of teaching the young, as they were in the medieval universities, and consequently one never encounters in Goodman's writings that bogus cultural democracy which denounces as elitism any regard for high culture or for the literary tradition. The culture and the tradition are there for those who wish to pursue them, but the elimination of compulsory education would make it a matter of free choice. It is true that as an artist Goodman was not notably experimental, and he was inclined to identify with Wordsworth's "simplification of vocabulary, and the connection of this with the speech of unsophisticated people and the expression of feeling." But he also remarked that the great thing about Wordsworth was something much more recondite, his "exquisite syntax," and he added a remark about the great Romantic poet that is germane to what I have been saying about his own views on the nature of a libertarian education: "In my opinion, his idea of pedagogy is true and primary; it *is* the beauty of the world and simple human affections, that develop great-souled and disinterested adults" (*Creator Spirit, Come*).

Anarchists, always seeking a way to liberate natural social urges other than the suicidal course of political revolution, have been greatly concerned with education, not merely as a means of drawing out the natural capabilities of young people in society as it exists, but also as one of the ways to transform society. It is significant that this preoccupation has been strongest among non-violent anarchists, like William Godwin and Leo Tolstoy, or among anarchists in general at times when the movement was not collectively dominated by myths of violence, as in France after terrorism died down during the later 1890s, when a notable libertarian educational movement arose under the leadership of Sebastian Faure and Elisée Reclus, and as in England during and after World War II, when Herbert Read published *Education through Art* and *The Education of Free Men*, and other anarchists like Tony Weaver, Tony Gibson, and Tom Earley — all of them involved in practical teaching — wrote extensively on free forms of education based on a re-immersion of the child in natural social processes.

In many ways Goodman's approach resembles that of the

English anarchists. He would certainly sympathize with Herbert Read's basic statement:

> To neglect the senses, either through ignorance of their signif-
> icance or from mere puritanical prejudice, is to neglect one
> half of our being. Neither in teaching nor in learning, neither
> in making things nor in our dealings with one another, can we
> afford to ignore the sensuous reactions that record the quality
> of experience. It follows that in any ideal system of education
> we should educate the senses, and to this end each of the arts
> should have its appropriate place in the curriculum.

Yet there are points at which Read's and Goodman's views do not entirely accord. Goodman's idea of educating the senses goes a good deal beyond the arts, which he would perhaps not give the over-riding importance they have in Read's rather more systematic proposals for the reform of education, largely, I think, because though he would agree that the education of the senses should precede the education of the intellect, Goodman recognizes that there are many people who can get along and live a full and happy life without being even minimally involved in the arts. They can, for example, be immersed from the beginning in all-absorbing occupations like farming or certain forms of craftsmanship or even the kind of mechanical work that demands intelligent attention. Here Goodman perhaps also differs from Read in the stress that — like Kropotkin and Fourier and Proudhon — he lays on the importance of productive work, as distinct from toil, in giving meaning to human life. Though I have found no mention of it in Goodman's writings, he must have found little to disagree with in William Morris's *Useful Work versus Useless Toil.*

Goodman's views on education show, admirably, the nature of both his conservatism and his traditionalism. He recognizes and lives by the great philosophies and the great poetry of the past, and what he perceives with apprehension is the way modern methods and systems of education have broken the lines of connection by which mankind's total achievement over the centuries can remain a living part of the present. One alarming result of this kind of alienation is that science has escaped from the modifying and moralizing influence of the humanities. And so he commends not the invention of new systems, but experiments in simplification, for, as he has said, "A free society cannot be the substitution of a 'new order' for the old order; it is the extension of spheres of free action until they make up most of the social life "(*Drawing the Line*). And often freedom can involve a stepping back rather than a stepping forward so that it becomes appropriate to consider how the medieval universities operated without the crushing superstructures of modern academic institutions, and how the guild systems of apprenticeship produced not merely good workmen but also well-rounded intelligences, so that we owe to the free cities of the middle ages so many of the innovations that led to the enlargement of life during the modern era.

This seems an appropriate place to turn from conservative aspects of Goodman's views on education to this relationship with anarchist traditionalism in the larger sense. Anarchists often deny tradition, since the appeal to the past seems to them a way of admitting the validity of authority. Yet no observer of the movement can fail to note how interested they are in the ancestry of their teachings, and how much attention those among them with a historical bent — like Kropotkin, Max Nettlau, and Rudolf Rocker — have given to the constructions of family trees reaching back not merely to the French Revolution or to the Diggers in the English Revolution but to distant forebears like Zeno the Stoic and Lao-Tse and Jesus Christ, whose apostles, according to one French historian of the movement, formed "the first anarchist society."

In attempting to give a scientific and historical basis to anarchism that might help it compete with the 'scientific socialism' of Marx, the two great anarchist geographers, Peter Kropotkin and Elisée Reclus, formulated the doctrine of mutual aid, which held that one of the great factors of evolution was a social instinct which made cooperation within the species as important in the scheme of nature as the struggles with adverse conditions and between species that neo-Darwinists like Thomas Henry Huxley had stressed. In a way, the theory of mutual aid was an extension into the whole animal world of Proudhon's earlier teaching of mutualism, which had already posed the existence of a natural social order that was weakened by the imposition of artificial institutions like the State and other forms of government.

In the historical, as distinct from the biological sense, what the theory of mutual aid gave to anarchism was a ready-made substitute for a tradition; a positive outlook on the past; and a reason for conservatism in the sense that Goodman meant when he said, "Edmund Burke had a good idea of conservatism, that existing community bonds are destroyed at peril; they are not readily replaced, and society becomes superficial and government illegitimate." Kropotkin and his followers taught that the urge to cooperation existed among the animals, so that people did not become social beings at the point where they emerged into social consciousness as we know it; sociability was one of the gifts he inherited from our animal ancestors, as were those complementary urges towards free cooperation and towards authority, which we see Kropotkin evoking with a curious Manichean vision when he claimed for anarchism a record as long as that of mankind and of the opposing current of government and coercion:

> It is evident that Anarchy represents the first of these two currents, that is to say, the creative constructive force of the masses, who elaborated common-law institutions in order to defend themselves against a domineering minority. It is also by the creative and constructive force of the people, aided by the whole strength of modern science and technique, that today Anarchy strives to set up institutions that are indispensable to the free development of society, in opposition to those who put their hope in laws made by governing minorities. We can therefore say that from all times there have been Anarchists and Statists.

Kropotkin observes that in human societies there have been certain periods when the nature of society has extraordinarily liberated the cooperative spirit in constructive ways, such as the time when the barbarians established their village communes all over Europe, and the later era when the free cities of Europe flourished as centers of medieval civilization. The village communes of the barbarians became subordinate to the patterns of graduated authority introduced by feudalism, and the free cities were largely robbed of their liberties and their originative vision by the rise of the Nation-State in the seventeenth century.

In much of this kind of interpretation of history, Goodman follows Kropotkin, and especially in his evaluation of what he called the "high Middle Ages," which he regarded as a period of searching and seminal thought and practice rather than — as it has so often been represented — of mental stasis. The picture he gives in *New Reformation* is, if anything, even more favorable than Kropotkin's, since Goodman was versed in areas of medieval philosophy which had comparatively little meaning for his more scientifically minded predecessor:

> . . . the organization of society was pluralistic and pragmatic; the moral sciences came alive, and in the physical sciences, there began to be widespread experimentation.
>
> In the heterogenous political structure of feudalism, national states, city states, municipal councils, craft guilds, trade associations, the international church, and the ghost of the international empire, there was a thriving moral philosophy and law, inventive and probing. Today, in every kind of moral inquiry, religious or secular, the medieval analyses reappear, in commercial transactions, craft regulation, sexual morality, rules of war, university polity and privilege, discussions of sovereignty and legitimacy.
>
> In form, medieval moral philosophy was apparently systematic rather than experimental, aiming at the *summum bonum* of salvation. But in the great variety of occasions and

jurisdictions, casuistry made moral inquiry concrete and pragmatic. Scholasticism and legalism provided a consensual language that made thought precise, rather than stifling. Arts and crafts, technology, were, like all other activities, personal, moral and responsible, e.g. in determining quality and just price and in guild and building-gang organization. Indeed, the free-city guilds were the closest we have yet come to workers' management.

On to this pluralistic and pragmatic scene appeared the dramatic new force of experimental science; but the opposite of our situation, it was in the context of prudence and morals. *Prima facie*, experimentation was making and doing, a branch of moral philosophy, liable to moral judgment and not merely a means of knowing; nor were its findings acceptable in style to orthodox academic natural philosophy. One important source of experimentation was the arts and crafts revived or newly invented by self-directed artisans who were both highly cooperative and highly competitive, producing for their own purposes and judging what they were doing, an excellent set-up for learning new science without bookish scientific preconceptions, and strictly prudential.

If the Middle Ages, where so much was "personal, moral and responsible," as well as genuinely experimental, fitted into Goodman's sense of a libertarian tradition as much as it did into Kropotkin's, he diverged into the history of his own environment to find the same virtues at the roots of the American experiment in liberation. He had very little to say, indeed, about the native American anarchists who in many ways were his intellectual forebears, like Josiah Warren and Lysander Spooner and Benjamin Tucker, but this was mainly because he saw in the whole American tradition a libertarian impulse that was far broader than the movement which the theoreticians I have mentioned represented. Here, for example, is one of his mental pictures of the early years of the United States:

During the first thirty years of the Republic only 5 to 10 per cent were enfranchised and as few as 2 per cent bothered to vote. But the conclusion to be drawn from this is not necessarily that society was undemocratic. On the contrary, apart from the big merchants, planters, clerics and lawyers, people were likely quite content, freed from the British, to carry on their social affairs in a quasi-anarchy, with unofficial, decentralized and improvised political forms. It was in this atmosphere that important elements of our American character was developed (*Creator Spirit, Come*).

And elsewhere he sketched out a pluralistic network of social forms which arose in revolutionary America and enjoyed an existence parallel to but independent of the formal structures that were created to replace the British apparatus of rule:

When the revolution of 1776-83 removed the top structure of British authority from the American colonies, this country was fundamentally organized as a network of highly structured face-to-face communities, each fairly autonomous; town-meetings, congregational parishes, gentry families and yeoman families. These had hierarchical structures: master and apprentice, indentured servants, family slaves, professionals and their clients, pastors and parishes; but each person was in frequent contact with those who initiated and decided.

For the first twenty-five years of the republic, in important respects there was virtually a community anarchy with regard to the central and state governments.

For immigrants and for the poor who felt too disadvantaged in the existing structured communities, the frontier was an open area for independence (*Drawing the Line*).

In Goodman's view, this healthy, pluralist, early American society was destroyed by the trend towards centralization, in government and industry alike, set into motion by the Civil War, and it is notable that he sees its last forlorn fling, not in the native or immigrant anarchists, but in the Populist movement:

> More than the beginnings of the modern labor movement during the same period, and certainly more than Reform politics, Populism clearly saw the closing trap of interlocking centralization. . . . Now the free market was restrained by trusts and ever higher tariffs. . . . The political parties became increasingly massified and distantly controlled, and there were alliances between government and the monopolies. To all this the Populists responded with heroic self-reliance, and tragic paranoia and political confusion.
>
> In my opinion, this was the last American political movement to face squarely the crucial dilemma of modern society: how to preserve practical democracy in high industrial conditions. For a couple of decades, Populism saw the answer: the Jacksonian Party democracy could not work; one had to start anew from below (*People or Personnel*).

The facets of any seminal work change in relative importance according to the times. When *Mutual Aid* was published, its immediate significance lay in its correction of the Huxleyan distortions of evolutionary doctrine, but it also had importance in giving scientific support to anarchist arguments about the possibility of human societies existing and succeeding without coercive institutions. In our day, when most anarchists no longer foresee the destruction of government ushering in a completely free society, *Mutual Aid* is most inspiring for its revelation that, even in times when authoritarian structures dominate society, the institutions created by voluntary cooperation still survive and prevent the collapse of society. Kropotkin's words, when he chronicled the decline of the once splendid free cities of Europe, carry the seed of the hope that has inspired contemporary writers like Paul Goodman and Colin Ward who seek within our society the elements that can be preserved and nurtured with a view to evolving a free and more natural way of living:

> And yet, the current of mutual aid and support did not die out in the masses; it continued to flow even after that defeat. It rose up again with a formidable force, in answer to the communist appeals of the first propagandists of the reform, and it continued to exist even after the masses, having failed to realize the life which they hoped to inaugurate under the inspiration of a reformed religion, fell under the dominions of an autocratic power. It flows still even now, and it seeks its way to find out a new expression which would not be the State, nor the medieval city, nor the village community of the barbarians, nor the savage clan, but would proceed from all of them, and yet be superior to them in its wider and more deeply human conceptions (*Mutual Aid*).

The recognition that Kropotkin was right in his assessment of the tenacity of mutual aid as a manifestation of human sociality led Colin Ward to declare in *Anarchy in Action* that anarchism exists already in our society and Paul Goodman to explore ways in which — even without any recognizable evolution — constructive social tendencies can be liberated by piecemeal change, by what he often wryly called "tinkering." Here, in this desire to foster and to revive social manifestations so constant in history that they can be called traditional, lies the essence of Paul Goodman's conservatism, the necessary conservatism of an anarchist in our own day.

This conservationist conservatism is manifest in aspects of Goodman's thought and action too varied and too broad to be more than mentionable in the present essay; in his advocacy for decentralization, meaning the breaking down of structures too large for the human scale; in his demands for a readjustment of the balance between rural and urban ways of living through repopulating the country, reviving village life, bringing the marginal land back into

cultivation through new forms of mixed farming; in his many proposals for the humanizing of city life; in his preference for guild over
trade union ethics; in his preference for the college over the multiver-
sity, for the storefront school over the massive modern educational
plant, and for apprenticeship over the barren perversion of academic
education that turns the schools into detention places for young people who would be better off and of more use to the community if they
were put to work. All these proposals involve piecemeal changes,
major or minor, and in most cases the idea is to return to a simpler
state of affairs in which a freer form of action can be initiated.

Perhaps Goodman is most differentiated from the old-style
fundamentalist anarchist in his recognition that the changeover to a
totally free society is not a possible revolution, and that the gradualism which earlier anarchists contemptuously rejected has to be
accepted for anything to be achieved in the real world. He constantly
uses phrases like "adjustments and transformations of historical conditions," and he recognizes that no process which is not gradual can
hope to carry the people with it, which is necessary if one is not to
resort to Bolshevik methods: "The best period is one in which every
new work destroys the convention of predecessors, yet advancing to
just the next step — the result of an achieved habit and assimilated
tradition — it carries its audience along" (*Creator Spirit, Come*).

It is, Goodman believes, of the essence of anarchism that its
principle is always manifested in relation to the actual situation, and
so remarks that "there *cannot* be a history of anarchism in the sense
of establishing a permanent state of things called 'anarchist' "
(*Drawing the Line*). In the foreseeable future, a mixed society seems
inevitable, and what the anarchist must do is to decide where to
"draw the line," where to go beyond "tinkering," where to disturb
the peace, for "Useful services must not be neglected because they
are inappropriate to the dominant style, and basic necessities must
not depend on the smooth working of the economy" (*People or
Personnel*).

The nature of anarchism is to resist change that reduces the naturalness of a society (which is a conservative act) and to promote change that makes society more free (which is a radical act). The process of anarchism "is always a continual coping with the next situation, and a vigilance to make sure that past freedoms are not lost and do not turn into the opposite, as free enterprise turned into wage-slavery and monopoly capitalism, or the independent judiciary turned into a monopoly of courts, cops and lawyers, or free education turned into School Systems."

In the end, it was the conservative in Goodman, his impulse to found everything in tradition, his recognition that people live largely by anarchist principles even in the most authoritarian society, his knowledge that small starts in the direction of simplification often immensely enlarge the scope of freedom, and his realistic awareness that in the foreseeable future the best we can expect is a vigorously pluralist society. This perspective preserved Goodman from the despairing inertia of the purist anarchist or the idealist futility of those who, as Herbert Read did in his last years, see the fulfilment of anarchist expectations as a distant point on a far horizon. Goodman saw it as part of the personal struggle of day-to-day living, permeating everything he did and said and wrote, and nourished by all that remains natural and free in human living. It was this that made him, by any standards, so interesting and stimulating a social critic. He was never afraid of the apparent contradictions of his position; he knew that in our era the anarchist and the true conservative must live within the same mind and work upon each other.

1986

9

Michael Archangel:
Encounter with a Doukhobor

I first knew the Doukhobors as shadowy figures of legend in my English childhood, when my father would compensate for a dull life in a small town beside the Thames by weaving nostalgic threnodies on his young manhood in the Canadian west. Evenings on the prairies, with the great pink-bellied hawks settling down; Cobalt in the silver boom; fishing camps on the pristine shores of the northern lakes; and the great winter fires of the cities where burntout buildings became palaces of ice. Against such scenes the necessary characters moved in the cinema of my brain with the exaggerated gesticulation of Japanese actors. Lefty Louis and Zip the Blood shot it out with the police from a Winnipeg streetcar; Charlie Chaplin clowned through the one-elevator hamlets with Fred Karno; Chinese in blue gowns and pigtails scurried along Portage Avenue; strange Russians cleared snow in the prairie towns and were given to stripping in public, regardless of sex.

I realized the Doukhobors were something more than eccentric shovellers of snow when I read Tolstoy and Kropotkin and discovered that for these great Russians the Doukhobors were a group of admirable peasant radicals — Nature's anarchists. During the thirties I found in Doukhobor anti-militarism a strain that appealed to my own pacificism, and I accepted Tolstoy's impression of a libertarian sect who took their Christianity neat and had turned their settlements into Utopian communities. Like Tolstoy, I was unaware that this simple view took no account of certain fundamental aspects of Doukhobor philosophy and practice. Unlike Tolstoy, I learnt my error.

When my wife and I returned to Canada in the spring of 1949, I found that on Vancouver Island, where we settled, there was a small group of Doukhobors who had migrated from the interior of British Columbia and had founded a colony at Hilliers, sixty miles north of the village where we were clearing land and carpentering a house in search of that Tolstoyan *ignis fatuus*, the marriage of manual and mental work.

The people of our village talked reluctantly about the Hilliers community, yet even their hostile comments told us something. The leader of the group — a heretical offshoot — was a prophet who called himself Michael the Archangel. He openly preached the destruction of marriage, and this our neighbors vaguely envisaged as a complex and orgiastic pattern of shacking-up which provoked and offended their Presbyterian imaginations at one and the same time.

Since Hilliers was near, we could easily go there to see for ourselves, but we knew already that chronic bad relations with the Canadian authorities had made the Doukhobors distrustful of strangers. However, I wrote to the community, and by return I received a letter from the secretary, whose name was — almost predictably — Joe. He not only welcomed my interest, but invited us to stay at Hilliers as long as we wished. I was a little surprised at the enthusiastic tone of his letter, but the reason became evident once we reached Hilliers.

One day in August we set off northward, hitch-hiking, and it was late afternoon when the last driver turned off the seacoast road into the broad valley, hot and still of air, where Hilliers lies in the lee of the hard mountain spine that runs down the length of Vancouver Island. The older, non-Doukhobor Hilliers was a whistle-stop on the island railway, and the entrance to the community stood opposite a siding filled with boxcars. A high cedar fence faced the road. A large board was nailed to it. *Union of spiritual communities of Christ*, it said, in Russian and English. The wide gates stood open; looking between them, the eye encompassed and then recognized with some surprise the unconscious faithfulness with which a Russian village of the Chekhov era had been reproduced. Low cabins of logs and unpainted shacks were scattered along a faintly marked trail that ran between grass verges to end, a furlong on, at two larger two-storeyed houses standing against the brown background of the mountains, with the gray bubble of a communal baking oven between them. Each cabin was surrounded by a picketed garden, where green rows of vegetables and raspberry canes ran over the black earth in neatly weeded symmetry, and ranks of sunflowers lolled their brown and yellow masks towards the light.

An old woman with a white kerchief shading her face was hoeing very slowly in the nearest garden. She was the only person in sight, and I went up to her fence. Could she tell me where to find Joe? Her English was so broken that I could not follow what she was trying to tell me. By this time our arrival had been observed in the cabins, and a little wave of younger women in bright full petticoats, and of blond, crop-headed small boys, came towards us hesitantly. There was nothing of the welcome we had expected. My wife Inge spoke to one of the women. "Joe ain't here," she answered. "He's at the other place." She waved vaguely northward. A pick-up truck drove in through the gates, and two young men got out. The women called to them, and they talked together in rapid, anxious Russian. Then one man got back into the truck and drove off, while the other came up to us. He was dark and nervous, dressed in an old blue serge suit, with chaff whitening the wrinkles. "I'm Pete," he said, "Joe's brother. Joe's coming." He paused. "Afterwards . . . you'll see Michael . . . Michael Archangel," he added hesitantly, and then fell silent. The small boys gave up interest and went to play in the boxcars.

Joe was so different from Pete that it was hard to believe them brothers — blue-eyed, wiry, jumping out of the truck to run and pump our hands. "Michael Archangel knew you were coming. A long time ago," he shouted. I had written only a week before. "A long time ago?" I asked. Joe looked at me and then laughed. "Yes, before you wrote!" Then he grabbed our rucksacks, helped us into the truck, and drove wildly for a couple of miles along a rough track beside the railway to a large old farm house in a quadrangle of shacks and barns surrounded by propped-up apple trees that were ochre-yellow with lichen. "This is the other place," Joe explained. "Most of the young people stay here. The old 'uns live up there with Michael Archangel."

We went into the kitchen. Two young women, fair and steatopygous as Doukhobor beauties are expected to be, were preparing the evening meal. A small girl showed us to our room and stood, avid with curiosity, while we unpacked our rucksacks and washed our faces. Then Joe took us around the yard, showed us the new bakehouse on which a hawk-faced man like a Circassian bandit was laying bricks, and tried to entice us into the bathhouse. I looked through the doorway and saw naked people moving like the damned in the clouds of steam that puffed up whenever a bucket of water was thrown on the hot stones. In a couple of seconds I withdrew, gasping for breath. The bricklayer laughed. "You never make a Doukhobor," he said. "Add ten years to your life," said Joe, coaxingly.

When everyone stood in a circle around the great oval table for the communal meal we began to see the kind of people the Doukhobors were. There were twenty of them, singing in the half-Caucasian rhythm that penetrates Doukhobor music, the women high and nasal, the men resonant as bells. Most had Slavonic features, their breadth emphasized among the women by the straight fringes in which their hair was cut across the brow. But a few, like the bricklayer, were so un-Russian as to suggest that the Doukhobors had interbred with Caucasian Moslems during their long exile in the mountains before they came to Canada. They sang of Siberian and

Canadian prisons, of martyrs and heroes in the faith. "Rest at last, ye eagles of courage, rest at last in the arms of God," they boomed and shrilled.

The singing was solemn, but afterwards the mood changed at once and the meal went on with laughter and loud Russian talk; now and then our neighbors would break off repentantly to translate for our benefit. The food was vegetarian, the best of its kind I have ever tasted; bowls of purple borscht, dashed with white streaks of cream, and then casha, made with millet and butter, and vegetables cooked in oil, and pirogi stuffed with cheese and beans and blackberries, and eaten with great scoops of sour cream. Slices of black bread passed around the table, cut from a massive square loaf that stood in the middle, beside the salt of hospitality, and the meal ended with huckleberries and cherries.

Afterwards Joe and Pete took us to drink tea in a room they used as an office. It was furnished with a table and benches of thick hand-adzed cedar, but a big blue enamel teapot served instead of a samovar. This was the first of a series of long conversations in which the ideas of the community were imparted to us, principally by Joe, who spoke English more fluently than anyone else at Hilliers. Except for a few phrases, the details of the dialogues have become blurred in my memory during the years that have passed since then, but this, in substance, is what we were told on the first evening.

The community began with the experiences of Michael Verigin, a backsliding Doukhobor. Michael had left his home in the mountains, opened a boarding-house for Russians in Vancouver, and prospered there. After a few years Michael began to feel the malaise which many Doukhobors experience when they go from their villages into the acquisitive outside world, and he returned to the mountain valley of Krestova. Krestova is the Mecca of the Sons of Freedom, the fire-raising and nude-parading radical wing of the Doukhobor sect. Michael rejoined the Sons of Freedom and was regarded with deference because he bore the holy name of Verigin and was a distant cousin of Peter Lordly, the Living Christ who presided over the Doukhobors' first years in Canada, and died mysteriously in a train explosion during the twenties.

"Then Michael had a vision."

"A dream?"

"No, a vision. He was awake, and he said there was a voice and a presence."

"He saw nothing?"

"That time he didn't. The vision told him he was no longer Mike Verigin. Michael the Archangel had gone into him. He was the same man, but the Archangel as well."

"How did he know it was a real vision?"

"He just knew." Joe looked at me with the imperturbable blue-eyed confidence of a man used to assessing the authenticity of supernatural messages. "The vision said Michael must prepare the world for the Second Coming."

The Second Coming did not mean the return of Christ. According to Doukhobor belief, Christ is returning all the time in various forms. The Second Coming meant the establishment of God's earthly kingdom and the end of time and mortality.

As the chosen pioneers in this great mission, the Doukhobors must purify themselves. The Archangel began by proclaiming that they must renounce not only meat and vegetables, but also tobacco and musical instruments. Joe himself had abandoned playing the violin, which he dearly loved. As he told me this, a radio was playing loudly in the kitchen. "That's O.K.," Joe reassured me. "A radio ain't a musical instrument."

Above all, the lust for possession must be rooted out. This meant not only a return to the traditional communistic economy from which the Doukhobors had lapsed under evil Canadian influences, but also the destruction of that inner citadel of possession, marriage. No person must have rights over another, either parental or marital. Women must be liberated, sexual relations must be free, families must wither away.

Two or three hundred of the Sons of Freedom, mostly seasoned old veterans of the nude marches and the pre-war internment on Piers Island, accepted the Archangel's teaching. Their neighbors showed disagreement by burning down the houses of those who followed Verigin. At this point the Archangel very conveniently had another vision.

Two of his followers must visit Vancouver Island. There they would find a town where a clock had stopped at half past two, and then they must proceed eastward until they saw a white horse by the gate of a farm. Joe and another man went on the expedition. They found the clock in Port Alberni, and the horse by the gate of a three-hundred-acre farm that was up for sale at a knockdown price. And, for what the fact is worth, I should record that after I had heard Joe's story I happened to visit Port Alberni, and there, on the tower of a fire-hall, I saw a dummy clock whose painted hands stood unmoving at half-past two.

The farm was bought with the pooled resources of the faithful, and Michael the Archangel led two hundred of his disciplines on the exodus to Vancouver Island. Immediately after leaving the mainland he added to all the other prohibitions a ban on sexual intercourse — to conserve energies for the great task of spiritual regeneration. Complete freedom was only to be won by complete self-control. So much for the stories of Free Love rampant!

I wanted to find out the actual nature of the power that enabled Michael the Archangel to impose such restrictions. Tolstoy once thought that, because they opposed the state, the Doukhobors lived without rulers. Other writers had suggested that the Living Christs, like Peter the Lordly Verigin and his son Peter the Purger, had been rulers as powerful as any earthly governor.

"Michael is just our spiritual leader," Joe explained blandly.

"But he still seems to have a great say in your practical affairs."

"It depends on what you mean by *say*. He gives no orders. We are free men. We don't obey anybody. But he gives us advice."

"Do you always accept?"

"If we know what's good for us, we do."

"Why?"

"Because we know Michael the Archangel is always right."

"How do you know?"

"We just know."

The next day we met the Archangel. He had sent a message early that morning summoning us to his presence, and Joe drove us to the hamlet where we had arrived originally. The Archangel's house was one of the larger buildings, but we were not allowed to go in. We waited outside. The Archangel would meet us in the garden.

A tall man in his late fifties came stepping heavily between the zinnia borders. A heavy paunch filled his knitted sweater, and his shining bald head loosened into a coarse, flushed face with a potato nose, a sandy moustache, and small eyes that glinted out of puffy sockets. It was a disappointing encounter. The Archangel bowed in the customary Doukhobor manner, but without the warmth most Doukhobors put into their greeting. He shook hands limply. He spoke a few sentences in Russian, welcoming us and wishing us good health, and he affected not to understand English, although we learned later that he was effectively bilingual. He picked two small pink roses from a briar that ran along the fence and gave one to each of us. In five minutes he was gone, retiring with dignified adroitness and leaving our intended questions about archangelic power unanswered. Joe led us away, loudly declaring that the Archangel had been delighted with us, and that he had given many messages which he, Joe, would transmit in due course. Our whole relationship with the Archangel took on this elusive, indirect form, with Joe acting like a voluble priest interpreting and embellishing the laconic banalities of the oracle.

For the rest of the second day we wandered around the community, talking to the people we encountered. I pumped the handle of a primitive hand washing-machine, and learned from the girl I helped a curious instance of Doukhobor double-think. A spaniel bitch trotted over the yard, followed by a single pup. "She had four," the girl volunteered. "Did you give the rest away?" "No, they were drowned." "I thought you didn't believe in killing." "We didn't kill 'em. The Mountie sergeant drowned 'em for us." She chuckled, and quite obviously felt no guilt for merely condoning a killing someone else had carried out.

Under the prophetic discipline there were certain signs of strain. I found empty beer bottles in a corner of one Doukhobor field, and in the shelter of the ten-foot plumes of corn which were the community's pride a young man begged a cigarette and smoked in hasty gulps to finish it before anyone came in sight. Yet there was also an atmosphere of dogged devotion. Much of the land had been irrigated, and it was growing heavier crops of corn and tomatoes and vegetables than any of the neighboring farms, while the houses were surrounded by rows of hotbeds and cold frames where melons and gherkins ripened. The younger people talked constantly of schemes for new kinds of cultivation and for starting light industries, but the younger people were so few. There were too many children, too many old visionaries.

Sunday was the climax of our visit. Our arrival had coincided with the community's first great festival. In the afternoon the only child so far born there was to be handed over to the care of the community as a symbolic demonstration against conventional ideas of motherhood and the family. Since the Archangel had forbidden fornication we were rather surprised that a being whose very presence seemed to defy his will should be so honored. From my attempts to discuss the situation I gained an impression that the Doukhobors applied a rather Dostoevskian equation — considering that, if the ban itself was sacred, so must be the sin against it. "Free men ain't bound by reason," as one young man rather unanswerably concluded a discussion on this point.

The day began with morning service in the bare meeting house. Flowers and plates of red apples had been brought in, and the sunlight played over the white head-shawls and bright cotton dresses of the women. Bread and salt stood symbolically on the small central table, and also a great ewer of water from which anybody who happened to feel thirsty would stop and drink as the service went on. The women ranged to the right of the table and the men to the left. On entering the hall each person bowed low from the waist, and the bow was returned by the whole assembly; the salutation was not to the man, but to the God within him. The Archangel stood at the head of the men, benign and copiously sweating; despite his celestial nature, he did not attempt to offend Doukhobor precedent by acting like a priest. Today, in fact, as a child was to be the center of the festival, the children led off the service, choosing and starting in their sharp, clear voices the Doukhobor psalms and hymns for the day. Almost every part of the service was sung, and the wild and wholly incomprehensible chanting of the two hundred people in the small meeting house produced in us an extraordinary sense of exaltation such as I have only experienced once since then, in a church full of Zapotec peasants at a festival south of Oaxaca. At the end of the service, we all linked arms at the elbows and kissed each other's cheeks, first right then left, in traditional token of forgiveness.

Later in the day we reassembled in the open air, forming a great V with the bread and salt at the apex. The singing rose like a fountain of sound among the drooping cedar trees, and between lines of women waving flowers and men waving green boughs the mother carried her child to the table. She was one of the young women we had met at the farmhouse on our arrival. As she stood there, her fair face grave and melancholy within the white frame of her head-shawl, she looked like the dolorous Mother of some naive ikon. The singing ended, the old hawk-faced bricklayer prayed before the table, and the mother, showing no emotion, handed the child to another of the women. The Archangel began to speak, in high, emotional tones; Pete, standing beside me, translated. The child would be named Angel Gabriel. The fruit of sin, he contained the seed of celestial nature. It was he who would fulfill the great destiny of the Doukhobors and lead mankind back on the great journey to lost Eden.

The women brought out pitchers of kvass and walked among the people as the orators began to speak. Emblematic banners were unfurled before the assembly. One, representing women dragging the ploughs that broke the prairies during the hard early days of the sect in Canada, was meant to celebrate the coming liberation of the sect from all forms of bondage. Another, covered with images of clocks and other symbols of time, was carefully expounded by the Archangel, who found it in the fatal dates that charted the destiny of the world. Then everyone spoke who wished — elders and young women; a Communist lawyer who had come in from the blue; even I, under moral coercion, as the enquiring Tolstoyan I then was. It was hot and tedious work as the sun beat down into the bowl among the mountains, and Sunday trippers from Qualicum Beach gazed in astonishment through the palisades.

We walked back to the farmhouse with a Canadian woman who had married into the Doukhobors. "You've seen what Mike wants you to see," she said bitterly. "You don't know all there is to know about that girl. Now she'll go up to stay in Mike's house. They won't let her talk to anyone, and they'll pay her out in every way then can for having a child by her own husband. Purification! That's what they talk about. I call it prison!" The mother of the Angel Gabriel was not at the evening meal, and we never saw her again. We asked Joe what had happened to her. She had gone willingly into seclusion, he answered; for her own good, of course.

Indeed, Joe had more important things to talk about in that last conversation. "You have a great part to play in the future of mankind." He fixed me with a sharp, pale eye. "Michael's vision has told him that the end of the world is very near. Now we have to gather in Jerusalem the hundred and forty-four thousand true servants of God mentioned in Revelation. This time Jerusalem will be right here."

"Here? On Vancouver Island?"

"On this very spot."

"But how do you know?"

"We ain't worrying. We just know. And the Archangel had a vision about you. He knew you were coming a long time ago. He knew you were a writer. He knew you were being sent here so you could tell the world what we're doing."

I must have looked at him very dubiously, for he flapped his hands reassuringly. "I ain't asking you to do it. Nor is Archangel. We just know you will. You'll write about us, and people will come to us, and then you will come back and be marked with the sign and live for ever among the servants of God."

We left the next day. The Archangel saw us once more in the garden, gave us a white rose each, and said we should meet again before long. "It's a prophecy," Joe whispered.

And indeed it was. One day, months later, I was broadcasting in Vancouver when Ross McLean, who was then a radio producer, said he had heard Joe was locked up in the court house. I went over, but I could not see him. The Mounties were holding him incommunicado. But as I was leaving the station Michael the Archangel was brought in, and for a couple of minutes, in that grim barred room, I was allowed to talk to him. He was pleased to be recognized, and even willing to talk a little English. "I am free soon," he said, as he was led away to the cells. Not long afterwards he and Joe were sentenced to some rather nebulous charges of disturbing public order. And a few months later Michael the Archangel died in jail.

Ten years afterwards we drove through Hilliers, turning off our road on a nostalgic impulse. The palisade was still there, opposite the railway siding, and for a moment everything looked unchanged. But inside, where Jerusalem should have been rising, there was only the ghost of what we had seen on the day the Angel Gabriel was named. Most of the buildings had gone, but falling fences and squares of thistles still marked out the theocracy where the Archangel had ruled.

1963

ACKNOWLEDGEMENTS

"The Advent of Anarchism and the Revolutions of 1848" appeared as "1848: The Year of Revolution" in the Introduction to *A Hundred Years of Revolution*, edited by George Woodcock (London: Porcupine Press, 1948).

"Anarchism Revisited" appeared in *Commentary* (August 1968) and in *The Rejection of Politics and Other Essays on Canada, Canadians, Anarchism and the World* (Toronto: new press, 1972).

"Democracy, Heretical and Radical" appeared in *The Case for Participatory Democracy*, edited by C. George Benello and Dimitri I. Roussopoulos (New York: Grossman Publishers, 1971).

"The Rejection of Politics" is abstracted from *Anarchy and Chaos* (London: Freedom Press, 1944) and also appears in *The Rejection of Politics*.

"Anarchy Now" appeared as "Anarchy" in *PPU Journal* (December 1946).

"The Folly of Revolutionary Violence" appeared in *Adelphi* (January–March 1947).

"The Tyranny of the Clock" appeared in *War Commentary* (Mid-March 1944) and in *The Rejection of Politics*.

"Anarchist Living and the Practice of Art" appeared in *Black Moss* (Fall 1976).

"Anarchism and Ecology" appeared in *The Ecologist* (March-April 1974).

"The Prospects for Anarchism" appeared as "The Ending Century: Prospect and Retrospect" in *The Raven* (March 1990).

"Pierre-Joseph Proudhon: An Appreciation" appeared as "Proudhon: An Appreciation" in *Dissent* (Autumn 1955).

"Michael Bakunin: The Destructive Urge" appeared as "Bakunin: The Destructive Urge" in *History Today* (July 1961).

"Alexander Herzen: Ancestor in Defeat" appeared in *Dissent* (Winter 1960).

"Peter Kropotkin: A Libertarian Life" appears as an undated typescript in the Woodcock papers at Queen's University Archives, Kingston, Ontario, Canada.

"Henry David Thoreau's Anarchism" appeared as "Thoreau as an Anarchist" in the Introduction to *Civil Disobedience* (Chicago: Charles H. Kerr, 1989).

"Herbert Read: The Philosopher of Freedom" appeared as "The Philosopher of Freedom" in *The Malahat Review* (January 1969).

"Noam Chomsky's Anarchism" appeared as "Chomsky's Anarchism" in *Freedom* (16 November 1974).

"Paul Goodman: The Anarchist as Conservator" appeared in *The Anarchist Papers*, edited by Dimitri I. Roussopoulos (Montreal: Black Rose Books, 1986).

"Michael Archangel: Encounter with a Doukhobor" appeared as "Encounter with an Archangel" in *The Tamarack Review* (Winter 1963).

SELECTED BIBLIOGRAPHY:
POLITICAL WRITINGS BY GEORGE WOODCOCK

Anarchism: A History of Libertarian Ideas and Movements. Cleveland: World, 1962; Harmondsworth: Penguin; 1963; Pelican edition with postscript, 1975; with new preface, 1986.

The Anarchist Prince: A Biographical Study of Peter Kropotkin. With Ivan Avakumovic. London: Boardman, 1950; New York: Schocken Books, 1971.

The Anarchist Reader. Edited by Woodcock. London: Fontana, 1977.

Anarchy or Chaos. London: Freedom Press, 1944.

The Basis of Communal Living. London: Freedom Press, 1947.

Civil Disobedience. Toronto: Canadian Broadcasting Corporation, 1966.

The Crystal Spirit: A Study of George Orwell. Boston: Little, Brown, 1966; London: Jonathan Cape, 1967; Harmondsworth: Penguin, 1970; London: Fourth Estate, 1984, with a new introduction; New York: Schocken Books, 1984, with a new introduction.

The Doukhobors. With Ivan Avakumovic. London: Faber and Faber, 1968; Toronto: Oxford University Press, 1968; Toronto: Carleton Library, 1977, with a new introduction.

Gandhi. London: Fontana, 1972.

Homes or Hovels: The Housing Problem & Its Solutions. London: Freedom Press, 1944.

A Hundred Years of Revolution: 1848 and After. Edited by Woodcock. London: Porcupine Press, 1948.

Letter to the Past, An Autobiography. Toronto: Fitzhenry & Whiteside, 1982.

New Life to the Land. London: Freedom Press, 1942.

Now. Edited by George Woodcock. London, 1940-41, 1943-47; Nendeln, Liechtenstein: Kraus Reprint, 1968.

Pierre-Joseph Proudhon: A Biography. London: Routledge & Kegan Paul, 1956; New York: Schocken Books, 1972, as *Pierre-Joseph Proudhon, His Life and Work;* Montreal: Black Rose Books, 1987.

Railways and Society. London: Freedom Press, 1943.

The Rejection of Politics and Other Essays on Canada, Canadians, Anarchism and the World. Toronto: new press, 1972.

What is Anarchism? London: Freedom Press, 1945.

William Godwin: A Biographical Study. London: Porcupine Press, 1948; Norwood, Pennsylvania: Norwood Editions, 1976; Montreal: Black Rose Books, 1989, with a new introduction.

The Writer and Politics: Essays. London: Porcupine Press, 1948; Montreal: Black Rose Books, 1990, as *Writers and Politics.*